Understanding LIVING TRUSTS®

How You Can Avoid Probate,
Save Taxes and Enjoy Peace of Mind

Fifth Edition

By Vickie Schumacher and Jim Schumacher

Published by
 Schumacher Publishing
Los Angeles

PLEASE READ THIS: We have done our best to give you useful and accurate information concerning the subject matter covered in this publication. However, please be aware that laws and procedures are constantly changing and are subject to differing interpretations. Also, variations in local laws and customs can affect the issues discussed in this book. This book is intended to give an overview with the understanding that the publisher and the authors are not engaged in rendering legal, accounting or other professional service. If legal advice or other expert assistance is required, the services of a competent professional should be sought.

First edition published March, 1988 as *A Will Is Not The Way—The Living Trust Alternative* and *Avoid Probate—The Living Trust Alternative*
Second edition published May, 1990 as *Understanding Living Trusts*®
Third edition published October, 1994 as *Understanding Living Trusts*®
Fourth edition published February, 1996 as *Understanding Living Trusts*®
Fifth edition published January, 1998 as *Understanding Living Trusts*®

This publication is available for bulk purchase. For information:
Schumacher Publishing
P.O. Box 64395
Los Angeles, CA 90064-0395
1-800-728-2665
http://www.estateplanning.com

ISBN 0-945811-22-5

Library of Congress Catalog Card Number: 97-062268

Printed in the United States of America

This book is lovingly dedicated to our sons

James Price Schumacher II
Charles Beckwith Schumacher

who every day help us to remember which things are truly the most important—like the first day of school, bedtime stories, pillow fights, birthday parties, Friday nights (pizza and movie night), baseball, pancakes, camping and swimming pools.

JJ (on the left) is now eight and in third grade. He is a blue belt in Tae Kwon Do (he just passed Dad) and is one high-powered first-baseman. (Dad's the coach, but JJ had to earn the position.) Charlie (on the right) is six and in kindergarten. His soccer team (also coached by Dad) was undefeated this year. Our days are now filled with Tae Kwon Do, piano lessons, sports of every kind—and homework.

Thanks, guys, for reminding us that work can often wait— and for understanding when we feel that it can't.

(JJ and Charlie would like to personally thank you for buying this book and contributing to their college fund.)

P.S. Mom is not in this picture because she took it!

MEET THE AUTHORS, VICKIE AND JIM SCHUMACHER

No one explains the benefits of Living Trusts and estate planning to the American public as clearly and as honestly as the Schumachers.

They have a unique perspective on what consumers want, what they understand, and what confuses, frustrates, and motivates them when it comes to estate planning—because they are consumers, too.

"When we first heard about Living Trusts," says Jim, "we were shocked we hadn't known about them before. We consider ourselves educated and intelligent, and we read financial publications. How could it be that we knew so little about something that was so important to our family?"

For over ten years, Vickie and Jim Schumacher have been helping consumers understand the complex issues of estate planning.

As they learned more, they became convinced that others needed to know this information, too. So, they combined their talents, started asking a lot of questions (many to Jim's brother, an attorney), and began to write about Living Trusts. Vickie, formerly a regional head of communications for a major employee benefits firm, was already an award-winning writer, nationally recognized for her abilities to communicate "legalese" in accurate, understandable English. Jim, a former sales and marketing executive with a Fortune 100 company, applied his business skills and Missouri "horse sense." As Jim puts it, "I'm just like any other consumer. It's got to be plain and simple—and it's got to mean something to *me*."

In 1988, they proudly finished the first edition of their book—and were promptly rejected by more than 20 publishers. "They all said consumers were not interested in this information. But we just didn't believe that," says Vickie. They decided they would have to publish it themselves. "We had put so much time and energy into this book—and we really believed this information would be as important to other families as it was to ours. So Jim got on the phone and convinced a couple of corporate clients to place advance orders so we could pay for the printing."

The rest has been nothing short of remarkable. The first edition sold more than 50,000 copies. With subsequent editions, that figure has now topped 300,000. *Understanding Living Trusts*® is in all major bookstores, selling well to consumers *and* professionals.

In the process, the Schumachers have become full-fledged consumer advocates. Their Los Angeles-based publishing company is solely dedicated to educating the American public about estate planning strategies.

"We want to help people understand the most effective ways to avoid unnecessary legal fees and taxes, and to provide for their loved ones—so they can have peace of mind," explains Jim.

Consumers know and trust the Schumachers when it comes to estate planning and Living Trusts, as evidenced by the crowd at this seminar.

The Schumachers are not affiliated with any law firm or financial institution. As a result, they remain independent and objective in their reporting. Because of this, and because of their ability to explain this complicated information in clear, conversational English, the Schumachers are frequent guests on radio and television talk-shows, and are keynote speakers at standing-room-only seminars. They have appeared on the American Association for Retired Persons' (AARP) *Prime Time*, been mentioned in numerous publications like *Modern Maturity,* and shared the seminar "billing" with such notables as Louis Rukeyser of *Wall Street Week.*

In addition to their book, the Schumachers have created the *Understanding Estate Planning System* for professionals. Their easy-to-understand brochures, special reports, multi-media/slide presentations and Web Site are used by thousands of banks, attorneys and financial professionals nationwide.

The Schumachers also host *The Estate Planning Learning Center* at their Web Site: **www.estateplanning.com**. This unique resource of educational information is available to both consumers and professionals. Free on-line services include: a database of estate planning attorneys, rated and reviewed by consumers; estate tax and probate calculator; frequently-asked questions; online presentations; and up-to-the-minute tax and legal news.

What's next? According to Jim, "We'll keep researching estate planning strategies and report to consumers. These are complicated and confusing issues—not just for consumers, but for professionals as well. Laws change constantly. And much of what is written is very difficult for consumers to understand. I don't think we'll run out of things to talk about anytime soon."

CONTRIBUTING EDITORS

The authors would like to thank the following individuals who acted as technical advisors and reviewers for this book. Their willingness to share their knowledge and experience with us—and with our readers—has greatly contributed to the balance and content of this publication. We thank them for their patience as we sometimes struggled to keep things accurate *and* understandable. As truly gifted teachers, they have guided us and offered suggestions—yet allowed us to reach our own conclusions. We hold them, their ethics, and their standards in the highest regard—and they inspire us to keep our own standards high.

 **Roy M. Adams** is head of the Trusts and Estates Practice Group of the Law Firm of **Kirkland & Ellis** based in Chicago, New York, Los Angeles, Washington, DC and London. Mr. Adams is an Adjunct Professor of Estate Planning and Taxation at Northwestern University School of Law, where he has taught estate planning and taxation for 20 years. He is the Senior Professor and Dean of Faculty of the American Bankers Association National Trust School and National Graduate Trust School, counseling and teaching bankers and others in related professions at the schools for 24 years. Mr. Adams is a Fellow of the American College of Trusts and Estates Counsel, and Director of multiple family companies and private foundations. He is Editorial Consultant and Chairman of the Editorial Advisory Board of *Trusts & Estates* Magazine, and he writes a popular bi-monthly column on estate planning, tax and trust law questions. His book, *Estate Planning Manual*, was published by the American Bankers Association in 1982, and it is supplemented annually. Additionally, he is the co-author of a two-volume text, *Illinois Estate Planning, Will Drafting and Estate Administration* (2nd Edition) published in 1994. Mr. Adams is also contributing author to the four-volume treatise published by Clark Boardman Callaghan, *Estate And Personal Financial Planning*, and he is a contributing editor to *Understanding Living Trusts.*® Mr. Adams chairs the Schumacher Publications Estate Planning and Tax Advisory Board and in that capacity reviews publications in estate, tax and related fields and responds to readers' questions. Mr. Adams conducts an extensive national and international practice in the areas of estate and tax planning, advising wealthy families and individuals with significant assets which often include substantial business interests. He lectures nationally and internationally in his areas of expertise and is a much sought-after speaker. He is admitted to practice in the states of New York and Illinois.

Theodore (Ted) J. Cranston is a Partner specializing in Trusts and Estates at the law firm of **Gray Cary Ware & Freidenrich** in La Jolla, California, and he chairs the firm's Tax and Trust Practice Group. He is a member of the San Diego, California, and American Bar Associations, and has served as Chairman and Vice-Chairman of the San Diego Bar Association's San Diego and La Jolla Probate Section Committees, as well as Chairman of the Law Office Economics Section Committee. Mr. Cranston has also served on various other committees of the San Diego Bar Association including the Real Property Section, the Tax Section, the Legislation Committee (Probate, Trusts & Estates), and the Speakers Bureau for local junior and senior high schools. Mr. Cranston has specialized in Trusts and Estates since 1965. He is a Fellow of the American College of Trust and Estate Counsel. He has lectured on Trusts and Estates at various Bar functions such as the San Diego Bar Association Estate Planning Clinic and the San Diego Bar Association Orientation Program on Estate Planning for New Lawyers. Mr. Cranston has lectured to other attorneys on various estate planning issues as part of California's Continuing Education of the Bar program, and speaks to other groups as well, including classes at the University of San Diego Law School and Tax Program, Internal Revenue Service organizations, and numerous private groups. He is a member of the Presbyterian Church (where he has served as junior high school teacher, trustee and elder), and has served on the Board of Directors of numerous organizations, including the San Diego Legal Aid Society, Girl Scouts of San Diego, United Cerebral Palsy Foundation of San Diego, San Diego Center for Children, San Diego Repertory Theatre, National Conference of Christians and Jews, School of Theology at Claremont, and Planned Parenthood. He has also served as Chairman of the National Council and Planned Giving Committee for the Salk Institute.

Edward A. Setzler is a Partner in the Kansas City, Missouri law firm of **Spencer Fane Britt and Browne**. He is a co-founder and past President of the Estate Planning Society of Kansas City, past Chairman of the Probate and Trust Committee of the Kansas City Bar Association, past Chairman of the Estate Planning Symposium, and is a member of the court-appointed Probate Manual Committee. He is a Fellow of The American College of Trust and Estate Counsel and is currently serving as its Chairman for the State of Missouri. Mr. Setzler has been a frequent lecturer on estate planning and probate matters for the Continuing Legal Education Department of the University of Missouri at Kansas City Law School and for the Missouri Bar Association. He is co-editor or co-author for the Missouri Bar Association Deskbooks on Estate Planning, Missouri Estate Administration, and Missouri Guardianship and Trust Law. Mr. Setzler is a member of the Board of Directors, Board of Governors, and an Ambassador of the American Royal and is serving on the Business Council of the Nelson Atkins Museum of Art. He is listed in the books *Best Lawyers in America, Who's Who in American Law, Who's Who in America, and Who's Who in the World*.

OUR PERSONAL THANKS TO:

Our Staff and Associates

Jasmine Murata Clouser—for art direction, design, illustrations and all-around "stuff." (During the last major revisions, she planned her wedding and got married. This time, we've had baby Dalton here in the office with us. Life does go on!)

Irene Allin, David Davidson, Darrin Dennis, Robert Fite and Sarah Lin—for "thinking consciously" and keeping the office running while we write.

Lynne Mackechnie, Sharon Sides, Alex Yuchongtian, Gayle Leonard, Kent Komae—for being there when we need you.

Professionals

For sharing your knowledge and expertise, for offering suggestions, and for patience in answering our questions—especially the "dumb" ones!

Debra Ashton	Millie Basden	Elton Brooks
Shela Camenisch	Natalie B. Choate	Dick Drummond
Michael Ettinger	Charles D. "Skip" Fox IV	Adrienne George
Jerry Gottlieb	Richard Gottlieb	Ronald Greening
John Hartmann	Carter Howard	Howard Lang
Marr Leisure	Kenneth Leventhal	Gary McFatridge
Susan B. Porter	Allen Reid	Jim Schreier
Cecil Smith	Steven E. Trytten	Anita Medina Tyson
Patrick Vaughan	Roy Weitz	Steven M. Wellner
Michael D. Whitty	Jerome L. Wolf	

Our Readers

Thank you for taking the time to call, write and e-mail us. While we cannot answer each individual personally, please know that we do read every letter and message. Many of the changes in this edition are a direct result of your comments, suggestions, questions and concerns. We sincerely hope this book is helpful to you and your families.

Our Parents

Your actions and teachings helped shape us into the individuals and parents we are today.

TABLE OF CONTENTS

Part Seven—
THE FINAL STEPS TO YOUR PEACE OF MIND 191

INTRODUCTION

Congratulations! You are about to read the book that has changed and enhanced the lives of over 300,000 people, as well as their families and loved ones.

It's a book that will unravel the often complex subject of estate planning and Living Trusts in a clear, understandable manner. And, as you'll see, it's a book that is not afraid to expose and clarify many of the common myths and misconceptions people have about estate planning and Wills.

Since you are reading this book, you are probably starting to think about how to transfer your assets to your loved ones after you're gone. Everyone wants to do the right thing. (What parent or grandparent doesn't?) But things are so much more complicated today. You probably have many concerns that your parents didn't have to face. For example:

- With people living longer, you may worry about what will happen if you become incapacitated.
- With second (and even third) marriages so common, you may worry about how to provide for your surviving spouse without disinheriting your children and grandchildren.
- With the high rate of divorce and lawsuits, you may worry about your assets ending up in the hands of your children's spouses or creditors.
- With current "spend now, save later" attitudes and values so different from yours, you may worry that your children will not be responsible with the assets you have worked so hard all your life to accumulate.
- With so much of our personal information available to others through giant computer databases, you may worry about how to protect your privacy.
- And with tax rates and legal fees so high, you may be concerned about how much of your assets your loved ones will actually receive.

A Living Trust can provide the solutions to all these concerns and more. In fact, as you will see in this book, a Living Trust fits the needs of today's families far better than any other plan.

You will learn how you can lose control when you have a Will, when you don't have a Will, when you use joint ownership, give away assets, or use beneficiary designations to transfer your assets—and how a good portion of your assets can be lost *unnecessarily* to court costs, legal fees, unintended heirs, and taxes.

You will also learn how you can keep control—while you are living, if you become incapacitated, and even after you die—with a Revocable Living Trust. You will learn that a Living Trust not only avoids probate and saves taxes, but also gives you more flexibility and control, and preserves your privacy.

We wrote this book because there is so much confusion and incorrect information about estate planning. People are frustrated by books, articles, and professionals they can't understand. They make bad decisions based on incorrect or incomplete information. And many risk the assets they spent a lifetime acquiring with inadequate do-it-yourself forms and fly-by-night promotions.

Before we tell you more, there are a few things we'd like you to know:

1. We wrote this book for you, the consumer. We have written it in clear, conversational English, and have intentionally avoided the use of technical legal terms wherever possible. We want you to understand this information—so you can be in control and tell your attorney what *you* want.

2. This edition of *Understanding Living Trusts*® is the most complete and up-to-date ever. We keep in touch (almost daily) with our readers nationwide to find out their most current questions and concerns. We then interview some of the nation's top estate planning attorneys—our Contributing Editors—and other experts to find the answers for you.

3. We are presenting this information as a general overview. We haven't gotten bogged down with specific laws and local customs, complicated tax discussions, or every conceivable situation that could come up. You may find some minor variations in your state's laws, but generally these will only be technical and won't affect the overall message.

4. This book is not a "do-it-yourselfer." Generic form books and kits can't address the unique needs of different families in different states. We believe you need assistance from an experienced and conscientious attorney—and we'll help you find one.

5. This book is your personal "action plan" for setting up a Living Trust. Inside, you'll learn:
   - what a Living Trust is, how it works, and the steps you'll need to take to set up one;
   - what to consider when deciding how you want your loved ones to inherit from you;
   - how to find the right attorney to prepare your Living Trust;
   - how to organize information your family will need; and
   - step-by-step instructions for what your family needs to do if you become incapacitated and after you die.

Our "mission" in writing this book is to educate and empower you. Our hope is that you will not only better understand the many benefits of a Living Trust, but that you will also take this knowledge and secure the financial future of your loved ones.

We know the value of a Living Trust. It has changed our lives and given us peace of mind. When properly set up, it can do the same for you and your family.

WHAT'S NEW IN THIS EDITION!

Tax Law Changes

On August 5, 1997, President Clinton signed *The Taxpayer Relief Act of 1997*. This legislation included the first major federal tax cuts in 16 years, as well as major changes to gift and estate tax laws.

This new, fifth edition of *Understanding Living Trusts®* incorporates relevant changes from this new legislation, which include:

NEW Increase in the individual federal estate tax exemption—from $600,000 in 1997 to $1 million by 2006. (See page 75.)

NEW New family business exclusion that will exempt a total of $1.3 million from estate taxes for family-owned businesses that qualify. (See page 76.)

NEW Several changes to make taxation of income in trusts and probate estates more equal. (See page 227.)

Non-Tax Changes

We have also made several "non-tax" changes, many of them a direct result of comments from our readers. These include:

NEW More information on who should be Beneficiary of your IRA and other tax-deferred plans (401(k), 403(b), pension, profit sharing, Keogh). (See page 180.)

NEW More on using separate Trusts to save estate taxes. (See pages 83 and 98.)

NEW More on funding your Living Trust. (See page 163-189.)

NEW More on benefits and "disadvantages" of a Living Trust. (See pages 48-66.)

NEW Updates on laws in specific states—including Florida and Pennsylvania—that affect your Living Trust. (See pages 48, 62, 63 and 166.)

NEW Up-to-the-minute information about Medicaid. (See page 94.)

NEW More on tax-reducing strategies of America's richest families that you can use. (See page 239.)

NEW Plus new charts, examples, and much more, including...

NEW **SPARRS— Schumacher Publishing's Attorney Rating and Review Site.** This new service, available free via our Web Site (www.estateplanning.com) lets you quickly locate attorneys in your area, learn about their background and areas of expertise, and read unedited ratings and reviews written by actual clients of the attorney. (See page 142.)

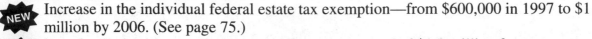

If you need more information, we have good news!

Special Report — Because of the many requests we receive for additional information on Living Trusts and other estate planning and wealth building strategies, we are writing a number of Special Reports. Whenever you see this icon in the book, it means we have written or are preparing a Special Report on that subject. If you'd like to order one, or would like a complete up-to-date listing of our publications, contact us at:

Schumacher Publishing

P.O. Box 64395, Los Angeles, CA 90064-0395

TOLL FREE ✆ 1-800-728-2665

www.estateplanning.com

GOOD PLANS CAN GO WRONG

GOOD PLANS CAN GO WRONG

To avoid probate after she died, Edith, an elderly widow, decided to give her home to her daughter Susan. They had always gotten along very well, and Susan assured her mother she would be able to live in the house for the rest of her life. She even stated so in her Will, just in case anything happened to her first. Unfortunately, Susan did die in a car accident. Not long after, Edith was shocked when she received an eviction notice. As it turned out, Susan had made her husband joint owner of the house with her, and when Susan died he became sole owner. He had never cared about Edith and decided to sell. Susan's Will didn't make any difference, because her share had transferred to her husband immediately upon her death.

Over the years, John and his wife Eleanor had planned carefully, saved and invested wisely for their retirement. They made sure their Wills, which left everything to each other, were always up to date. They even had Trusts in their Wills for extra protection. Unfortunately, John developed Alzheimer's Disease. As his condition worsened, Eleanor needed to sell some of their investments. But John was no longer able to conduct business, and Eleanor soon learned she couldn't sign for him—only a *court appointee* could sign for him. It was hard enough dealing with John's situation, but now Eleanor also had to deal with the court. She didn't know the court would *stay* involved to "protect" John's share of the proceeds. She had to keep detailed records of everything—the court insisted upon approving all expenses *and* the sale of their jointly owned assets. When John died several years later, Eleanor found herself back in court again—this time to probate his Will.

Claire was very lonely after Fred, her husband of 40 years, died. To fill her time, she started taking ballroom dancing lessons. Her instructor, a much younger "gentleman," was very quick to provide her with the companionship she was missing. And Claire, with a new sense of self-esteem, soon fell head over heels in love. Fred's and Claire's children were shocked when their mother announced she had married her instructor. But the real shock came seven months later when Claire died—and the children learned their mother had placed everything in joint ownership with her new husband. As the new sole owner, he decided to sell everything and leave town. Because their mother had made her new husband joint owner, the children had been completely disinherited. And everything Fred and Claire had built over the years was gone.

When George and Betty moved to Florida, they gave their home in New York to their daughter Anne, a divorced mother of three. Anne later remarried and, as a wedding present to her new husband, she changed the title on the house from her name to both their names, as husband and wife. Not long after, Anne suddenly became ill and died. Her husband, now the sole owner, promptly booted the children (all teenagers) out of the house. George and Betty will undoubtedly have many sleepless nights—and regrets—over this situation.

Louise only had one child, a grown son named David, and to make things easier for him when she eventually died, Louise added his name on the title of her house. David was very good to his mother, but he was irresponsible when it came to money. Eventually, he got so far behind in payments to his creditors that they sued him. Louise was shocked when she was forced to sell her home to pay his debts.

When Edward and Beth married, they both had children and assets from previous marriages. They had new Wills prepared, with each leaving their separate assets to their own children. When Edward died ten years later, Beth's attorney advised her that, as a surviving spouse in that state, she was entitled to a percentage of all of Edward's assets—including the 300-acre farm that had been in his family for generations. Although she knew Edward had wanted the farm to go only to his children, she felt that she and her children had a right to part of it. She decided to claim her share, prompting a bitter battle within the family. Eventually Beth won. But the farm ended up being sold to pay the expenses—and the closeness the family had developed during Edward's lifetime had been destroyed.

Mary was a widow with no children or immediate family. In her Will, she left everything in equal shares to three institutions which had been a big part of her life—to her husband's university for scholarships in his memory, to her neighborhood church, and to a children's hospital, where her only child had been treated for a terminal illness many years earlier.

When Mary died, her Will had to be probated before her assets could be given to the institutions. As required by law, a notice of her death was published in the newspaper and a list of her assets was made public. Some distant relatives Mary barely knew saw the notice in the paper, hired an attorney, and contested the Will. The institutions had to hire attorneys to try and uphold Mary's Will, and Mary's estate also had to be represented by an attorney. A nasty and expensive legal battle began. Finally, more than four years later, the institutions agreed to give Mary's relatives half of her estate, just to end the fight. This was obviously not what Mary had wanted.

Betty, recently divorced, had a 3 year old daughter named Sarah. She had heard she should have a Will (especially since she had a child), and when she saw an advertisement for a Will kit, she ordered one through the mail. In her Will, she left everything directly to Sarah. She didn't have that much in assets, so she increased her life insurance and listed Sarah as Beneficiary. She named her sister Linda as Sarah's Guardian, thinking Linda would be able to use the insurance money to raise Sarah if something happened to her.

A few years later, Betty died unexpectedly and her Will went through probate. Because Sarah was a minor, the court had to establish a guardianship for her. The court did allow Linda to be Sarah's Guardian, but the court kept control of the inheritance—everything Betty left Sarah in her Will *and* the money from the insurance company. When Sarah turned 18, the legal age in that state, the court guardianship, by law, ended. And Sarah received her entire inheritance in one lump sum, which she quickly spent in just one year of expensive living.

Dorothy, a widow, put all of her property, including her house, into joint ownership with her married son. She did this thinking that, when she died, her property would automatically go to her son without the need for probate. Several years later, her son and his wife separated and Dorothy decided to sell her house so she could move in with her son. But she soon discovered she could not sell it without her *daughter-in-law's* signature on the deed.

The daughter-in-law was still legally married to her son and was entitled by law to a "marital interest" in the property. The title company would not insure clear title to the buyer without the daughter-in-law's signature because it wasn't clear what her "interest" would be—and she refused to sign unless she got part of the money when the house was sold. Dorothy was stuck—she didn't know that joint ownership with a married person can include *that person's spouse*. And because Dorothy had placed her house in joint ownership, she lost control of her own home.

On the advice of a neighbor, Frank and Elizabeth, an elderly couple, put everything they owned, including their home and stocks, in their adult daughter's name. They believed this would avoid probate and that all their assets would pass directly to their daughter—their only child—when they were both gone. A year later, Frank died of a heart attack. Several months after that, their daughter died in a car accident.

Elizabeth *never* thought she would survive both her husband and daughter. To add to her distress, Elizabeth now owned nothing in her own name— everything was in her daughter's name. She was forced to probate her daughter's estate to get back her own property. During this long process she had to rely on the court to grant her living expenses. Sometimes the court would approve them, sometimes not. And during a declining stock market, she helplessly watched the value of her stocks fall to only a fraction of their previous value—because the court could not react in time for them to be sold quickly enough. Elizabeth lost her financial independence plus a substantial portion of her assets to probate—just trying to get back what was hers in the first place.

John and Ellen had each been married before and had young children from their first marriages. When they married, they considered it a fresh start and one family. They put all of their assets in both their names (joint ownership), with the intention that when they died, all the children would receive an equal share. They didn't have Wills because they thought joint ownership would serve the same purpose.

When John died, everything went to Ellen and she continued to raise and care for all the children. When Ellen died many years later, her assets went through probate. But because she did not have a Will, under the probate laws of that state Ellen's property could only be distributed to *her surviving blood children*. Since John's children had never been legally adopted by Ellen, they received nothing. Even though John and Ellen thought of all the children as being their own, the probate laws did not. Because they relied on joint ownership, they unknowingly disinherited John's children.

Doris and Bob owned a family-style restaurant. They had been moderately successful for years, and put everything they made back into the business. When Bob died, one of their competitors went down to the probate court and looked up his file. In it he found much of Bob and Doris' financial information, a competitor's dream. He also saw in the file that Doris had requested a living allowance from the court, indicating she was short on cash. He offered to buy Doris out—at 50% of what he knew the restaurant was worth. To his amazement, she accepted, without any negotiation. This competitor had "inside information"—courtesy of the probate files.

Marie, an elderly widow, had a Will which left everything in equal shares to her five grown children. When she learned she had cancer, she put everything she owned into joint ownership with her oldest son, thinking this would avoid probate and make things easier for her family when she died. She discussed it with her son and was sure that he would carry out her wishes and divide everything equally among the five children.

When she died, ownership did immediately go to her son. But he died suddenly in a construction accident a few weeks later, *before* the property could be

A *Living Trust would have prevented these situations*

distributed. His wife, only recently married to Marie's son, claimed everything as his surviving spouse, and she decided to keep it all herself! Marie's Will (which, remember, left everything in equal shares to her children) could do nothing, because as soon as she died *she no longer owned anything.* Marie's joint ownership plan did avoid probate, but it also disinherited her children!

Stella, recently divorced, added her 12-year old son as joint owner on the deed to her house, thinking it would automatically become his if something should happen to her. A year later, she needed to sell the house. But she couldn't, because her 13-year old son (her joint owner) could not legally sign the papers. She had to put her own son in a court guardianship and the court insisted on approving the sale. By that time, the buyers were long gone—but the court was still there. Eventually she was able to find another buyer, and this time the sale went through. But the court kept control over her son's share of the proceeds until he turned 18—at which time he promptly spent it all on a sports car, a motorcycle and "good times." In the meantime, Stella couldn't afford to buy another house with just her share. She found out the hard way that joint ownership with a minor does not work.

Olivia wanted to make sure her daughter Jill and her new granddaughter would be provided for if something happened to her, so she purchased a new insurance policy and named her daughter Jill as the Beneficiary. Not long after, Olivia suddenly became ill and died. The insurance proceeds were paid directly to Jill, who deposited the check into her joint checking account. A few days later, Jill's husband withdrew all the money and left town—leaving Jill and her baby with nothing.

. . . .

A Living Trust would have prevented these good plans from going wrong.

Part One

WHY GOOD "PLANS" CAN GO WRONG

Part One —
WHY GOOD "PLANS" CAN GO WRONG

People want to do the right thing for themselves and their families. But, as you've just seen, all too often their good intentions have tragic results. The really sad part is the unhappy endings are often *avoidable*. If they had just *known* what could happen, chances are many people would have done things differently.

What we're talking about is called *estate planning*. It's not just for "wealthy" or "old" people (whatever those are). It's something we *all* need to do—regardless of age, marital status, or wealth—if we want to keep control of our assets (our estates) when something happens to us. And it's important to plan now, while we can. Because with estate planning, no one gets a second chance.

In this section, we'll look at five basic ways most people "plan" their estates. (You're probably already using at least one of them now, even if you think you haven't done any estate planning.)

We'll explain how you can easily lose control of your assets while you are living, if you become incapacitated, and after you die when you use one of these "plans." Then, in Part Two, we'll show you how one plan—the Revocable Living Trust—gives you far more control than the others.

And we'll explain it all in clear, conversational English—*so you can under-stand it*. Because we want *your* good intentions to have a happy ending.

▉ LOSING CONTROL WITH A WILL

A Will is one of the most widely used legal documents and is probably what first comes to mind when you think about how to plan your estate and transfer your assets to your loved ones. (After all, we've been told for years that we should have a Will.)

In a Will, of course, you name who you want to receive your assets when you die and who you want to handle your final affairs for you (often called an Executor or Administrator).

But contrary to what you've probably heard (and been led to believe), a Will may not be the best plan for you and your family. That's because a Will:

■ Does not avoid probate when you die;
■ Does not prevent the court from taking control of your assets if you become physically or mentally incapacitated; and
■ Probably does not give you the control you think it does if you have minor children or grandchildren.

Let's see how much control you really have with a Will in each of these situations.

A Will Does Not Avoid Probate When You Die

A Will is simply an expression of your wishes—what you want to happen to your assets after you die. All Wills must go through some kind of probate court process before they can go into effect. How complicated that process will be will depend on the laws in your state.

You've probably heard of probate, read about it, or perhaps even experienced it when a relative died. Let's take a brief look at it now.

What Is Probate?

Probate is the legal process through which the court makes sure that, after you die, your Will is legally valid, your debts are paid, and your assets are distributed according to the instructions in your Will.

Probate has existed in one form or another for hundreds of years. It was created with the best of intentions to protect your creditors, assets, and your family by providing an orderly method of paying bills and transferring ownership of your assets after you die—all under direct supervision of the court system.

A Will does not avoid probate

Why Do We Have To Go Through Probate?

You may be wondering why you can't just appoint someone to pay your bills and distribute your assets after you die—*without* involving the probate court. (If you have a Living Trust, you *can*, as we'll explain in Part Two.)

Well, very simply, if your name is on the title of an asset and you die, probate is the *only legal way* to take your name off the title of an asset and put the new owner's name on.

In most states, a Will by itself is not enough authority to retitle assets or release account balances—a court order is required to do this. So, after you die, your family will not be able to change titles on assets that are titled in your name without a court order—and that can only be done through the probate court.

Also, your Will must be validated as being authentic before ownership of your assets can be transferred to your heirs—and the probate court is the only way this can be done.

What Assets Go Through Probate?

Not everything you own will automatically go through probate. For example, jointly owned assets that transfer to the surviving owner generally do not go through probate. Nor do assets that have a valid beneficiary designation (like an insurance policy). But there can be some significant problems with both, causing you to lose control of your assets, even while you are living. You'll want to finish reading this section if you currently rely on these.

Assets in a Trust also avoid probate, as we'll explain in Part Two. However, if you have a Trust *in your Will* (called a Testamentary Trust), it does *not* avoid probate. The Will has to go through probate *before* the Trust can go into effect.

What Happens In Probate?

Probate doesn't happen automatically. Someone, usually a relative or the Executor you name in your Will, must petition the court for probate proceedings to begin—for example, when checks need to be written, or when an asset needs to be sold or transferred to a new owner.

Probate procedures will vary slightly from state to state, and even from court to court. A traditional "formal" probate will usually include the following general process.

When probate proceedings begin, the probate court takes control of your estate, supervising payment of your debts and distribution of your assets. In most states, the court will require that a notice of your death appear in local newspapers, giving your creditors and anyone else who feels he/she has a right to part of your estate a certain length of time (several weeks or months) to present their claims.

At the first hearing, the judge will make sure your Will is valid—that it is the correct one (if you had more than one Will), that you were competent when you signed it, and that it is properly signed and witnessed. Otherwise, he/she will declare that you died without a Will (see "Losing Control by Doing Nothing" later in this section). The judge will then officially appoint your Executor and open a file on your estate.

You may have named an attorney in your Will. If not, your family or Executor can usually choose one. Although having an attorney is not always a legal requirement, the paperwork can be complicated. Also, most judges prefer to deal with someone who is already familiar with the process.

Your Executor will compile an inventory of your assets (with formal appraisals of valuable assets) and pay your final bills. These are then submitted to the court for approval. Your Executor also applies for and collects any death benefits to which your estate is entitled, and has your final tax returns prepared.

A second notice is usually given for a final hearing to settle your estate. At this hearing, the judge will review the paperwork and order your debts paid (including all probate expenses). If there is not enough cash in your estate to pay your expenses, the judge may order some of your assets sold. Your remaining assets will then be distributed according to the terms in your Will.

If there are any disputes, the judge will make the final decisions, holding additional hearings if necessary. Finally, your Executor will be released from his/her duties and your file will be closed.

Probate

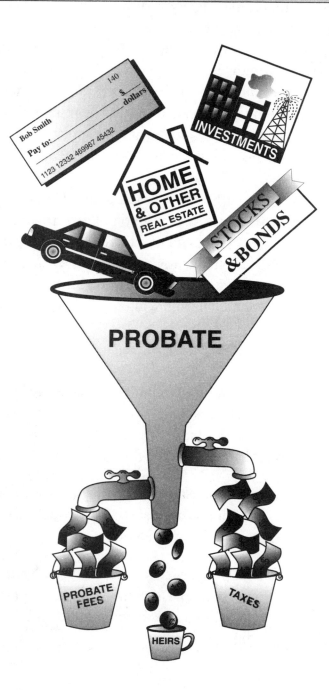

Without a Living Trust, assets titled in just your name must go through a probate process, and all expenses must be paid, before the assets can be fully distributed to your heirs.

Probate can be expensive

■ Exception—Small Estates
Most states allow very small estates to bypass probate. But few qualify because the limits are typically very low—in some states, as low as $15,000 in assets that are subject to probate.

■ Informal Probate
In an attempt to simplify the probate process, many states now allow informal probate proceedings (also called independent administration). A few states also have special processes for surviving spouses. Generally, these require fewer court appearances and accounting procedures.

However, these are still probate proceedings. The American Association for Retired Persons (AARP) recently completed a survey of probate files in several states. In its findings, entitled *A Report on Probate*, AARP concluded that informal probate frequently does not save the time and money it was intended to save—because the processes and forms are often still too complicated for most people to handle without substantial attorney involvement.

So, What's Wrong With Probate?
■ It can be expensive.
The same survey by AARP found that probate is big business. In fact, AARP estimates that probate costs could top *$2 billion* a year—$1.5 billion for attorneys, and hundreds of millions more for Executors, bonding companies, appraisers and probate courts.

The costs to probate your estate must be paid before your assets can be fully distributed to your heirs. These costs vary widely from state to state, but usually are estimated at 3-8% of an estate's gross value.

Some states calculate probate fees on the total *gross* value of an estate—*before* debts are paid. So, for example, if your home is valued at $100,000 when you die, probate fees would be calculated on the full $100,000—even if the mortgage is $95,000.

Some states even allow probate fees on the entire value of the estate—including assets (like life insurance) that do not go through probate!

If someone tells you probate is not expensive where you live, ask for a written estimate of what it would cost to probate your estate if you died today and, if you are married, what it would cost if your spouse died tomorrow—then you can decide if it's expensive or not.

Who gets most of this money?

The biggest expenses are legal and Executor fees. A family member who serves as Executor may waive the fee (although AARP estimates, in its survey, that fully one-third of Executors *do* take a fee). Also, in many states, if the attorney who probates your estate is also named as your Executor, the attorney is entitled to *both* fees.

Some states have regulated (statutory) fee schedules for attorneys and Executors—so you can actually look up a chart and determine what it should cost to probate an estate. Some states use hourly fees—$100 to $200 per hour is not an unusual attorney rate. And quite often the Executor will be paid at the same rate as the attorney. Other states use what is called a "reasonable" fee system. The problem with "reasonable" fees is there is no way for you to know what the cost will be until the entire process has been completed.

The following chart shows fees in California, Florida and New York for the attorney and Executor. (Probate fees in your state may be higher or lower.)

Examples of Probate Fees

Estate Value	Combined Fees For Attorney and Executor*		
	California	*Florida*	*New York*
$100,000	$6,300	$6,000	$10,000
$200,000	$10,300	$12,000	$18,000
$500,000	$22,300	$30,000	$36,000
$1,000,000	$42,300	$60,000	$63,000
$2,000,000	$62,300	$110,000	$113,000
$5,000,000	$122,300	$250,000	$263,000

*Statutory fees for California and Florida. Statutory executor fees and estimated legal fees in New York. Filing, appraisal, and publication fees, bonds and legal fees for "extraordinary" services (Will contest, tax advice, tax returns, and real estate transactions, for example) are in addition.

Probate takes time and is a public process

Regardless of how fees are initially calculated, a judge usually can (and often will) allow higher fees, depending on the time and/or circumstances involved. Initial fees often do not include legal fees for real estate transactions, completing tax returns, or if someone contests the Will—these are often considered "extraordinary" fees.

Generally speaking, the more time the attorney and Executor have to spend probating an estate, the more it will cost.

Why should I care about probate fees in other states?
If you own assets (especially real estate, like a vacation home) in other states, your family will probably face *multiple* probates, each one according to the probate laws and costs of that state. They will also probably need to hire an attorney in each state.

But I don't own that much. Why should I be concerned about probate?
Generally, probate costs take a larger percentage from smaller estates (which can least afford it) than from larger ones.

■ Probate takes time.
It usually takes nine months to two years to complete the process. During part of this time, your assets will probably be frozen so an accurate inventory can be taken, and nothing can be distributed or sold without the court's and/or Executor's approval. If your family needs money to live on, they must request a living allowance, which may or may not be approved. Also, assets could drop in value if the court and/or Executor cannot react quickly enough to sell them—for example, if your family wanted to sell stocks in a declining market.

Why does it take so long? Keep in mind that probate moves on the court's schedule and the attorney's schedule—not your family's schedule. In most cases, you can't just call the judge and say "we would like to probate Grandpa's Will on Monday." It can take weeks to get a hearing. And, remember, you are not the only client the attorney has. So your family has very little say in how quickly things can happen.

■ Your family has no privacy.
Probate is a public process. Any "interested party" can find out details about your estate—including who the heirs are, what they will receive, their addresses, etc.

It's surprising how easy it is in some states to have access to probate files of *anyone*—usually all you need to know is the name of the person and the year in which he or she died.

For example, a perfect stranger can look up actress Natalie Wood's file and see all the details of her almost $6 million estate—including her interest in the television series *Charlie's Angels* (valued at $2.3 million); royalties from movies; investments in real estate, oil and gas leases; artwork; a yacht; and at least nine separate bank accounts. It's amazing how detailed the records are—even her half of an $83.31 refund from the telephone company is included in her assets. You can also see exactly how much she left her mother, sisters, daughters and husband—and their addresses at the time of her death.

And just recently, details about Jacqueline Kennedy Onassis's Will were published in *The New York Times*, *Money* magazine, *Fortune* magazine, and others. (On a recent trip to New York, Jim paid a visit to the Surrogate Court and very easily obtained a copy of her probate file—which included her Will and John F. Kennedy's Will, her death certificate, a list of specific items she gave to certain people, etc.) Why are we all able to know such private information about someone who, during her lifetime, kept her personal and financial affairs so carefully guarded? Because of probate, her Will is part of the public records—and available for *anyone* to see.

Now, you may not be as wealthy as Natalie Wood or Jackie Onassis. But probate files can make for some pretty interesting reading for the curious (or nosy). Do *you* want people you know—and even total strangers—to be able to find out what you owned and to whom you left it?

Some people think, "I won't be around then anyway, so why should I care?" Maybe you don't care about yourself, but think about the ones you leave behind.

It might surprise you to know that there are people who go through probate files and compile lists of new widows/widowers and Beneficiaries. These lists are then sold as leads to people who sell investments or want to manage the new inheritances.

Some are legitimate, but many are outright scams—unscrupulous solicitors who prey upon bereaved survivors, especially spouses, who are at a particu-

The probate process, not your family has control

larly vulnerable time in their lives. Many of these surviving spouses have never had to handle finances before and are not only emotionally upset about the loss of their partners, but are understandably terrified about being alone and on their own. If your estate goes through probate, some of these solicitors may call on your family.

If you are a business owner, the lack of privacy can be devastating to your business. Competitors can get valuable "inside information" about your financial records and personal family affairs—courtesy of the probate system.

Also, you may have intentionally left one or more heirs out of your Will. But the probate process invites them to contest, and *the court*—not you or your family—will decide what (if anything) they will get.

■ You and your family lose control.

The probate process—not you or your family—has ultimate control over how your Will is interpreted, how much probate will cost, how long it will take, and what information is made public. Families are used to handling their affairs privately and independently. Suddenly losing that control to a legal process and having to pay for it can be *very* frustrating.

Summary

Probate was, and in many cases still is, a very slow, cumbersome, and public process. It is a product of the "horse and carriage days," when it took months to locate and notify relatives (and creditors) of a death or illness in the family. Back then it didn't matter that probate took a long time or was so public—but today it does.

Things move much more quickly today in this age of "instant" communications. We can contact friends and relatives anywhere in the world in just minutes. Today, financial decisions must often be made within hours—sometimes minutes. And with so much of our financial information already available through giant computer databases, we often find ourselves struggling to hold on to whatever privacy we have left.

Quite simply, the world in which we live has changed faster than probate. Many people today are more sophisticated and knowledgeable, and they value their privacy. Many are quite capable of handling the responsibilities when a family member dies—perhaps still with professional assistance, but only *as they need it*, not as the court *dictates*.

A properly prepared Revocable Living Trust lets your family—instead of the court—control the process of settling your estate.

Okay, now you know how you can lose control with a Will after you die—because a Will does not avoid probate. Now, let's look at how you can lose control when you have a Will—*while you are still living*.

A Will Does Not Prevent Court Control At Incapacity

Many people are surprised to learn that a Will does not prevent the court from taking control of their assets if they become incapacitated. They don't realize that a Will only goes into effect *after* you die. A Will *cannot* go into effect if you become incapacitated—*because you are still living*.

Becoming incapacitated and losing control of their financial affairs is a valid concern of millions of older Americans—and those who will care for them. With advancements in health care, people are living longer. But this also means that more of us will reach the point where we can no longer take care of ourselves.

Of course, incapacity doesn't just happen to older people. Without warning, any of us at any age could be critically injured in an accident or stricken with a devastating illness.

However, few people plan for this possibility—or they mistakenly think a Will is all they need. As a result, many people end up under control of the court *before* they die—and their families must find a way to cope with it.

Why Would The Court Take Control Of Assets At Incapacity?

Think about this for a few moments. If you can't handle your affairs because of mental or physical incapacity—for example, if you have a stroke or a heart attack, develop Alzheimer's Disease, or are injured in an accident—who will conduct business for you?

Sooner or later, your signature will probably be required for something—to withdraw savings, sell or refinance assets to pay your expenses, etc. Of course,

Your Will can't help if you become incapacitated

you may still be able to physically sign your name but, in the opinion of others, may be unable to make sound decisions.

The person you have named as Executor in your Will can't step in and take care of your affairs because your Will can't go into effect. And your family or friends can't just take over and sign your name for you. Someone (a relative or friend) will have to petition *the court* to appoint someone to act for you.

What Happens When The Court Gets Involved?

Here again, procedures will vary from court to court, but most will be similar to this explanation. A public hearing will be held to determine your ability to handle your affairs. In some states, they refer to this as your "competency." If the court agrees that you need someone to act on your behalf, or finds you incompetent , you may lose many of your rights as a citizen. And you and your family will lose control. Because once the court gets involved, it usually stays involved—to "protect" your interests—until you recover or die.

In some states, this court-controlled process is called a "conservatorship." In others, it's called a "guardianship." Some people refer to it as a "living probate" because it's similar to probate at death—but you're still alive.

The original intent was, of course, an honorable one. To prevent someone from taking control of your assets and squandering them, the court steps in and takes control, making financial decisions for you and looking after your welfare.

But there are many things people do not like about this process. It can be *embarrassing*—because records and proceedings are open to the public. It can be *expensive*—because of court costs, examinations and testimony by qualified physician(s), attorney fees, auditor fees, and bonds. It can be *time consuming*—because the person the court appoints to act for you must keep detailed records and submit all expenses to the court for approval.

Also, most people prefer that a family member or friend take care of them. But if the court takes control, the court—not you—will decide who will act for you. The court could appoint someone you would want—like your spouse. But it could also appoint a relative you dislike or one who has only selfish motives, or even a "professional guardian or conservator" who is a stranger to you. If more than one person wants this position, there could be an expensive court battle—and guess who would pay all the costs? *You* would.

You may remember what happened to Groucho Marx not too many years ago. Toward the end of his life, the court found him incompetent. The woman who lived with him battled members of his family for control over Groucho and his money. Everyone had attorneys, of course—and they were *all* paid with Groucho's money. The hearings were lengthy, expensive, very public and probably taxing on Groucho who was wheeled in and out of court (he died soon after the hearings ended). Like many people, Groucho had a Will—but he didn't plan for incapacity.

Sometimes, the court may not have the resources to properly monitor the financial records. In these situations, the assets can (and often do) simply disappear without a trace—with no record of how the money was spent.

If you recover, you must prove to the court that you are now competent and can handle your own affairs (which may be difficult, since the court has already found you *in*competent). And finally, this process does not replace probate at death. So after you die, your family will still have to go through probate to have your Will enforced.

Wouldn't A Power Of Attorney Prevent Court Control Of Assets At Incapacity?

Maybe—but then, maybe not. A power of attorney is a legal document that gives someone authority to conduct business for you if you are unable to. However, most general powers of attorney become *invalid* at incapacity, so they won't work then.

So professionals often recommend using a *durable* power of attorney, which *does* remain valid through incapacity. But even a durable power of attorney may not work when it's needed.

That's because some financial institutions will not accept *any* power of attorney. Others will only accept one if it is on *their* form *and* they know this is what you want. The reason is they have no way of knowing if you have changed your mind. And they don't want to be held liable for giving your assets to someone you may not want to have them. This can be good protection—but it can also be a big problem if you are depending on a durable power of attorney to work for you.

The court, not the guardian, controls your child's inheritance

If the durable power of attorney does work, it may work *too well*. In many states, giving someone power of attorney is like giving that person a "blank check" to do whatever he/she wants with your assets. You could even recover to find you own nothing in your own name.

A durable power of attorney has benefits when used under proper circumstances, but relying on one to prevent the court from taking control of assets at incapacity is risky at best.

If you have a Revocable Living Trust and you become incapacitated, the person you have selected will be able to pay your bills, manage your investments, and take care of your financial affairs for as long as necessary—without interference from the court. And, unlike a Durable Power of Attorney, with a Living Trust this person has more legal responsibilities to you and your loved ones.

Now you know how you can lose control when you have a Will after you die and even while you are living. Let's look at one more way you can lose control with a Will—when you have minor children or grandchildren.

A Will—And Minor Children (Or Grandchildren)

Many parents and grandparents are very surprised to learn how little control they actually have with a Will when it comes to their minor children and grandchildren.

For example, many parents think if they name a Guardian for their minor children in their Wills and something happens to the parents, that person will automatically be able to use the inheritance to take care of the children. But that's not what happens.

Instead, when the Will is probated, the court will set up a guardianship for a minor child. It will appoint a Guardian to raise the child (usually the person named in the parent's Will, but it could appoint someone else).

However, *the court, not the Guardian, will control the inheritance* until the child reaches legal age (18 or 21). At that time, the child automatically receives the *entire* inheritance. Most parents prefer that their children inherit at a later age, but with a simple Will (which is what most parents have) you have no choice.

Note: In some states, the Executor can transfer the minor's inheritance to a "custodial account" under the Uniform Transfer to Minors Act or the Uniform Gifts to Minors Act. These accounts are usually set up at a bank and a "Custodian" is named to manage the funds. Laws will vary from state to state, but generally if the inheritance is more than $10,000, court approval is still required. In any event, the child will still receive the full amount at legal age.

What happens in a court guardianship for a minor is very similar to what happens when the court takes control for an incompetent adult—things move very slowly and it can be very expensive. Every expense must be documented, audited and approved by the court. And because the court must do its best to treat everyone equally under the law, it is difficult to make exceptions for each child's special and unique needs.

Note for Divorced or Separated Parents: Courts typically prefer to see a natural parent as Guardian whenever possible so, even if you name someone else, the court will probably appoint your "ex" as Guardian. A disinterested or irresponsible parent may suddenly become *very* interested in the child when he/she learns that Guardians are entitled to be paid for their services. Also, many courts simply do not have the resources to monitor all guardianships carefully. So it's possible your "ex" may have unsupervised access to the child's inheritance.

Can The Court Take Control Of Assets I Leave A Minor Grandchild?

Many grandparents, other relatives (aunts, uncles, etc.) and even parents leave money, real estate, stocks, certificates of deposit (CDs), and other investments directly to a minor child. If the child is still a minor when the person dies, the court will usually get involved, especially if the inheritance is substantial.

That's because minor children can be *on* a title, but they cannot *conduct business* in their own names. So as soon as the owner's signature is required to sell, refinance, or transact other business, the court will have to get involved. (Sometimes, depending on the value and type of asset, this happens even before the child can receive the money or be listed on the title.)

The court has to make sure the child's interests are "protected," even if both parents are alive and well. Of course, this protection isn't free, and the child's inheritance (or the parents) will have to pay for it. An attorney will need to represent the child in court and the court will probably insist that a guardian (usually a parent) is added to the titles when they are transferred to the child.

Establishing the guardianship is a relatively simple process, but once it is in place the court will stay involved. Until the child reaches legal age, none of the assets can be sold (or the money spent) without the court's approval. And this guardianship could go on indefinitely if the child is physically or mentally incapacitated when he/she reaches legal age.

Wouldn't A Children's Trust In A Will Prevent The Court From Controlling The Assets?

If your Will includes a Children's Trust in it, you can name someone to manage the inheritance after you die instead of the court. But keep in mind that your Will must go through probate *first*. The Children's Trust is funded with your assets after your Will is probated. You should also realize that a Children's Trust in a Will *cannot* go into effect if you become incapacitated—because *your Will* cannot go into effect until *after* you die.

With a Living Trust, the person(s) you select—not the court—will control the inheritance for your minor children or grandchildren until they reach the age(s) at which you want them to inherit—even if you become incapacitated.

Summary

That was a lot of information, but now you know why a Will may not be the best plan for your family. Remember, a Will:

- Does not avoid probate when you die;
- Does not prevent the court from taking control of your assets if you become physically or mentally incapacitated; and
- Does not give you as much control as you may have thought when you have minor children or grandchildren.

Now, let's look at how other "plans" can cause you to lose control.

2 LOSING CONTROL BY DOING NOTHING

If you don't have a Will, your state has one for you

Doing nothing is another *very* common "plan." Many people procrastinate and don't do anything for any number of reasons. They think they're too busy. Or they don't own enough. Or they're not old enough. Or they're confused and don't know what to do or who can help them.

What happens if you don't do anything? If you own assets in your name and you become incapacitated, the court can take control just as we explained. And when you die, your estate will go through probate.

The only difference is that your assets will be distributed according to state law. Every state has laws for the distribution of assets for those who die without a Will. So, if you haven't written a Will, or if your Will is not accepted by the court, the state has a Will *for* you. The problem is that it probably is *not* what you would have wanted.

For example, in many states if you are married and have children, each will receive a share of your estate. This means your spouse could receive only a fraction of your estate, which may not be enough for him/her to live on. Also, the laws in most states allow for the inheritance of property only by blood-line—so a companion, special friend, or charity would not receive anything.

If you have minor children, the court will control their inheritances and it will appoint their guardian(s)—without knowing who you would have chosen.

And, finally, it can be expensive and time consuming to look for heirs. (All costs, of course, are paid from your assets.) And if no heirs are found, the state in which you live will become your heir.

Doing nothing—for whatever reason—is probably the worst possible "plan." Because you have absolutely NO control.

If you have been procrastinating, we hope the information in this book will be your "call to action"—that you will finally be motivated to do something. A Living Trust does not have to be complicated or expensive. But even if you decide not to have one, we hope you at least get a Will so you'll have some say over who receives your assets.

3 LOSING CONTROL WITH JOINT OWNERSHIP

Joint ownership is probably the most commonly used estate "plan"—although you may not have thought about estate planning at the time you purchased the asset. If you are married, you and your spouse may own many of your assets jointly. After all, that does seem like the fair thing to do, doesn't it? (The fact that it doesn't cost anything to set up also contributes to its popularity.) Joint ownership is also frequently used between parents and their adult children.

The type of joint ownership most people use (and the one we will be discussing here) is called "joint ownership (or joint tenants) with right of survivorship."

Many people have come to rely on joint ownership as an alternative to Wills and probate. Even some professionals recommend it as a way to avoid probate.

Doesn't Joint Ownership Avoid Probate?

Not really—usually it just *postpones* it. When one joint owner dies, ownership *will* transfer to the other owner without probate. (Because that person's name is already on the title, the court does not have to get involved.) But when the surviving owner dies without adding another owner (which often happens), or if both owners die at the same time, the asset *must* be probated before it can go to the heirs.

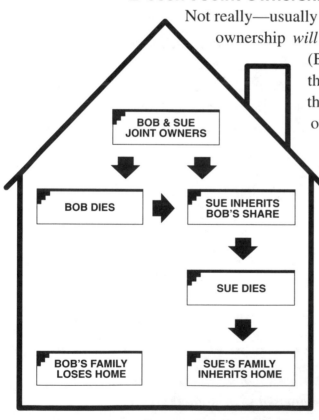

When one joint owner dies, his/her share immediately goes to the other owner. Using joint ownership can cause you to unintentionally disinherit your own family.

Are There Other Problems With Joint Ownership?

Joint ownership probably causes more problems than any other estate plan. It can even cause you to unintentionally disinherit your own family, as this illustration shows.

That's because, if you die first, you have no way of controlling what happens to your jointly owned assets. They are not controlled by your Will because the transfer of ownership takes place *immediately* upon your death. So, even if your Will says you want someone else to receive your share of a jointly owned asset, it will still go to the surviving owner—who can then do whatever he/she wants with it.

If you and your spouse own assets jointly, this would cause you to disinherit any children you have from a previous marriage. Your spouse could include your children in his/her Will now, but you still can't be sure they will inherit. Your spouse could always write a *new* Will and disinherit your children. Or your spouse could add a new co-owner (like a new spouse), who would then own the asset when your spouse dies.

Disinheriting can be a problem even if you don't have children because if you die first, your co-owner's family (not yours) will eventually inherit your jointly owned assets—even though the assets had once been half yours.

There are other risks when you use joint ownership. For example:

- It's very easy to *add* a co-owner. But taking someone's name *off* the title can be very difficult. If your co-owner doesn't agree, you could end up in court.
- Your assets are exposed to your co-owner's debts and obligations. For example, if you add your adult son on the title of your home and he is successfully sued, you could be forced to sell your home.
- Your co-owner could transfer his/her share to someone else without your knowledge or approval. (This would change the type of joint ownership to "tenants-in-common" which is explained later.)
- If you add a minor as a joint owner of an asset (especially real estate, automobile, boat, stocks, etc.), the only way to sell or refinance the asset later is through a court guardianship, which will not end until the minor becomes an adult.
- There could be gift and/or income tax problems. (We'll explain both of these later—gift taxes in Part Nine, income taxes later in Part One.)
- If your estate is larger, you could be limiting your tax planning options.
- And if your co-owner becomes incapacitated, you could find yourself with a new "co-owner"—the court!

Why Would The Court Get Involved If My Co-Owner Is Incapacitated?

Many people mistakenly think that joint ownership of all assets is the same as a joint bank account, on which *either* owner can sign checks, make deposits

Joint ownership causes all kinds of problems

and withdrawals, etc. But on many assets, especially real estate, *all* signatures are required to transact business. If you need your co-owner's signature to sell or refinance and he/she is incapacitated, you'll have to ask the court to appoint someone to act for your co-owner—even if the ill owner is your spouse. And, remember, once the court gets involved, it will usually stay involved to protect that owner's interests.

Other Kinds Of Joint Ownership

While "joint owners (tenants) with right of survivorship" is the most commonly used form of joint ownership, there are others.

■ Tenants-in-Common

One kind of joint ownership is called "tenants-in-common." Even though it works very differently from "joint tenants with right of survivorship," people often confuse them. Under tenants-in-common, when one of the owners dies, that owner's share will be distributed as directed in his/her Will (or to the heirs if there is no Will). It will not go to the other owner unless the Will says so—and it will not avoid probate.

■ Community Property

Nine states—Arizona, California, Idaho, Louisiana, Nevada, New Mexico, Texas, Washington, and Wisconsin—have a form of joint ownership between spouses commonly called "community property." Community property automatically goes to your surviving spouse—unless your Will states otherwise.

The problem with both tenants-in-common and community property is that you could find yourself with *several* new co-owners when your co-owner dies and the heirs inherit the property. Sometimes it's hard enough to get two people to agree. Imagine how difficult it could be to get *several* owners to reach an agreement, especially if you are trying to sell a piece of real estate. You could also have the same problems we mentioned earlier (incapacity, lawsuits, etc.). But with *several* owners involved, your risks and problems are multiplied.

■ Tenants-by-the-Entirety

Some states have another form of joint ownership between spouses called "tenancy-by-the-entirety." Just like joint tenants with right of survivorship, when one spouse dies his/her share *automatically* goes to the surviving spouse, even if the Will says otherwise. So you have many of the risks we mentioned earlier, like unintentional disinheriting and court interference if one spouse becomes incapacitated. But, as tenants-by-the-entirety, neither spouse can transfer his/her half to someone else without the other's approval—which joint tenants with right of survivorship and tenants-in-common can both do.

Is Joint Ownership Worth The Risks?

Maybe joint ownership will work for you—but then again, maybe it won't. With joint ownership, you're playing a kind of "estate planning roulette" with your family. Your assets could still end up in probate, your co-owner could become incapacitated, you could be sued—you could even disinherit your own children. If joint ownership is starting to sound complicated, that's because it can be. Just remember that whenever you have a co-owner, you could easily lose control.

With a Living Trust, you don't have these risks. Even if you die first, you can keep full control of your assets—including who inherits them after you die.

4 LOSING CONTROL BY GIVING AWAY ASSETS

Some people actually re-title assets in their children's names while they are living (which, as the owner, you can certainly do), thinking it will make things easier for their children when something happens to them. This *will* avoid probate of the assets after you die and prevent the court from taking control of them if you become incapacitated. But it can create *all kinds* of problems.

The first problem with giving away an asset is—it's gone. What if you want or need it back? You may think your children would give it back to you. But things change in families, you know. Your children could sell the asset against your wishes, lose it to their creditors, or be influenced by a spouse. If you outlive your children or they divorce, a daughter (or son)-in-law could end up owning the asset. Would he/she give it back to you?

The second problem has to do with taxes. Currently, whenever you give someone other than your spouse more than $10,000 in one year, a *gift tax* may be involved. (We'll explain gift taxes in Part Nine.) And when your children sell the asset, there will probably be a substantial *capital gains tax*.

That's because the asset would not receive a *stepped-up basis*. The *basis* of an asset is the value used to determine gain or loss for income tax purposes—in other words, what you paid for it. If you give an appreciated asset to your

Giving away assets can cause tax problems

children while you are alive, it keeps *your* basis (what you paid for it). But if they receive it as an inheritance (through a Will or Trust), it receives a new *stepped-up* basis—and is re-valued as of the date of your death.

Here's what this can mean to your children. Let's say you purchased your home in 1955 for $20,000 and it's worth $150,000 when you die. If your children receive it as an inheritance after you die, the basis would be $150,000. And if they sell it for $150,000, they would pay no capital gains tax. But if you give it to your children while you are alive, the basis would be $20,000 (what you paid for it). If they then sold the house for $150,000, they would pay $26,000 capital gains tax on the $130,000 gain. (The top capital gains rate on assets held longer than 18 months is now 20%; 20% of $130,000 = $26,000).

Gifts Do Not Receive A Stepped-Up Basis

	Transfer By Gift While You're Living (No Stepped-Up Basis)	Transfer By Inheritance Through Your Will Or Trust (Stepped-Up Basis)
Selling Price	$150,000	$150,000
Basis	-20,000	-150,000
Gain	$130,000	$0
Capital Gains Tax (20%)	$26,000	$0

If you give away an appreciated asset while you are living, it keeps your basis. If the asset is transferred by inheritance through your Will or Trust after you die, it receives a new stepped-up basis and is re-valued as of the date of your death. This can save the new owner a considerable amount in capital gains tax when the asset is eventually sold.

Substantial gifts may also disqualify you from receiving Medicaid and Supplemental Security Income (SSI) benefits for a significant period of time.

You could "sort of" give away an asset—by placing it in joint ownership with your children. But you've just read about the risks of joint ownership. Plus you may have a gift tax liability. (Remember, more about gift taxes in Part Nine.)

Gifting can be a great way to reduce estate taxes if your estate is larger and you can afford to give away an asset. (We explain estate taxes in Part Three and gifting in Part Nine.) But never give away an asset you may need later. And make sure you get assistance from an experienced professional. Otherwise, there could be some serious tax consequences for both you and your children.

A Living Trust will make things easier for your family when something happens to you—without having to give away your assets and losing control.

5 LOSING CONTROL WITH BENEFICIARY DESIGNATIONS

Using beneficiary designations to transfer assets is becoming more and more common. That's because many assets today—like insurance policies, IRAs, retirement plans, and some bank accounts (like pay-on-death accounts)—let you name a Beneficiary. And when you die, these assets will be paid directly to the person(s) you have named as your Beneficiary(ies)—without probate. At least that's the way it's *supposed* to work.

Here are some examples of situations you may not have considered:

■ If your Beneficiary dies before you (or you both die at the same time), the proceeds will have to go through probate so they can be distributed with the rest of your assets.

■ If your Beneficiary is incapacitated when you die, the court will probably take control of the funds through a "living probate." That's because most institutions (an insurance company, for example) will not knowingly pay to an incompetent person, and will probably insist on court supervision.

■ If you list a minor child as a Beneficiary, you could be setting up a court guardianship for the child. That's because most institutions (again, like an insurance company) will not knowingly pay these funds directly to a minor—nor will they pay to another person (like a parent) *for* the child. They just do not want the potential legal liabilities, and will usually require proof of a court-supervised guardianship.

■ If you list "my estate" as the Beneficiary, the court must determine who "my estate" is. The funds will go through probate and will be distributed with the rest of your assets.

Even if the funds *are* paid to the Beneficiary you have named, things may not work out as you had intended. For example:

■ It's possible the person you name as Beneficiary may not be responsible enough to handle such a large sum of money. For example, he/she could be too easily influenced by a spouse or others, make bad investment decisions, or could lose the funds to a creditor.

■ If you name someone as a Beneficiary *with the understanding* that the funds will be used to care for another or will "be held" for that person until a later time, you have no guarantee your wishes will be followed. For example, if you name the parent of a minor grandchild as Beneficiary with the understanding that the money is for the child, you cannot be sure the child will ever see the money.

■ If your estate is larger, you could be limiting your tax planning options. This could cause serious tax consequences later on for your family.

Using beneficiary designations to transfer assets directly to your loved ones after you die may seem simple. But you can easily lose control.

With your Living Trust as the Beneficiary, you—not the courts or Uncle Sam— will keep control over the full proceeds, even if your loved one is irresponsible, a minor, incapacitated or has died before you.

SUMMARY

Now you know about the five "plans" most people use:

1 **Wills**
2 **Doing Nothing**
3 **Joint Ownership**
4 **Giving Away Assets**
5 **Beneficiary Designations**

And you know how you can lose control when you use them. We could go on about potential problems, but you've probably got the general idea by now.

Let's move on to the sixth plan—the Revocable Living Trust—and see why it gives you far more control over your assets than any of these other plans.

Part Two

....

KEEPING CONTROL WITH A REVOCABLE LIVING TRUST

Part Two—
KEEPING CONTROL WITH A REVOCABLE LIVING TRUST

Now that you know how you can lose control with other "plans," let's look at how you can *keep* control with a Revocable Living Trust.

In this section, you will learn what a Living Trust is and how it works. You'll learn about the many benefits of a Living Trust—which go far beyond avoiding probate. We'll even tell you what a Living Trust does *not* do, and if there are any disadvantages of having one.

And, finally, we'll tell you why Living Trusts have become so popular and why you may not have been told about them before.

WHAT IS A REVOCABLE LIVING TRUST?

A Revocable Living Trust is a legal document that, to many of us, looks much like a Will. And, like a Will, it includes your instructions for who you want to handle your final affairs and who you want to receive your assets after you die.

But, *unlike* a Will, a Living Trust:
- Does not go through probate.
- Prevents the court from controlling your assets at incapacity.
- Gives *you*—not the courts—control over the assets you leave to your minor children or grandchildren.

And it does *much* more, as you will soon see.

Compare a Will and a Revocable Living Trust

	Will	Revocable Living Trust
Used 100s of Years	✔	✔
Names Someone To Handle Final Affairs	✔	✔
Names Who You Want To Receive Assets	✔	✔
Avoids Probate		✔
Prevents "Living Probate"		✔

Before we go much further, we want to make clear that there are different *kinds* of Trusts. For example, an *Irrevocable Trust* is frequently used in tax planning. Usually, after an Irrevocable Trust has been set up, you cannot change it or remove assets that have been transferred into it. We'll explain some of these in Part Nine.

A *Testamentary Trust* is created after you die by a provision in your Will. It can be used in tax planning or to manage assets for minors or other Beneficiaries. However, a Testamentary Trust does *not* avoid probate and it provides *no* protection if you become incapacitated—because it is part of your Will. Also, in some states, a Testamentary Trust is subject to ongoing court supervision.

The kind of Trust we are discussing in this book is a *Revocable Living Trust.* (To keep things easy, we will often refer to it simply as a "Living Trust," and even sometimes just as "the Trust" or "your Trust.") The legal name for a Living Trust is a *revocable inter vivos trust. Inter vivos* means that it is created while you are living. *Revocable*, of course, means that it can be revoked—changed, or discontinued.

Why Does A Living Trust Avoid Probate And Prevent Court Control At Incapacity?

When you set up a Living Trust, you transfer *ownership* of your titled assets (home, other real estate, bank accounts, stocks, etc.) from your individual name to the name of your Living Trust—which *you* control.

For example, you would change the titles on your assets from "John and Mary Smith, husband and wife," to "John and Mary Smith, Trustees of the Smith Family Trust dated January 1, 199_."

Technically, *you* no longer own anything—everything is now in the name of your Trust. So there is nothing for the courts to control when you die or if you become incapacitated. The concept is very simple, but *this* is what keeps you and your family out of the courts.

> *With a Living Trust, you'll have more control over your assets.*

Do I Lose Control Of The Assets I Put In My Living Trust?

No—you keep full control. You can continue to do *everything* you could do before, including buying and selling assets. You can make changes or even cancel your Trust—remember, it's a *Revocable* Living Trust. In fact, the Internal Revenue Service considers putting assets in a Revocable Living Trust to be a "non-event" because you can take them out at any time. *Nothing changes but the names on the titles.*

As you'll see in the next few pages, not only do you *not* lose control—you'll actually have *more* control over your assets when they are in a Revocable Living Trust than you do now.

Are Living Trusts New?

No, Living Trusts are not new—and they are not tax shelters or gimmicks. They have been used successfully, in one form or another, for hundreds of years and, in fact, go back at least to the Middle Ages.

The concept was used by knights and other nobility who received land in exchange for providing services to the king. For the knight, this usually meant going off to fight wars. To keep the land, the knight had to keep providing his services. After years of fighting the king's wars—and with the increasing availability of money taking the place of the barter system—the weary knight started paying the king a fee instead. And the king would then hire a mercenary to fight in the knight's place.

Eventually the knights got pretty smart and figured out they could transfer the *title* of their land to individuals (like clergymen and church members) who were exempt from paying fees to the king—but the knights retained the *use* of the land for their lifetimes or for several generations to come. This became

Putting Your Assets into a Living Trust Avoids Probate

ASSETS TITLED IN YOUR NAME

ASSETS TITLED IN YOUR TRUST'S NAME (NO PROBATE)

CHANGE TITLES
(Nothing left to probate)

PROBATE

LIVING TRUST

HEIRS

BENEFICIARIES

Assets titled in just your name must go through a probate process before they can go to your Beneficiaries. But assets that you re-title in the name of your Trust completely avoid probate and can go straight to your Beneficiaries. Final income taxes will still have to be paid, but a Living Trust (like a properly prepared Will) can reduce or eliminate estate taxes.

known as a *Trust*, because the knight *trusted* the clergymen to allow him to continue *using* the land. So the knight kept the *use* of his land, the clergymen got title to it—and the king didn't get his fees. This was the beginning of the Living Trust concept as we know it today. (Now, wasn't that interesting?)

Only you can make changes to your Trust

How a Living Trust Works

Your Living Trust Team

To understand how a Living Trust works, you need to understand the roles of the people involved with your Trust and their legal names. The accompanying *Living Trust Team* chart will also be helpful.

■ The Grantor

When you set up your Trust, you become what is called in legal terms the *Grantor* (also called *Creator, Settlor* or *Trustor*). This is the person *whose Trust it is*. If you are married, you and your spouse can be Co-Grantors of one Living Trust, or you can be Grantors of your own separate Trusts. *Only the Grantor (you) can make changes to your Trust. That's the key. That is how you keep control.*

■ The Trustee

You will name a *Trustee* to manage the assets in your Trust. This can be anyone you wish, including yourself. If you are your own Trustee (as many people are), you will continue to handle your affairs for as long as you are able. If you are married, you and your spouse can be *Co-Trustees*. This way, either of you can automatically act for the other (just like a joint checking account) and, if one of you becomes incompetent or dies, the other *instantly* has control of all Trust assets—*with no court involvement*.

You don't have to be your own Trustee if you don't want to or don't feel you are capable. There are many qualified institutions which manage Trusts professionally (these are called Corporate Trustees), or you can name another individual (like an adult son or daughter). In Part Four, we'll discuss your options in detail.

Even if you name someone else as Trustee, *you're still in control*. As long as you are competent, you can replace your Trustee at any time—because you are the *Grantor* of your Trust.

Your Successor Trustee steps in when needed— with no court interference

■ **The Successor Trustee**

You need to name someone you know and trust as your *Successor Trustee* to step in and manage your Trust if the Trustee becomes incapacitated, dies, or decides he/she no longer wants to be Trustee.

For example, if you are the only Trustee, someone will need to step in and manage your Trust if you become incapacitated and when you die. Even if you and your spouse are Co-Trustees, eventually you will both die and you may both become incapacitated before then. So you need to have a "back-up," someone you trust who can step in and take over for you.

Successor Trustees can be individuals (trusted friends, adult children, other relatives) and/or a Corporate Trustee.

■ **The Beneficiaries**

In a Living Trust, the people and/or organizations who will receive your assets and possessions when you die are called your Beneficiaries. Most people leave their assets to relatives, but you can leave them to anyone or to any organization(s) you wish—many people like to include a favorite charity, foundation, religious group, or fraternal organization.

Now, let's look at the roles these people have when you die and if you become incapacitated.

What Happens When You Die?

Your Successor Trustee (or Co-Trustee) will have the same responsibilities an Executor would if you had a Will. But since he/she does *not* have to report to the court, everything can be done more efficiently and privately.

Your Successor (or Co-Trustee) collects any income, pays your final bills, sees that tax returns are filed, and then follows your instructions for distributing your assets—even selling assets, if that's what you wanted. Since all of your assets are titled in the name of your Trust, it's very easy for your Successor Trustee to conduct business.

What Happens If You Become Incapacitated?

Your Successor Trustee (or Co-Trustee) automatically steps in and handles your financial affairs for you for as long as necessary. He/she can write checks, make deposits, apply for disability benefits, pay bills, even sell assets.

Your Living Trust Team

Grantor(s): Person(s) creating the Trust—you (and your spouse). (Also called Creator, Settlor or Trustor.)

Trustee(s): Manages the Trust now. Usually you (and your spouse) and/or a Corporate Trustee (bank or trust company).

Successor Trustee(s): Will step in and manage the Trust for as long as necessary if you (and your spouse) become incapacitated. At your death(s), your Successor will distribute your assets according to your instructions. Successor Trustees can be adult children, trusted friends and/or a Corporate Trustee. You should name more than one, in order of your preference, in case your first choice is unable to act.

Beneficiaries: Persons and/or organizations who will ultimately receive the assets in your Trust when you (and your spouse) die.

Children's Trust: If you have minor children, you will want a Children's Trust set up *within* your Living Trust. If you (and your spouse) become incapacitated or die, your assets can then be used to care for your children without court interference.

Guardian: Person you have named to raise your children if you (and your spouse) are unable to because of incapacity or death. Must be an adult.

Children's Trustee: Manages the assets in your Children's Trust until the children reach the age(s) you specify they will inherit. Provides for education, maintenance, and support of your children from the assets in the Trust. Can be the same person you name as Guardian, another adult, and/or a Corporate Trustee.

GRANTOR(s)

TRUSTEES(s)

SUCCESSOR TRUSTEE(s)

BENEFICIARIES

CHILDREN'S TRUST

CHILDREN'S GUARDIAN

CHILDREN'S TRUSTEE

CHILDREN

Your Successor Trustee must follow your instructions

No courts or attorneys are required, and everything is done privately. If you recover, you simply start handling your affairs again and your Successor Trustee returns to being your Successor. There is no complicated paperwork or procedure to regain control. Plus, you have peace of mind knowing that, if this should ever happen to you or your spouse, you will be taken care of by someone *you* have selected, someone you know and trust—not someone a court appoints to take care of you.

■ Who Decides If You Are Incapacitated?

Actually, *you* can. Your Living Trust can include a provision that lets you specify who has the authority to determine your ability to manage your affairs. You can include how many and what kinds of doctors you want to examine you. You can even name certain doctors if you wish (just try to choose ones you think will be around longer than you). This will prevent any "conspiracy" to have you declared incompetent.

Why You Can Be Sure Your Successor Trustee Will Follow Your Instructions

Many Living Trusts state that when someone steps in for you and becomes your *acting* Trustee, he/she must keep the Beneficiaries (and sometimes, the other Successor Trustees) informed of all actions. So there can be a lot of "checks" on your acting Trustee's decisions.

In addition, a Trust is a *binding legal contract* when it is signed (unlike a Will, which becomes binding only after you die and it is accepted by the court). Trustees are *fiduciaries*. By law they have a legal duty to follow your Trust instructions and to act in a *prudent* (conservative) manner at all times for the benefit of the Trust Beneficiaries.

Of course, anyone you name as a Trustee, Co-Trustee or Successor Trustee should be someone you can trust. But if an acting Trustee were to "abuse" his/her fiduciary duties (for example, by failing to follow the instructions in your Trust document), he/she could be held legally liable.

What Happens If You Have Minor Children/Grandchildren

If you have minor children or grandchildren, you will need to set up a Children's Trust *within your Living Trust* to prevent the court from taking control of the inheritance. Here's why.

When you (and your spouse) die, your acting Trustee, following your instructions, will probably distribute your assets and dissolve your Trust. If you have minor children or grandchildren, your Trust needs to specify that their inheritance goes immediately from your Trust into one for the children. The Children's Trust "inherits" *for* the minor children—they do not directly receive the inheritance in their own names.

As long as the inheritance stays in a Trust—first in yours, then in one for the children—you will prevent the court from taking control of the inheritance.

You will name a Trustee to manage the inheritance and provide for the children according to your instructions until each reaches the age(s) you specify. If you are a parent (or legal Guardian), you will name a Guardian to raise your children. The Trustee and Guardian can be the same person or different people. The Trustee can also be a Corporate Trustee. The court must still approve the Guardian, but this is only a minor formality when compared to a court guardianship in which the court also controls the inheritance.

With a Children's Trust in your Living Trust, there does not have to be any court guardianship or delays involved with your children's inheritance—even if you become incapacitated. So the Trustee and Guardian will have much more flexibility, and will be able to respond more quickly, to meet your children's changing needs. And with your hand-picked Trustee controlling the money, there may be no real incentive for an irresponsible "ex" or other relative to oppose your choice for Guardian.

Having a Children's Trust in your Living Trust is better than having one in a Will because:

1. With a Living Trust, the assets can go into the Children's Trust without the delays or expenses of probate. But if the Children's Trust is part of your Will, the assets must go through probate *before* they can go into the Children's Trust.

2. A Living Trust can be written so that the Children's Trust can go into effect at your incapacity. But if the Children's Trust is part of your Will, the Children's Trust *cannot* go into effect if you become incapacitated—because *your Will* can only go into effect *after* you die.

Your Trust is prepared from your decisions

How a Living Trust is Set Up

The attorney you select prepares your Living Trust from *your* decisions about what you want to happen if you become incapacitated and when you die. *You* make the basic planning decisions—inventory your assets, decide who will manage them now (Trustee), who will handle your financial affairs if you become incapacitated and when you die (Co-Trustee or Successor Trustee) and who will eventually receive your assets after you die (Beneficiaries).

Trust documents are usually prepared from standardized Trust forms. Many commercial banks, trust companies and financial advisers have sample Trust forms if you want to look at some basic Trust provisions. Your attorney will probably not need to create something completely new and customized for you. In fact, many people only need one basic Trust document to handle all their needs and assets.

This may sound pretty simple and it is—*as long as* you use an estate planning attorney who is experienced in doing Living Trusts and can make the necessary modifications to handle *your* family's situation. It is *very important* that your Living Trust is done properly.

After your attorney has prepared your Living Trust document and you have read and approved it, you sign the Trust and it is usually notarized. Titles and account names for your assets (home, other real estate, bank accounts, investments, etc.)—and many beneficiary designations—will then need to be changed from your name to the name of your Trust. This is called "funding" your Trust.

Now, don't worry—we'll help you with all this. In Part Four, we give you information to help you decide who will be your Trustee, Successor Trustee(s) and how to provide for your Beneficiaries. There is also an Organizer in Part Ten to help you organize your assets. In Part Five, we'll help you find the right attorney to prepare your Trust for you. And in Part Six, we explain—asset by asset—how titles and beneficiary designations are changed to your Trust.

Don't Leave Your Living Trust Unfunded

Your Living Trust is unfunded if you have signed your Trust document but haven't changed titles or beneficiary designations. You do not want to leave your Living Trust unfunded—because anything you leave *out* of your Trust will probably have to go through probate when you die and would be subject to court control if you become incapacitated. *The only way to completely avoid probate at death and court control at incapacity is to put everything you own into your Trust.*

You should be suspicious if someone tells you that you only need to place one asset (or maybe one dollar) into your Living Trust to fund it.

Why It's Important To Change Beneficiary Designations

As we explained earlier, beneficiary proceeds (for example, from insurance policies or an IRA) are intended to be available immediately upon death, paid directly to the Beneficiary *outside* of the probate process.

You now know that doesn't always happen. And even when the proceeds are paid directly to your Beneficiary, what happens then is not always what you intended. Remember, this person may be easily influenced by others, could make bad investments, or could lose the money to a creditor (or spouse).

Making your Living Trust the Beneficiary will prevent the possibility of the court taking control of the proceeds, and give you maximum control over the proceeds, even after you die. For example:

■ If a loved one is incapacitated when you die, your Successor Trustee will be able to use the funds to care for him/her—*without* court involvement.

■ If you wish to provide for minor children or grandchildren, the funds will flow through your Living Trust into a Children's Trust. And the Trustee *you* select (not the court) will manage the assets until each child reaches the age(s) *you* want him/her to inherit.

■ You can keep the funds in Trust to provide for an adult Beneficiary and protect the money from bad investments, creditors, a spouse (or ex-spouse), or undue influence.

Also, having all of your assets—including beneficiary proceeds—flow through your Living Trust is a very convenient way to coordinate your total estate plan through one document.

■ Possible Exception

There may be valid tax reasons to name your spouse as first Beneficiary (and your Living Trust as second Beneficiary) on tax-deferred savings plans like your IRA, 401(k), pension plan, and Keogh. A discussion of your options (the pros and cons) is included in Part Six.

THE BENEFITS OF A LIVING TRUST TO YOU AND YOUR FAMILY

One of the main reasons people initially set up a Living Trust is to avoid probate. But, as they soon find out—and as you'll see in the following pages—avoiding probate is only *one* of the many benefits of a Living Trust.

Avoids Probate When You Die

Saves Money—By avoiding probate, you can potentially save thousands of dollars. So a big chunk of your hard-earned and carefully-managed assets can go to your Beneficiaries—instead of to unnecessary legal fees and court costs.

Takes Less Time—Without court interference, your Successor Trustee will be able to move more efficiently to wrap up your final affairs. So, especially with smaller estates (where no estate tax returns are required, as we'll explain in Part Three), Beneficiaries can receive their inheritances in as little as a few weeks, instead of months or years.

Maximum Privacy—A Living Trust is more private than probate. In most states, no announcements have to be placed in the paper (so no one is "invited" to contest your Trust), and your Trust is not part of the public court records.

If you live in Florida, your Trustee must file a "Notice of Trust" with the probate court after you die to let creditors (and any other "interested parties") know that your Trust exists and that its assets will be available to satisfy any claims they may have. But no information about your assets is required—just your name, when you died, the name and date of your Trust, and the Trustee's name and address.

If you live in California, as of January 1, 1998 your Trustee is required to notify your heirs and Beneficiaries after you die. However, nothing is required to be published or filed with the probate court.

Also, if your state has an inheritance tax, an inventory or summary of assets may be required to be filed with the tax return. But otherwise, no information about your assets, Beneficiaries, or Trustees will ever have to be made public. In fact, a Living Trust is usually so private that disgruntled heirs or opportunity seekers who might have contested your Will may not even know you have died.

So, while a Living Trust cannot guarantee *complete* privacy, it gives you the *maximum privacy possible*. And that is much more than you get with a Will—which is guaranteed to be made *public* through probate.

Minimizes Emotional Stress—With the court restrictions removed, your family can continue its normal daily routines. Your affairs can be handled more efficiently. Your family will be able to grieve your passing privately and get on with their own lives, without the frustration of prolonged court proceedings.

Avoids Multiple Probates

One Living Trust can control all your assets—even real estate you may own in other states. So there will be no need for additional probates in other states.

Prevents Court Control Of Assets At Incapacity

Your hand-picked Successor Trustee (or Co-Trustee) can immediately step in for you. There are no court delays or interferences, you save countless dollars in unnecessary attorney fees and court costs, and your situation stays private.

Prevents Court Control Of A Minor's Inheritance

Your Trustee can automatically step in at your death or incapacity and use your assets to provide for your minor children or grandchildren. Since the court cannot control the inheritance, there are no court delays or interferences.

Your Trustee can react more quickly to provide funds to meet the individual needs of each child. The money you save in attorney fees and court costs can go to provide for the children. No information about the inheritance will be made public. And since your hand-picked Trustee controls the money, relatives (or an "ex") who might only be interested in the inheritance will be discouraged from competing to be named as Guardian.

You Control When Your Beneficiaries Inherit

Maybe you can't take it with you, but with a Living Trust you can sure *keep control* of it after you're gone.

A Living Trust avoids probate and more

49

With a Trust, you control when your Beneficiaries inherit

One of the most powerful benefits of a Trust—unlike a simple Will—is that *you* control when your Beneficiaries will receive their inheritances. Assets can be distributed right away, *or* they can stay in the Trust until your Beneficiaries reach the age(s) you want them to inherit.

For example, you could give children or grandchildren their inheritances in installments—so they don't "blow it" all at one time. You can provide for a loved one with special needs. You can even keep assets in Trust for future generations. (More about this in Part Four.)

More Equitable (Fair) Distributions

Most parents want to treat their children fairly. This may mean giving each an equal share *or* it may mean giving more to one child than another. For example, you may want to leave more to your son who is a teacher than to your daughter who is a doctor. Or you may want to "compensate" a daughter who takes care of you during your last years.

This is often much easier to do with a Living Trust than with a Will. That's because many people who have a Will also own some assets that transfer *outside* the Will—like jointly owned assets that transfer automatically to the surviving owner and assets that will be paid directly to named Beneficiaries. The problem is that the *values* of these assets (home, stocks, savings, retirement plans, and others) *can fluctuate greatly* over time. So how can you be sure your children will receive the *amount* you want each one to have?

For example, let's say you add your daughter as a joint owner on some stocks and you name your son as the Beneficiary of an insurance policy. At the time you decide to do this, the values are approximately what you want each to receive. But when you die, the value of the stocks has *decreased* while the insurance proceeds have stayed the same. Your son receives what you intended—but your daughter receives much less.

If you want your son and daughter to receive equal shares, you could put both their names on all your assets—but what if one wanted to sell and the other didn't? Or you could have all your assets titled in just your name and paid to your estate, and then specify in your Will how much you want each one to receive—but then *everything* will go through probate.

When you change titles and beneficiary designations to your Living Trust and have all your assets in one "pot," your Successor Trustee can look at their values when you die and make sure each Beneficiary receives the amount you intended—without probate.

Prevents Unintentional Disinheriting

With a Living Trust, you don't have to worry about unintentionally disinheriting a loved one. Remember how easily you can unintentionally disinherit your own family when you use joint ownership? But joint ownership isn't the only culprit.

Unintentional disinheriting can happen anytime you give an asset to someone—through joint ownership, a beneficiary designation, or outright—with the understanding that the asset is really for someone else. You can't be sure your "intended receiver" will ever see the asset, because you have no control over what the "messenger" will do with it. He/she could sell the asset, spend the proceeds, give it to someone else—or even lose it to a creditor or spouse.

By contrast, when your assets go through your Living Trust, *you have complete control* over what *your Trust* will do with them. The instructions in your Trust *must* be followed—so there is no risk of unintentional disinheriting.

More Difficult To Contest

A Living Trust *can* be contested, but not nearly as easily as a Will. With a Will, *anyone* can come forward and claim to have a right to part of your estate—without having to hire an attorney. And it's very easy to find out about your estate when notices of the probate proceedings appear in the papers and the entire process is public.

By contrast, since a Living Trust is more private and the assets are not frozen (as they usually are for some time with a Will), the Trustee may have already made distributions to the Beneficiaries by the time a disgruntled "heir" finds out about the Trust. The contesting "heir" must then hire an attorney and sue each Beneficiary and/or the Trustee individually. This complicated, expensive and time-consuming process often discourages the more frivolous claims.

This could also be a valuable benefit if you want to provide for someone who is not related to you—a special friend or companion—or a charitable organization, and you think someone might try to contest your wishes.

You can change your Trust at any time

Effective Pre-Nuptial Protection

A Living Trust can even provide effective pre-nuptial protection. That's because any assets you put into your Living Trust *before you marry* remain the property of that Trust, and stay separate from property accumulated *during* your marriage—even in community property states. You just have to be careful not to combine assets acquired before and after the marriage.

It is not uncommon to see three Living Trusts in one family—each spouse has a separate Living Trust for property acquired *before* the marriage (usually giving it to his/her respective children from a previous marriage or to other relatives), and they have one common Living Trust for assets acquired *during* the marriage.

No Special Government Forms Required

As long as you are a Trustee of your Living Trust, you do not need a separate tax identification number or need to file a separate tax return. You continue to use your social security number and file the same personal income tax returns as before. When your Successor Trustee takes over for you, or if you decide to name someone else as your Trustee, he/she will need to apply for a tax identification number and file a separate tax return for the Trust. Your attorney, CPA or a Corporate Trustee can provide assistance if needed.

Flexible—Can Be Changed Or Cancelled At Any Time

Your Living Trust can change with you throughout your lifetime as your family situation and goals change.

For example, as minor children become adults, and as family members are born, marry, divorce, become ill and die, you will probably find you need to change something in your Trust. You may want to change the Trustee or Successor Trustee, or add a Beneficiary. You may decide to disinherit (or "re-inherit") someone. You may want to change how your Beneficiaries will inherit. You do not need to have your Trust completely redone to make these changes—your attorney will simply prepare an amendment for a nominal cost.

You can take assets out of your Living Trust and put new ones in. You could even cancel your Trust—because it's revocable. And since *all* of your assets (home, other real estate, bank accounts, investments, business interests, stocks, insurance) can be controlled by *one* set of instructions, when you want to make a change to your estate plan it's easy—you only have to change your *one* Trust document.

Easier For Your Family

When you set up a Living Trust, you're doing much of the work that will need to be done after you die—in effect, you are "pre-probating" your own estate.

The process makes you organize your assets, locate documents, and make sure everything is in order now—rather than paying for the courts and attorneys to help your family do it *for* you when you can't.

Taking the time now to get organized—and having all of your assets flow through your Living Trust with *one* set of instructions—will make things much easier for your family at what will be a very emotional and vulnerable time. And you'll feel very good about having done it.

Also, if it turns out that you uncover a problem with an account or a title, think how much better it will be for *you* to straighten it out *now*—instead of your family, attorney and the court trying to sort it out *without* you.

Professional Asset Management

With a Living Trust, you have the option of having a Corporate Trustee (bank or trust company) manage your assets for you. This can be especially valuable now if you don't have the time, ability or desire to manage your assets. It can also be valuable later on, if you become unable to manage them—and if you decide to keep assets in Trust for your Beneficiaries.

A Corporate Trustee has the experience, time and resources to help you achieve your investment goals—*without* you losing control. In Part Four, we'll give you more information so you can decide if you should name a Corporate Trustee as a Trustee of your Trust.

Reduces Or Eliminates Estate Taxes

A Living Trust can include provisions to reduce or even eliminate estate taxes. So can a Will—if it includes a Testamentary Trust. But, remember, with a Will you have probate and court control of assets if you become incapacitated.

We'll explain all about estate taxes—what they are, who has to pay them, how much they are—and how a Living Trust can reduce them in Part Three, which comes next.

Benefits of a Revocable Living Trust

- Avoids time and expense of probate when you die
- Avoids multiple probates if you own real estate in more than one state
- Easier, more efficient administration of your estate
- Prevents court control of assets at physical or mental incapacity
- Gives you maximum privacy
- Minimizes emotional stress on your family
- Can reduce or eliminate estate taxes
- Often allows quicker distribution of assets to Beneficiaries (especially with smaller estates)
- Lets you keep assets in Trust until Beneficiaries reach age(s) you want them to inherit
- Easier to make equitable (fair) distributions to Beneficiaries
- Prevents court from controlling assets when minor children inherit
- Can protect dependents with special needs
- Prevents unintentional disinheriting
- More difficult than a Will to contest
- Provides effective pre-nuptial protection
- Inexpensive, easy to set up and maintain
- Can be changed or cancelled at any time
- Professional asset management if you use a Corporate Trustee
- Lets you keep maximum control while you are living—even if you become incapacitated—and after you die
- Peace of mind

Gives You Maximum Control

The reason a Living Trust gives you all these benefits is simple.

Anytime a *person* is on the title of an asset or is named as a Beneficiary, things can happen over which you have no control. People—including you—get sick, they become injured, they die, they get divorced, they remarry, they go bankrupt—and they can be influenced by others.

This is why many good plans go wrong—and why assets end up in probate, conservatorships, and guardianships. It's why loved ones unintentionally get disinherited. It's why assets end up with children's ex-spouses, creditors and other unintended heirs. It's why the court can take control of your assets if a Beneficiary is a minor, incapacitated, or dies before you. And it's why you can end up paying too much in taxes.

When you transfer your assets to your Living Trust, you don't have these problems. *A Trust is not a person*—it doesn't get sick, die, marry or divorce. Regardless of what happens to the *people* you care about, you can keep control over what happens to the *assets* in your Trust—who gets them and when.

A Revocable Living Trust may not be perfect—few things are. *But no other plan can give you all these benefits and this much control.*

Peace Of Mind

Once you set up your Living Trust, you get the best benefit of all—peace of mind. We all know that this is something we *should* do. And once you've finally taken the time to put your plan in place, you can relax with your family and friends, knowing you've done the best you can do for yourself *and* those you love.

WHAT A LIVING TRUST DOES *NOT* DO

As much as a Living Trust does, it does not do *everything* you might want. For example, a Revocable Living Trust:

Does Not Control Medical Decisions

Many people confuse a Living Trust with a Living Will. Although the names are similar and they are both legal documents, they do very *different* things.

With a Living Trust, you have peace of mind

A Living Trust, which we are discussing in this book, is for keeping control of your *assets*. A Living Will is for keeping control over *medical* decisions. It lets others know how you feel about life support in case of terminal illness. In Part Five, we discuss Living Wills and the Durable Power of Attorney for Health Care, another health care document.

Does Not Protect Assets From Creditors While You Are Living

Because a Living Trust is *revocable*, you still have control of your assets and have access to them at all times. Remember, even the IRS considers a Revocable Living Trust to be a non-event because you can put assets in your Trust and take them out at any time. So, a Living Trust does *not* shield your assets from creditors while you are living.

However, after you die, creditors only have a certain length of time to file claims—so there is some protection then. (More about the creditor claims period later in this section.)

If you are concerned about protection from creditors while you are living, your attorney will be able to suggest some options for you to consider, like a Family Limited Partnership or an Asset Protection Trust (These are explained in Part Nine.)

Does Not Affect Your Income Taxes

A Revocable Living Trust has no effect on your income taxes while you are living. You still must report any income you earn each year and any taxes owed must be paid.

Remember, as long as you are a Trustee of your Trust, you continue to file your same income tax return and use your own social security number. If you are not a Trustee (you name someone else as your Trustee or your Successor has taken over), the Trust will need a separate tax identification number and a separate tax return will need to be filed.

Does Not Help You Qualify For Medicaid

Medicaid is a federally funded health care program that was created primarily to provide health care services for the poor. It also pays for an unlimited number of days of nursing home care, which makes it appealing to many who are *not* poor.

To qualify for Medicaid, you can only have a certain amount of assets and receive a certain amount of income. As a result, many people who want to qualify have only two choices: 1) spend most of their assets, or 2) give away their assets which, depending on the values and when the assets are given away, could cause them to be ineligible for Medicaid benefits for some time.

Some people have thought that putting their assets in a Revocable Living Trust would help them qualify for Medicaid—because the assets would no longer be titled in their individual names. But, because a Living Trust is *revocable*, you still have full control and access to your assets at all times—you haven't really "given them away." The assets in your Living Trust will be considered "available" when either spouse applies for Medicaid. So, putting your assets in a Revocable Living Trust will not qualify you for Medicaid.

> **Note:** Under current law, if you give away assets directly from your Living Trust, it could take longer to become eligible for Medicaid benefits. If you find you need to give away some assets in order to qualify for Medicaid *after* you have put them in your Living Trust, be sure to transfer those assets *back* into your own name *first*. However, before you do anything about trying to qualify for Medicaid, consult with an attorney who specializes in Elder Law.

An alternative to Medicaid is long term care insurance, which was specifically created to help pay for the costs of long term care. You don't have to spend or give away your assets to receive benefits—so you keep your independence.

ARE THERE ANY "DISADVANTAGES" OF A LIVING TRUST?

You may be thinking that a Living Trust sounds too good to be true. Surely, there must be *something* wrong with it.

You will, undoubtedly, hear some negative things about Living Trusts. When you do, consider the source. Does this person have something to gain by my not using a Living Trust? Is this person trying to sell me something? Could this person simply be misinformed?

What some people may think is a disadvantage usually turns out to be either bad or outdated information or, at the most, only a minor inconvenience that pales when compared to the many benefits a Living Trust can provide. Let's take a look at some objections and "disadvantages" you may have heard.

"Probate Isn't Expensive Here, So There's No Reason To Have A Living Trust."

If someone tells you probate is not expensive, ask this person to help you understand how "inexpensive" it is. After all, what is not expensive to a $150 (or more)-per-hour attorney may be very expensive to you.

Ask this person to give you a written estimate of what it would cost to probate your estate—including attorney and executor fees—if you died today. If you are married, ask him/her to write down what the probate would cost if your spouse dies tomorrow.

If you live in a state that has statutory fees (a set fee schedule), this will be fairly easy. The person will be able to determine what the costs will be, depending on the value of your assets. (Make sure you know if the attorney and executor fees apply to assets that do *not* go through probate.)

However, if you live in a state that has "reasonable" fees, this will be more difficult, if not impossible. There will be no way to know how much the probate will cost until the entire process is over. (And when was the last time you bought something without knowing what it would cost?)

Next, ask this person to write down what the attorney and court costs would be if you became incapacitated today—and, if you are married, what they would be if your spouse becomes incapacitated tomorrow. No one should be able to give you a good estimate—because no one can predict how long an incapacity will last and what complications might arise.

And keep this in mind—avoiding the *cost* of probate is only *one* reason to have a Living Trust. Don't forget about the other benefits, which include maximum privacy and control. For many people, the fact that a Living Trust prevents court control of assets if you (and your spouse) become incapacitated is, in itself, worth the entire cost of the Trust.

"A Living Trust Is More Expensive Than A Will."

It will probably cost more *initially* to set up a well-drafted Living Trust than to have a Will prepared. One reason is that a Living Trust usually has more provisions than a Will because it deals with issues while you are living as well as after you die. A Will, of course, only deals with issues after you die.

There may also be some costs to transfer assets into your Living Trust when you set it up, and from your Trust to your Beneficiaries after you die. However, these will be minimal if you and your Successor Trustee do much of the work yourselves. By contrast, with a Will, you will be paying the courts and attorneys to do this *for* you *after* you die. (Which do you think will cost less?)

Of course, with both a Living Trust and a Will, final income tax returns (and estate tax returns, if required) must be prepared.

When comparing costs, don't forget that the true cost of a Will must include the costs of probate when you die, the costs of a possible conservatorship if you become incapacitated, and the costs of a guardianship if you leave assets to minor children. When you make a true comparison, a Living Trust is really quite a bargain.

"With A Living Trust, You Have To Pay Management Fees."

Trustees are entitled to receive a reasonable fee for their services. However, if you are your own Trustee (which is what most people choose to do), you will pay *no* management fees while you are able to manage your Trust yourself. Your Successor Trustee is only entitled to receive a fee when he/she actually steps in for you—but many family members do not accept a fee.

If you name a Corporate Trustee as your Trustee or Successor Trustee, they will charge a management fee only when they start to act for you. Usually this fee is quite reasonable when compared to the services they provide and the experience they have. And often their fee is offset by their investment performance—in other words, the higher earnings they are able to generate on your assets often more than compensates for their fee.

"It Takes Time To Change Titles And Beneficiary Designations."

Yes, it does take some time to change titles and beneficiary designations to your Living Trust. But, remember, you can either do it now or you can pay the courts and attorneys to do it *for* you later.

Most "disadvantages" are just incorrect or outdated information

It's best to just make this process a priority and don't stop until everything has been changed to your Trust. If you only do a few assets now and then, it could take you a long time—or worse, you may never get it done. Stay positive and focused. Remember, you'll probably only have to do this once. Remind yourself *why* you are doing it. Think how much easier things will be for your family. And look forward to the peace of mind you'll have when you're done!

"Refinancing Real Estate Can Be Difficult."

As Living Trusts have become more popular, this isn't the problem that it used to be. However, depending on where you live, you still may encounter some difficulty if you want to refinance property that is in your Trust. Here's why.

Local banks, and savings and loans, often re-sell their mortgages to institutions in the secondary lending market. And they have been reluctant to refinance property in the name of a Living Trust because these secondary lenders did not have any guidelines for whether or not a Revocable Living Trust would be considered an "eligible borrower."

However, since Living Trusts have become so widely accepted and used across the country, the major secondary lenders (Fannie Mae, Freddie Mac and Ginnie Mae) have published guidelines under which they will accept a Revocable Living Trust as an eligible borrower.

If you find refinancing becoming a problem for you, you may want to check with another lender. Or you can transfer the title back to your name *temporarily* (just until the loan has been approved and closed). Then transfer the property *back* into your Trust as soon as possible. This entire process can often be done all at one time when you sign the new loan.

"It's Better To Have The Probate Court's Supervision."

Many people who set up a Living Trust name a family member as Successor Trustee. But some forget to inform this person about his/her responsibilities. As a result, their Successor Trustees don't know what they are supposed to do when the person dies. Some simply do nothing, which can eventually cause some problems and unnecessary expenses. For example, there can be penalties if tax returns are not filed when they are due.

Probate advocates argue that people *need* the supervision of the probate court in order to do things right. *But the solution is not probate—it's education.*

Your Successor Trustee needs to know that, even with a Living Trust, some things *do* need to be done after you die—and *you* need to choose your Successor with care. Remember, your Successor Trustee has the same responsibilities as an Executor—paying final bills, having tax returns prepared, getting appraisals if needed, distributing assets. The only difference is that your Successor Trustee does these things *without* court interference.

In Part Seven, we have included step-by-step instructions for what your Successor Trustee needs to do if you become incapacitated and when you die.

"A Living Trust Is A Waste Of Time And Money Because Most People End Up Going Through Probate Anyway."

If your Living Trust is properly prepared and funded, your assets will *not* go through probate. There are only three reasons your assets would go through probate if you have a Living Trust:

1. *Your Trust is not fully funded.* This can happen if you procrastinate and don't finish changing titles and beneficiary designations, or if you simply forget an asset. It can also happen if you acquire additional assets and don't title them in the name of your Trust.

2. *Your Trust is not properly written.* This can happen if you use a do-it-yourself kit or software program and don't have it reviewed by an experienced attorney. It can also happen if your Trust is prepared by an out-of-state attorney who is not familiar with your state's laws. And it can happen if you use an attorney who is not experienced specifically in Living Trusts. (If you need help finding an attorney, see Part Five.)

3. *You do not have a Revocable Living Trust.* Some attorneys write Testamentary Trusts (in a Will) even when the client asks for a Living Trust. Some attorneys have even written Living Trusts that make all the assets go through probate before they go to the Beneficiaries.

How can you know what you have? If you have a Trust but did not change titles, you either have a Testamentary Trust or a Living Trust that is not funded. If you have any questions about your Trust, read your document. If you can't understand it, it might be worth it to have it reviewed by another attorney. (A Trust officer at your local bank or trust company may also be able to provide some assistance.)

If your Revocable Living Trust has been properly prepared and funded, your assets will avoid probate. We can't say it often enough—it is very important that your Living Trust is prepared by an attorney who has experience in Living Trusts. And your Living Trust must be funded—it can only control the assets that you put in it.

Now, having said all that, in a few states there may be some *procedures* your Beneficiaries will want or need to have done through the probate court—like getting a shorter time limit on creditors' claims or a homestead determination in Florida. (Both are explained below.) Even so, your assets will *not* have to go through probate if they are in your Living Trust.

"Creditors Have Less Time In Probate To Submit Claims."

Probate proponents have long argued that one of the disadvantages of a Living Trust is that creditors have a much longer time during which they can present claims (including lawsuits) after you die than in probate.

With probate, creditors usually have only a few months to present their claims. After this time, they are "forever barred" and the Executor can distribute the assets without fear of any future claims. In some states, the normal statute of limitations is the only time limit that applies if you have a Living Trust.

Because of this, you may have heard that professionals and business owners who are concerned about the risk of a lawsuit after they die should have Wills instead of Living Trusts.

Well, times—and the laws—are changing. California and Missouri recently passed laws so that a Living Trust can have the same time limit for creditors' claims as probate. Similar legislation is pending in other states.

But even if you live in a state that doesn't have this, there is no reason for all your assets to go through probate. You can still have a Living Trust *and* get the shorter time limit on creditor claims that probate provides. Here's how.

You set up a Living Trust just as we have explained and transfer your assets into it. Then, after you die, a probate can be opened to see if any creditors have claims to present. If they do, then *just enough assets to satisfy the claim(s)* can be transferred out of your Living Trust—the rest are protected from probate. And all your assets are protected from any future claims from creditors.

A good example is Florida. When there is no probate (because all your assets are in your Trust), creditors have up to two years to file their claims. But, with probate, they can be limited to just three months. So, if your Beneficiaries are concerned about creditors and don't want to wait for two years, they can open a probate proceeding and start the creditor clock running. No assets have to go through probate—but all creditor claims can be cut off within three months.

Any inconvenience usually pales when compared to all the benefits

"You'll Lose Your Homestead Exemption."

Most states have laws that protect a certain amount of homestead property (house, other buildings and surrounding land used as your residence) from creditors. You might also get a deduction on your property taxes.

In most states, there is a limit on the *value* of property that can be claimed as a homestead. But in some states—including Florida and Texas—there is no *dollar* limit. There is only a limit on the *number of acres* you can own.

For example, in Florida, homestead property can be up to one-half acre within a municipality or up to 160 acres outside a municipality. In Texas, a homestead can be up to one acre in an urban area and up to 200 acres in a rural area. (When John Connally, the former governor of Texas, filed for bankruptcy, he got to keep 200 acres of his ranch—plus the house!) So you can see that homestead exemptions can be very valuable.

In Florida and Texas, putting your home in a Living Trust will *not* cause you to lose your homestead exemption—and it should not in other states.

> **Note:** In Florida, if your Beneficiaries want to sell your homestead property after you die, the title insurance underwriter will probably require a "homestead determination" from the probate court before it will issue a title insurance policy to the new owner. The property will *not* go through probate. Also, this is not something that is required because you put your homestead in a Living Trust—title companies require this *whenever* an inherited homestead is sold.

"You Can Lose Bankruptcy Protection On Your Home."

In some states, a portion or all of your home is automatically protected from creditors if you file for bankruptcy. In a few states, putting your home in a Living Trust can cause you to lose this exemption. But the amount of protection you forfeit (which varies, depending on the state in which you live) may be so insignificant that it doesn't matter. For example, in Missouri, only the first $12,500 of a personal residence can be protected from bankruptcy—certainly not enough to warrant leaving your home (the most valuable asset most people own) out of your Living Trust.

If you are considering filing for bankruptcy, you will want to find out if your state has a homeowner's exemption, how much it is worth and if you will lose any of it by putting your home in your Living Trust. You'll also want to find out about any options you may have.

"ATM Withdrawals Can Be Inconvenient."

If you use a credit card to withdraw cash from your personal checking account through an automatic teller machine (ATM), you may run into a problem. Most banks will not issue a credit card in the name of a Trust, and for the ATM to work, the names on the account and the credit card must match. So if your personal checking account is in the name of your Trust and your credit card is in your name, the ATM won't work. If this turns out to be a problem for you, you can make the withdrawal as a cash advance against the credit card itself, instead of against your checking account.

If your bank issues a separate ATM withdrawal card, you'll probably be okay—especially if you are your own Trustee. However, some banks may still be hesitant to issue an ATM card to a Trust account if they're not sure who is authorized to use it. So they may ask to see your Trust document before approving it. (A Certificate of Trust, explained in Part Five, may satisfy this requirement.) Of course, if you have a good relationship with your bank, you probably won't have a problem.

"A Trustee Has More Personal Liability Than An Executor."

Your Successor Trustee, just like an Executor, is not personally liable for any debts you owe when you die. In other words, their personal assets cannot be seized to pay your debts.

If the Trustee distributes all the assets to the Beneficiaries and Uncle Sam says more taxes are due, the Trustee will be liable for the payment of those taxes if the Beneficiaries will not give the money back to the Trustee. The Trustee can go ahead and distribute assets. But to protect themselves from this potential liability, most Trustees will hold back a "reserve amount" until the IRS sends written confirmation that the taxes have been paid in full. An Executor does not have this liability—but only because the probate court *will not allow* all the assets to be distributed until the confirmation has been received from the IRS.

A Trustee also has certain legal responsibilities. If a Trustee abuses his/her powers—for example, if your Successor Trustee does not follow the instructions in your Trust or uses your assets for his/her own benefit—he/she can be sued by the Beneficiaries and held personally liable. This, remember, is for your protection. And, most Trustees, even family members, take their responsibilities seriously—so this usually is not a problem.

"A Trustee Is Liable For Clean Up Of Contaminated Property."

In 1980, Congress passed a law that defined who is liable for the clean up of hazardous substances. This law is known as CERCLA—the Comprehensive Environmental Response, Compensation, and Liability Act of 1980. Responsible parties include past, and current, owners and operators of contaminated property. Other federal and state laws place similar liabilities on those responsible for clean up of petroleum products and other pollutants.

This means a Trustee can be personally liable for the clean up of any pollutant found on property that is in your Trust. If you are your own Trustee, this won't impact you since you (as the owner of the property) are already liable. However, your Successor Trustee(s) *and* your Beneficiaries could also be liable if the clean up has not been completed and paid for by the time of your death, and the contamination continues after they begin to "manage" the property.

If there is a possibility that property you own is contaminated—for example, if a gas station with underground tanks (or a printing facility or other business that may have used chemicals) was on property you now own—be sure to tell your attorney.

It's best to find out the extent of the contamination and estimated cost of clean up *before* transferring the property to your Trust. Your attorney can then help you with your planning options, which may include:

■ Compensating your Successor Trustee for the liability (life insurance on your life is one possibility). Your Successor Trustee should also be fully informed of the situation *before* agreeing to serve.

■ Leaving this property out of your Trust and letting it go through probate. Under existing law, there is some possibility that letting the property go through probate may reduce the risk of liability for the Executor and heirs.

■ If the cost to clean up the property exceeds its value, you could give it to the U.S. government or to an ex-spouse. (Just kidding!)

"Congress Will Probably Eliminate Living Trusts."

Anything's possible, but this is highly unlikely. Remember, Living Trusts have been around, in one form or another, for hundreds of years. Besides, neither the state nor federal government receives income from probate, so there's no incentive for them to eliminate Living Trusts and make people go through probate. In fact, the states have every reason to *encourage* Living Trusts as a way to reduce the already overcrowded court system.

"Probate Has Better Income Tax Planning Options After You Die."

There *used to be* some *differences* (not necessarily advantages) in how federal income taxes were determined—after you die—when an estate goes through probate and when you have a Living Trust.

Most families were not affected by these differences. However, attorneys (especially pro-probate attorneys) loved to debate the "importance" of these differences and, in some cases, they actually persuaded people *not* to set up a Living Trust because of them.

In recent years, pro-Trust attorneys pushed to make the taxation of Trusts and probate estates equal. Finally, in *The Taxpayer Relief Act of 1997,* the last remaining differences were all but eliminated.

We have included an explanation of these issues in Part Eight, including how they used to be different and how they are now the same—just in case you run into someone who is not current with the law!

Summary

As we mentioned earlier, many of these "disadvantages" simply turn out to be incorrect or outdated information. For most people, any disadvantages either never come up or can easily be planned around. However, if you are concerned about any of these, be sure to mention them to your attorney.

WHY HAVEN'T LIVING TRUSTS BEEN USED MORE IN THE PAST?

Probate is big business

If a Living Trust is such a wonderful thing, why did so many of us get a Will?

"It's The Way We've Always Done It."
We inherited Wills and probate from the English. And after several hundred years, this was a system that worked. Probate laws and procedures are pretty much set, and there are plenty of tested and proven cases to rely upon.

Many law firms have developed entire departments that do nothing but handle probate estates. And as new attorneys are brought into a firm, they are taught how things are done by the more experienced attorneys. So the traditional way of doing things—probate—has been handed down through generations.

"Trusts Are Only For The Wealthy."
Trusts have been around for hundreds of years, too. But they were mainly being done by the larger firms for wealthy clients who needed special tax planning. As a result, Trusts became associated with well-to-do families—like the Rockefellers and the Morgans—who used Trusts to transfer enormous amounts of wealth from one generation to the next.

Some Corporate Trustees, who only managed Trust assets of substantial value, also helped encourage the myth. Because it generally wasn't cost effective for them to handle smaller accounts, they often told people of moderate means they didn't need a Trust.

So, it's easy to see how the public—and many professionals—came to believe that Trusts are only for the wealthy.

Probate Is Big Business
Wills and probate were (and can still be) a lucrative business. Remember, AARP (American Association for Retired Persons) estimates that probating estates generates as much as *$1.5 billion* a year for attorneys, and hundreds of millions more for bonding companies, appraisers and the probate courts.

Building a "Will practice" was pretty simple—and profitable. Some attorneys would draft your Will for a nominal charge because they knew they had an

67

excellent chance of probating your Will when you died (and your spouse's Will when your spouse died). Frequently, the attorney would even be named in the Will to represent your estate(s) in probate.

And if you (and your spouse) became incapacitated, or died leaving minor children, the same attorney would also probably represent you or your children in the court proceedings (yet another source of attorney fees).

You Get What You Ask For

The public didn't know there was another way. And if all you know about is a Will, and you ask for a Will, then you'll probably get...a Will.

Resistance To Change

So, no wonder the legal profession has been reluctant to make changes. With Wills and probate, attorneys had a well established, often lucrative business doing something clients asked for. They were comfortable—why should they take the time to learn a different way? You know the old saying: "If it ain't broke, why fix it?"

So WHY ARE LIVING TRUSTS SO POPULAR NOW?

One simple reason—consumer demand.

With more than 65 million Americans now over the age of 50, more people than ever before are starting to think about how to transfer their assets and provide for their loved ones after they're gone.

They all want to do the right thing—what parent or grandparent doesn't? But things are so much more complicated today. This generation has concerns that most of their parents didn't have to face. For example:

■ With people living longer, they worry about what will happen if they become incapacitated.
■ With second (and even third) marriages so common, many worry about how to provide for their surviving spouses without disinheriting their children and grandchildren.

■ With the high rate of divorce and lawsuits, they worry about their assets ending up in the hands of their children's spouses or creditors.

■ With today's "spend now, save later" attitude and values so different from their own, many worry that their children will not be responsible with the assets they have worked so hard all their lives to accumulate.

■ With so much of our personal information available to others through giant computer databases, they worry about how to protect their privacy.

■ And with tax rates and legal fees so high, they are concerned about how much of their assets their loved ones will actually receive.

In their research (through reading our publications and others), people began to find out what can happen when they use Wills, joint ownership, and beneficiary designations to transfer assets. They learned that, without proper planning, much of their assets can be lost *unnecessarily* to court costs, legal fees, unintended heirs, and taxes.

They also began to find out about Revocable Living Trusts—and they liked what they learned. The Living Trust met their needs far better than any other plan. Here, finally, was a way that not only avoids probate and saves taxes, but also gives them more flexibility and control, and preserves their privacy.

Armed with this knowledge, this generation—one of the largest, and most powerful and influential we have ever had—started asking for Revocable Living Trusts instead of Wills. And the legal profession has been scrambling to meet the demand.

The progress in just the last few years has been nothing short of amazing. Many legal conventions now regularly include Revocable Living Trusts on their agendas. Local, state, and national bar associations sponsor seminars so more attorneys can learn how to draft them.

Thanks, in large part, to the efforts of this generation, it is now much easier than ever before to find an attorney who will offer you the choice of a Living Trust and can prepare one for you.

A Comparison At A Glance

	With No Will	With A Will	With A Living Trust
At Incapacity* (inability to handle your financial affairs)	*Court Control:* Court appointee (conservator/guardian) must keep detailed records, report to court, and usually post bond (even if appointee is your spouse). Court oversees financial affairs, approves all expenses.	*Court Control:* Same as with no Will.	*No Court Control:* Your Successor Trustee manages your financial affairs according to your instructions for as long as necessary.
Court Costs & Legal Fees	Impossible to estimate. Court and attorney usually involved until you recover or die.	Same as with no Will.	No court costs. Minimal legal fees if attorney assistance is desired.
At Death	*Probate:* Court orders your debts paid and assets distributed according to state law.	*Probate:* Debts paid and assets distributed according to your Will (if valid and no contests are successful).	*No probate:* Debts are paid and assets distributed to Beneficiaries by Successor Trustee according to your Trust's instructions.
Court Costs & Legal Fees	Your estate pays all court costs, legal and executor fees (often estimated at 3-8% or more of an estate's value).	Same as with no Will. Costs and fees can increase if Will is contested.	Usually none if no estate taxes (attorney can be helpful for larger estates). Successor Trustee is entitled to a reasonable fee.
Time	Usually 9 months to 2 years before heirs can inherit.	Same as with no Will.	Can be just weeks (larger estates may take longer for estate tax filings).
Flexibility and Control	*None:* Court procedures, not your family, have control at incapacity and death. When you die, assets are distributed according to state law (probably not what you would have wanted).	*Limited:* Same as no Will, except assets are distributed when you die per your Will (if valid and no contests are successful). Will can be changed until your incapacity.	*Maximum:* You can change/discontinue Trust until incapacity. Assets stay under control of your Trust, even at incapacity and after your death. More difficult to contest than a Will.
Privacy	*None:* Court proceedings are public record. Family can be exposed to disgruntled heirs, unscrupulous solicitors.	*None:* Same as with no Will.	*Maximum:* Living Trusts are not public record. Your family can take care of your financial affairs privately.
Minor Child	*Court Control:* Court controls inheritance, appoints guardian. All decisions and financial transactions require court approval. Child receives full inheritance at legal age.	*Court Control:* Same as with no Will. Children's Trust in a Will provides limited protection, but the Will must be probated first and cannot go into effect at your incapacity.	*Minimal Court Control:* Trustee you select manages inheritance and provides funds for expenses until child reaches age(s) you specify. Court approves guardian, but cannot overrule your choice of Trustee and has no control over inheritance.
Court Costs & Legal Fees	Impossible to estimate. Court and attorney usually involved until child reaches legal age. All costs are paid from child's inheritance.	Same as with no Will. Costs may be less with Children's Trust in Will.	Minimal.

*Durable Power of Attorney for Health Care/Health Care Proxy can prevent court interference in medical decisions.

Part Three

....

How to Reduce/ Eliminate Estate Taxes and More
(The ABCs Of A Living Trust)

Part Three—
How to Reduce/Eliminate Estate Taxes and More (The ABCs Of A Living Trust)

By now, you know about the many benefits a Living Trust offers you and your family. But so far we haven't talked much about estate taxes that may have to be paid when you die—and how your Living Trust can reduce or even eliminate them.

In this section, we'll explain what estate taxes are, who has to pay them and how much they can be. We'll explain how additional provisions in your Living Trust can give you powerful tax planning and other benefits—including how you can provide for your surviving spouse for as long as he/she lives, yet keep control over who will eventually receive your assets. So even if you don't have to worry about estate taxes, this may be valuable information for you.

Expenses That Can Reduce Your Estate

When you die, there are basically three ways your estate can be reduced before it can go to your Beneficiaries. One is probate which, as you know by now, can be avoided with a Living Trust. There are also two kinds of taxes—income taxes and estate taxes. Both of these are different from—and in addition to—any probate costs. Let's first look at the income taxes.

Regardless of whether or not you have a Living Trust, your estate must file a federal income tax return for the year in which you die—just as you do now every year. (Depending on the state in which you live, you may also pay state income taxes.) Any income you receive in the year you die must be reported and any taxes due on that income must be paid. A Living Trust has *no* effect on your income taxes.

Expenses That Reduce Your Estate

When you die, your estate can be substantially reduced in three ways:

1) **Probate**, which can be avoided with a Living Trust;

2) **Income Taxes**, which must be paid on any income you receive in the year you die; and

3) **Estate Taxes**, which can be reduced or even eliminated with a Living Trust.

The other tax is the federal estate tax. Fortunately, you can reduce or even eliminate your estate tax bill if you plan ahead. And, as you will see in this section, one easy way to do this if you are married is through your Living Trust. (In Part Nine, we explain other ways to reduce estate taxes that can be used by both married and single people.)

UNDERSTANDING ESTATE TAXES

What Are Estate Taxes?

The federal estate tax is a tax on the net value of your estate (your assets less your debts) at the time of your death. Some people call this the "death tax." Also, some states have their own death/inheritance taxes in addition to the federal tax.

The federal estate tax is expensive. It starts at 37% and quickly goes up to 55%. So, unless you plan ahead, Uncle Sam could become your biggest heir!

What makes the estate tax so *egregious* (that's a great word; it means "flagrantly bad") is that it is, in effect, a *double* tax. Over the years, you've already paid *income* taxes on the money and assets that now make up your estate. When you die, your estate may have to pay taxes on these assets *again*.

Also, estate taxes must be paid in cash—usually within nine months of your death. As a result, assets often have to be sold quickly—at depressed prices— just to pay estate taxes. Because of this, many family farms and businesses do not survive for the next generation. Families are often forced to sell in order to pay the estate taxes. (There is one exception to the nine-month deadline. If you are a business owner and your business is at least 35% of your taxable estate, you may be able to pay the estate taxes in installments, with Uncle Sam as your "banker.")

Uncle Sam could become your biggest heir!

Who Has To Pay Estate Taxes?

Your estate will have to pay estate taxes if the net value (assets minus debts) when you die is more than the "exempt" amount set by Congress at that time. From 1987 through 1997, this amount was $600,000.

In *The Taxpayer Relief Act of 1997*, Congress voted to increase the exempt amount—to $625,000 in 1998, and gradually to $1 million by the year 2006, as shown in the chart below. Also, family businesses that qualify are allowed an additional exemption, which we'll explain in just a moment.

Individual Federal Estate Tax "Exemption"

Year of Death	Estate Tax Exemption*
1998	$625,000
1999	$650,000
2000 and 2001	$675,000
2002 and 2003	$700,000
2004	$850,000
2005	$950,000
2006 and after	$1,000,000

*In 1998, the actual tax on the first $625,000 is $202,050. But everyone gets a tax credit of $202,050. So the first $625,000 is, in effect, exempt from estate taxes. To keep things simple, we refer to this as a $625,000 estate tax exemption.

Of course, an increase in the estate tax exemption is good news. But before you call your Congressman to thank him or her, let's put this one in perspective:

1) By the time it's fully phased in, the $1 million exemption will be about the same as if the $600,000 exemption had been adjusted for 3% inflation since its effective date in 1987.

2) The exemption is still not tied to inflation. Once it hits $1 million in 2006, it will stay there until Congress increases it again.

3) This can all change, of course, with the stroke of a pen. Notice that most of the increase occurs in 2004 and later. Between 1997 and 2003, there will

be one Presidential and three Congressional elections. Many of the current members of Congress will not be around in 2003, and it will be up to a new group of lawmakers to find ways to pay for their entitlement programs. Anything, including a repeal of this law, is possible.

Note: Since there is no way for us to know in what year(s) you will be reading this book, or in what year you (and your spouse) will die, all of the following examples and illustrations in this book were prepared using the 1998 federal estate tax "exemption" ($625,000).

Family Business "Exemption"

Starting in 1998, family-owned businesses and farms that qualify can get an additional exemption for a total estate tax exemption of $1.3 million. (Technically, the IRS calls this an "exclusion.") As shown in the chart below, the amount of this exemption will *decrease* as the individual exemption *increases*.

Family Business Federal Estate Tax "Exemption"

Year of Death	Individual Exemption	Add'l Business Exemption	Total Business Exemption
1998	$625,000	$675,000	$1,300,000
1999	$650,000	$650,000	$1,300,000
2000 and 2001	$675,000	$625,000	$1,300,000
2002 and 2003	$700,000	$600,000	$1,300,000
2004	$850,000	$450,000	$1,300,000
2005	$950,000	$350,000	$1,300,000
2006	$1,000,000	$300,000	$1,300,000

Of course, to qualify for the family business exemption, you will have to jump through a few hoops. Among the requirements:
- The business interest must make up at least 50% of your estate.
- The principal place of business must be in the United States.
- You (or a family member) must have owned and "materially participated" in the business for at least five of the eight years before your death.
- The business must be inherited by a "qualified heir"—a member of your family or a long-time employee (ten or more years).
- For the most part, the business must remain "in the family" and in the U.S. for ten years after your death. With few exceptions, if a qualified heir does not "materially participate" in the business, sells or otherwise disposes of

any portion of the business, loses U.S. citizenship or moves the principal place of business out of the U.S. within ten years after your death, your family will have to pay back some of what they saved in estate taxes from using this additional exemption—plus interest.

As you can see, determining whether you qualify for this additional exemption will not be easy. And, if you do, your family will almost certainly have to file some kind of form with the IRS every year for the next ten years after you die. Plus, by the time the increase in the individual exemption is fully phased in (in 2006), the family business exemption will only be worth an extra $300,000. So, for many families, it will not be worth the trouble and expense. If you think you may qualify, go slowly and discuss it *in detail* with your attorney.

Note: To keep things simple and understandable, we will assume, in the rest of this section, that you do not qualify for the family business exemption.

Planning For Appreciation

Now, if you think your estate isn't large enough to be affected by estate taxes, you *could* just skip over this section. But before you do, consider this: many people don't really know how much they are worth. Assets (especially real estate and stocks) may have appreciated greatly since you bought them. So by the time you add everything up, you may be worth a lot more than you think.

Also, estate taxes are based on the value of your estate *when you die*. Many assets (especially real estate and stocks) can appreciate greatly between now and then. As the following chart shows, even a modest estate can appreciate tremendously in value over time. So while you may not have an estate tax problem now, you could easily have one by the time you die.

Assets can appreciate greatly over time

How Your Estate Can Appreciate Over Time*

Today	In 5 Years	In 10 Years	In 15 Years
$300,000	$441,000	$648,000	$952,000
$400,000	$588,000	$864,000	$1,269,000
$500,000	$735,000	$1,080,000	$1,586,000
$600,000	$882,000	$1,295,000	$1,903,000
$700,000	$1,029,000	$1,511,000	$2,221,000

Assumes 8% growth

Determining Your Taxable Estate

To determine the current size of your taxable estate, you add up the current market value of everything you own and subtract any debts and mortgages. (The Organizer in the back of this book will help you do this easily.) Be sure to include assets you own outright and *your share* of any jointly owned assets.

Assets include real estate, checking and savings accounts, investments (including CDs, stocks, bonds and mutual funds), profit sharing balances, IRAs, pensions, investments in partnerships and/or businesses, notes payable to you, any personal property you own, automobiles, boats, campers, and any benefits to which your estate will be entitled when you die.

Your assets also include—this one may surprise you—the death benefits from *all* life insurance policies on your life for which you have any "incidents of ownership" as defined by the IRS. This would include policies you can borrow against, assign, or cancel, for which you can revoke an assignment, or for which you can name or change the Beneficiary—regardless of who actually *owns* the policy. For example, insurance provided by your employer would be included if you can name and/or change the Beneficiary.

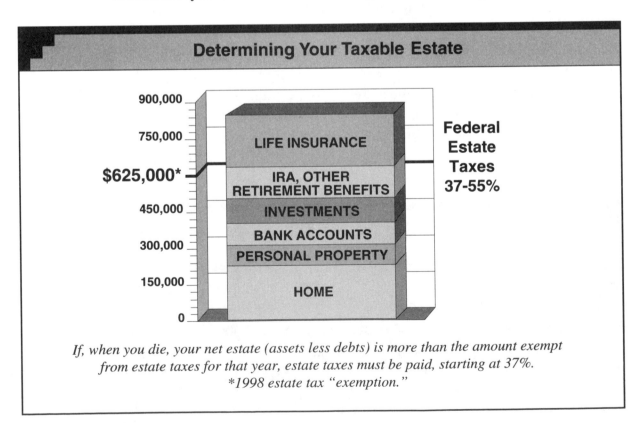

Determining Your Taxable Estate

If, when you die, your net estate (assets less debts) is more than the amount exempt from estate taxes for that year, estate taxes must be paid, starting at 37%.
1998 estate tax "exemption."

■ Add Taxable Gifts

There is one more thing you may need to do before calculating estate taxes: add back in any "taxable gifts" you have made since 1976.

What is a "taxable gift"? Generally, anytime you give anyone other than your spouse more than $10,000 in one year, you have made a taxable gift. If you are married, you and your spouse can each give $10,000, for a total of $20,000 per recipient per year. (Beginning in 1999, this amount will be tied to inflation.)

The gift does not have to be in cash. For example, if you give your son some stocks, or make your daughter a joint owner on your home, these are gifts. And if the value of the gift exceeds $10,000 in one year, the amount *over* $10,000 is a taxable gift—and Uncle Sam wants to know about it.

That's because Uncle Sam wants to make sure you don't give away some or *all* of your assets without paying *any* estate taxes. Otherwise, you could give everything away and have a taxable estate of "0."

In Part Nine we explain more about making gifts and gift taxes.

How Much Will *Your* Estate Have To Pay In Estate Taxes?

As we explained earlier, if you die in 1998 and the net value of your estate is less than $625,000, under current law your estate will pay no federal estate taxes. That's the good news.

But if your estate is over $625,000, here's the bad news. Every dollar over $625,000 will be taxed, starting at 37%. And as the value of your estate increases, the rate quickly jumps to 55%. This means that—unless you plan ahead—from 37¢ to 55¢ of every dollar in your estate over $625,000 will be confiscated by the federal government when you die!

The chart on the next page shows what estate taxes are on various size estates in 1998. Find the one closest to your net estate and see what the tax would be.

Now, what can you do about these estate taxes?

> *From 37-55¢ of every dollar over $625,000 could go to Uncle Sam!*

Federal Estate Taxes in 1998*

Taxable Estate	Estate Tax	% Tax on Amount Over $625,000
$625,000	$ 0	0%
$750,000	$46,250	37%
$1,000,000	$143,750	38%
$1,250,000	$246,250	39%
$1,500,000	$353,750	40%
$2,000,000	$578,750	42%
$2,500,000	$823,750	44%
$3,000,000	$1,088,750	46%

** Every dollar **over** the exempt amount ($625,000 in 1998) is taxed at 37-55%.*

How To Reduce Or Eliminate Estate Taxes

If you plan ahead, you can reduce or, depending on the size of your estate, even eliminate estate taxes. In the simplest terms, there are three ways to do this:

■ **Reduce the size of your estate *before* you die.** If you reduce the *size* of your taxable estate now (by spending or giving away some of it), you will reduce your estate tax *bill*. But you have to make gifts correctly—otherwise, you will end up paying too much in gift/estate taxes. In Part Nine, we explain some of the best ways to do this.

■ **Buy life insurance to pay estate taxes.** Depending on your age and health, buying life insurance can be an inexpensive way to pay any remaining estate taxes. However, if you are the owner of the policy, that will just increase the size of your taxable estate and the amount of estate taxes that must be paid. In Part Nine, we explain how to purchase insurance and keep it out of your taxable estate.

■ **But first, if you are married, include a special tax-planning provision in your Living Trust.** In the rest of this section, we'll explain how this works.

LEAVING EVERYTHING TO YOUR SPOUSE: UNCLE SAM'S PLAN

You may not know it, but if you are married (and your spouse is a U.S. citizen), you already have a "plan" to reduce estate taxes when you die. You didn't sit down and plan it—your dear old Uncle Sam already did it for you.

Here's how "Uncle Sam's plan" works. Currently, when you die you can leave *any* amount of assets (real estate, personal property, investments, etc.) to your spouse and there will be *no* estate taxes at that time. This is called the "unlimited marital deduction" for two reasons: 1) there is *no limit* on the value of assets one spouse can leave to the other, estate tax-free, and 2) the assets you leave to your spouse are *deducted* from your taxable estate. So, if you leave everything to your spouse, *your* taxable estate will be zero.

That sounds pretty good—so far. But when your surviving spouse dies, everything your spouse owns (including the assets you leave your spouse when you die) will be subject to estate taxes before the assets can be distributed to your Beneficiaries.

Of course, your spouse's estate will be entitled to its estate tax exemption. So, in 1998, there will be no estate taxes on the first $625,000 your spouse owns. But guess what? *Both* you and your spouse are entitled to an exemption. And if you leave everything to your spouse, you will *waste* yours.

Leaving Everything to Your Spouse Wastes One Exemption

Bob & Sue $1,250,000	Bob Dies (no estate taxes) →	Sue $1,250,000

Sue's Net Estate	$1,250,000
Sue's Federal Estate Tax Exemption	- 625,000
Sue's Taxable Estate	$ 625,000
Estate Taxes Owed	**$ 246,250**

When you die, you can leave an unlimited amount to your surviving spouse free of estate taxes. But when your spouse dies, the entire estate will be taxed—and only one estate tax exemption (your spouse's) will be available. (1998 exemption used.)

**An A-B
Living Trust
can save
$246,250
in estate taxes**

If you plan ahead, you and your spouse can use *both* your exemptions. In 1998, that will let you leave *up to $1.25 million estate tax-free* to your Beneficiaries—and save $246,250 in estate taxes.

Now you can see why we call this Uncle Sam's plan. Leaving everything to your spouse can cause you to pay a lot more in estate taxes.

It's unfortunate that so many couples do this. But it's understandable. They want to make sure the surviving spouse is provided for, and they want to avoid estate taxes when the first spouse dies. They think they're doing the right thing by leaving everything to each other through their Wills, joint ownership, beneficiary designations—and even their Living Trusts. Plus, it's easy—you don't have to plan ahead to use the unlimited marital deduction.

But planning ahead can be easy, too. With your Living Trust, you can avoid probate, provide for your surviving spouse *and* reduce or even eliminate estate taxes by using *both* exemptions. Here's how.

THE A-B LIVING TRUST SOLUTION

You and your spouse together can set up one "common" Living Trust (just like we've been discussing), of which each of you owns half. For as long as you are both living, you have *one* Living Trust with all your assets in it. Then, when one of you dies, this Trust will automatically split into two *separate* Trusts.

This is called an "A-B Living Trust" because the two separate Trusts are often referred to as Trust A (for the surviving spouse) and Trust B (for the deceased spouse). To help keep these straight, think of Trust A as the one "**A**bove the ground" (for the living person) and Trust B as "**B**elow the ground" (for the deceased person). It is a bit direct but, as a word association trick, it works.

As an alternative, you and your spouse can start out with separate Trusts (instead of one common Trust). While you and your spouse are living, both these Trusts are considered "A" Trusts. (Remember, you're both **A**bove the ground.) Then, when one of you dies, the deceased spouse's Trust becomes Trust B, and the surviving spouse's Trust remains Trust A. (More on separate Trusts later in this section.)

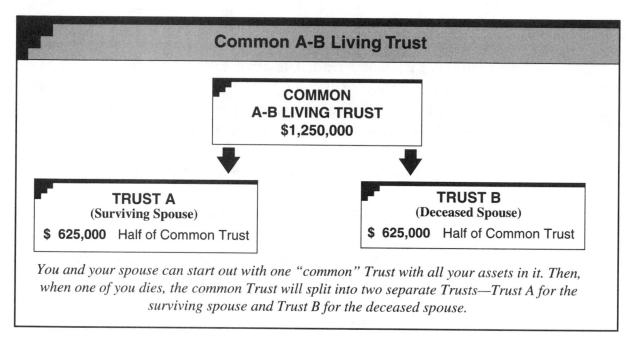

Common A-B Living Trust

**COMMON
A-B LIVING TRUST
$1,250,000**

TRUST A
(Surviving Spouse)
$ 625,000 Half of Common Trust

TRUST B
(Deceased Spouse)
$ 625,000 Half of Common Trust

You and your spouse can start out with one "common" Trust with all your assets in it. Then, when one of you dies, the common Trust will split into two separate Trusts—Trust A for the surviving spouse and Trust B for the deceased spouse.

If you live in a community property state, you and your spouse will probably have a common A-B Trust. If you live in a noncommunity property state, your attorney may feel more comfortable starting out with separate Trusts. Either way works. They are only different while you and your spouse are both living. After one spouse dies, they are exactly the same.

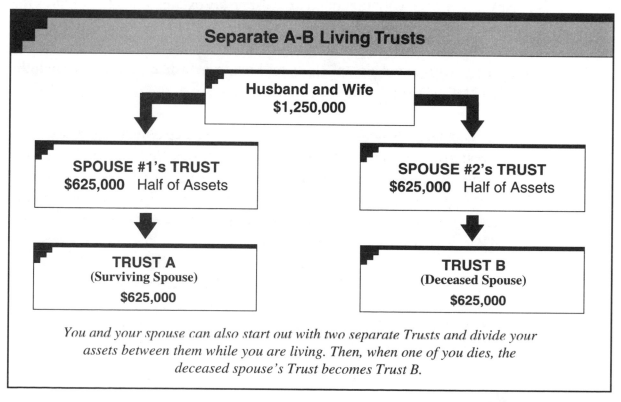

Separate A-B Living Trusts

**Husband and Wife
$1,250,000**

SPOUSE #1's TRUST
$625,000 Half of Assets

SPOUSE #2's TRUST
$625,000 Half of Assets

TRUST A
(Surviving Spouse)
$625,000

TRUST B
(Deceased Spouse)
$625,000

You and your spouse can also start out with two separate Trusts and divide your assets between them while you are living. Then, when one of you dies, the deceased spouse's Trust becomes Trust B.

Leave up to $1.25 million to your children estate tax-free— with no probate

Note: Your attorney may refer to this as a "Living Trust with an A-B provision." He/she may also use different names for the separate Trusts. For example, Trust A is often called a *Survivor's Trust* or *Marital Trust*, because it's for the surviving spouse. Trust B is often called a *Bypass Trust*, because it "bypasses" estate taxes, or a *Credit Shelter Trust*, because it "shelters" the estate tax "credit" ($202,050 in 1998, as explained earlier in this section). We prefer to call them Trust A and Trust B—we just think it's easier to understand.

How An A-B Living Trust Saves Estate Taxes

This is best explained with an example. To keep things simple, let's say you both die in 1998 when the estate tax exemption is $625,000. Also, we will assume that no assets have been left out of your Trust.

If you have a common Trust and its value is *not more than* $1.25 million when the first spouse dies, usually half of the value of the assets is placed in Trust A and half is placed in Trust B. If you start out with separate Trusts, you divide your assets between the two Trusts while you are living. So the assets will already be divided when one spouse dies.

Now, *each Trust* will be entitled to an estate tax exemption—Trust B uses the deceased's $625,000 exemption and Trust A will use the surviving spouse's $625,000 exemption when he/she dies. As the chart at right shows, this simple strategy will shield up to $1.25 million from estate taxes. Tax savings: *$246,250!*

This is not a tax shelter or some tricky way to avoid paying taxes. The estates *are* being taxed when both spouses die—*you are both simply using the exemptions to which you are entitled.*

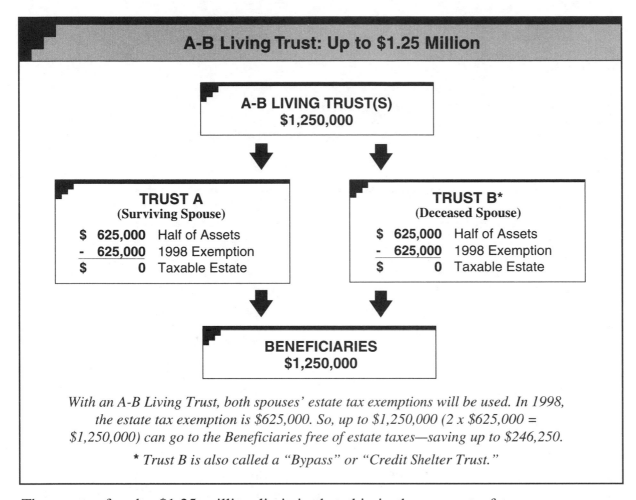

A-B Living Trust: Up to $1.25 Million

A-B LIVING TRUST(S)
$1,250,000

TRUST A
(Surviving Spouse)

$	**625,000**	Half of Assets
-	**625,000**	1998 Exemption
$	**0**	Taxable Estate

TRUST B*
(Deceased Spouse)

$	**625,000**	Half of Assets
-	**625,000**	1998 Exemption
$	**0**	Taxable Estate

BENEFICIARIES
$1,250,000

With an A-B Living Trust, both spouses' estate tax exemptions will be used. In 1998, the estate tax exemption is $625,000. So, up to $1,250,000 (2 x $625,000 = $1,250,000) can go to the Beneficiaries free of estate taxes—saving up to $246,250.

* Trust B is also called a "Bypass" or "Credit Shelter Trust."

The reason for the $1.25 million limit is that this is the amount of two exemptions in 1998 (2 X $625,000 is $1,250,000). This amount will go up as the estate tax exemption increases. For example, in the year 2000, the estate tax exemption will be $675,000. So you would then use this as an illustration of how an A-B Living Trust would work if the estate is not more than $1,350,000 (2 X $675,000 is $1,350,000).

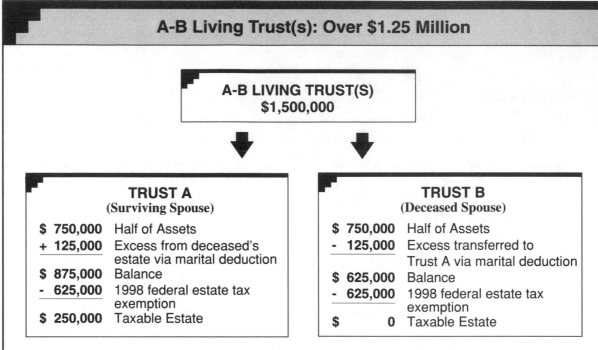

A-B Living Trust(s): Over $1.25 Million

A-B LIVING TRUST(S)
$1,500,000

TRUST A (Surviving Spouse)			**TRUST B** (Deceased Spouse)	
$ 750,000	Half of Assets		$ 750,000	Half of Assets
+ 125,000	Excess from deceased's estate via marital deduction		- 125,000	Excess transferred to Trust A via marital deduction
$ 875,000	Balance		$ 625,000	Balance
- 625,000	1998 federal estate tax exemption		- 625,000	1998 federal estate tax exemption
$ 250,000	Taxable Estate		$ 0	Taxable Estate

If the combined estate is more than two exemptions ($1.25 million in 1998), usually only an amount equal to one exemption ($625,000) stays in Trust B. The rest is added to Trust A (the surviving spouse's Trust). By making full use of both spouses' exemptions, estate taxes will only be due on $250,000 of this $1.5 million estate.

■ **If You Own More Than $1.25 Million**

If the value of the Common Trust is *more* than $1.25 million when the first spouse dies, usually only $625,000 (the amount of one exemption in 1998) is placed in Trust B. The rest, as shown above, is added to Trust A (the surviving spouse's Trust). If you already have separate Trusts and the deceased spouse's Trust (Trust B) is more than $625,000, the excess is usually transferred to the surviving spouse's Trust A.

Of course, you could have more in Trust B. But then estate taxes would have to be paid on everything over $625,000. By not having more than $625,000 in Trust B, there are no estate taxes on Trust B. And there are none due now on the rest of the deceased spouse's assets because they are transferred to Trust A using the marital deduction. So no estate taxes will be due until the surviving spouse dies. Then, his/her exemption will be used on the assets in Trust A.

So, in 1998, by making full use of both spouses' $625,000 exemptions, estate taxes will only be due on $250,000 of this $1.5 million estate.

Keep in mind that, since the estate tax exemption will increase over the next few years, how much should go into each Trust will depend on the total value of the estate and the amount of the exemption when the first spouse dies.

Provide for your spouse and keep control

Provide For Your Surviving Spouse

You may be thinking, "Saving taxes is great. But if our assets are divided and in separate Trusts, what happens if my spouse doesn't have enough in his/her Trust? Will my spouse be able to get money from my Trust after I die?"

Yes—and that's another reason why many couples find an A-B Living Trust so appealing. Even after you have died and the assets are in two separate Trusts, you can still provide for your surviving spouse *for as long as he/she lives*.

Let's assume, for ease of explanation, that the husband dies first. When the assets are divided into Trust A and Trust B (as shown in the chart on the next page), his wife now has complete control over Trust A and can do whatever she wants with its assets. (Remember, this is now her Trust.) In addition, she can receive any income generated by Trust B for as long as she lives and can even withdraw from the principal if needed for health, education, maintenance and support. And, if she is the Trustee, she could also change the investments.

There are some restrictions if she receives money from Trust B for other reasons, but these areas cover anything she would need for normal living expenses. She cannot have 100% control over the assets in Trust B, because that would legally give her ownership of them, causing them to be taxed when she dies. (Because of this, if you want your surviving spouse to be Trustee of Trust B, your attorney may want a Co-Trustee named to act with your spouse.)

The surviving spouse, then, has complete control over her own Trust (Trust A) plus, for the rest of her life, she can receive all the income from Trust B and principal from it when needed for the purposes explained above. Then, when she dies, the assets in both Trusts will go to the Beneficiaries without probate—and, in 1998, up to $1.25 million will be estate tax-free.

Keep Control

There is something else the A-B Living Trust does that a lot of people, even those who *don't* have an estate tax problem, like. It lets you keep control of your share of the assets—even if you die first.

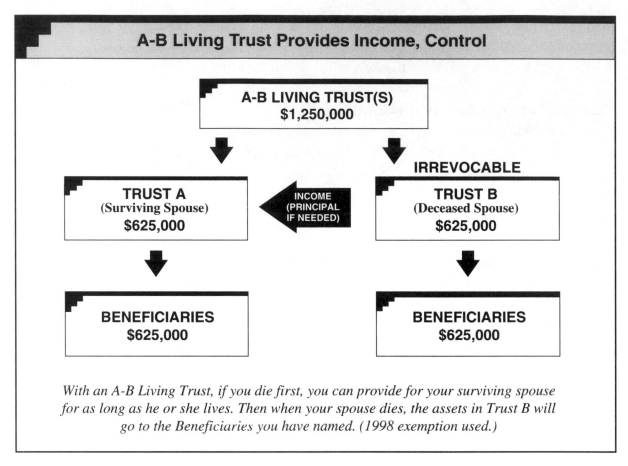

A-B Living Trust Provides Income, Control

A-B LIVING TRUST(S)
$1,250,000

TRUST A
(Surviving Spouse)
$625,000

INCOME
(PRINCIPAL
IF NEEDED)

IRREVOCABLE

TRUST B
(Deceased Spouse)
$625,000

BENEFICIARIES
$625,000

BENEFICIARIES
$625,000

With an A-B Living Trust, if you die first, you can provide for your surviving spouse for as long as he or she lives. Then when your spouse dies, the assets in Trust B will go to the Beneficiaries you have named. (1998 exemption used.)

As the chart above shows, when the first spouse dies, Trust B becomes *irrevocable*—the instructions cannot be changed by anyone (not even by the surviving spouse).

So, even if you die first, you can be sure your share of the proceeds will go to whomever *you* have named as Beneficiary(ies). *Your* Beneficiaries could be the same as your spouse's—or, as the chart shows, they could be *different*.

This could be important if either of you has children from a previous marriage and you want to provide for them—or if you want to make sure that, if your spouse later remarries, your part of the estate doesn't end up going to your spouse's new husband or wife!

If you wish, your spouse can continue to enjoy your assets while he/she is living. For example, if you die first, you may want your spouse to continue to live in the home you have owned together. Then, when your spouse dies and the house is sold, your share of the proceeds will go to whomever you have named as Beneficiary(ies)—your children from your first marriage, other relatives, etc.

You *can* give your spouse limited ability to change Beneficiaries of your Trust (Trust B)—if, for whatever reason, you want to do that. But unless this provision (called a "limited power of appointment") is specifically included in the Trust document, your surviving spouse will only be able to make changes to Trust A (his/her Trust).

Of course, there is no way for you to know now if your Trust will be Trust A or Trust B (because you don't know which of you will die first). It doesn't matter—you simply specify in the Trust document that, if you die first, certain instructions will apply to Trust B. Your spouse will do the same.

So an A-B Living Trust lets you reduce or even eliminate estate taxes, provide for the surviving spouse for as long as he/she lives, *and* keep control over your share of the assets—even if you die first.

Dividing Assets Between Trust A And Trust B

Remember, if you have a common A-B Living Trust, when one spouse dies the Trust will split into two separate Trusts. At this time, the Trustee (probably the surviving spouse) will need to decide which assets to put in Trust B and which ones to put in Trust A.

If you have separate Trusts, your assets will already have been divided. But, depending on how your document is written, you may be able to "swap" assets between Trust A and Trust B.

How do you know which assets to place into which Trust? It would be smart to place into Trust B assets that will appreciate the most in value over the next few years. That's because the assets in Trust B are only valued and taxed *when the first spouse dies*. They are *not* re-valued later when the second spouse dies—and they may be worth much more.

For example, let's say you die in 1998 and you own some investments that are worth $625,000. They are placed in Trust B. No estate taxes will be due at this time because the value of Trust B does not exceed your $625,000 exemption. Now, let's say that by the time your spouse dies, these assets have appreciated

Put appreciating assets in Trust B

in value to $1,300,000. *The full $1,300,000* will go to your Beneficiaries *estate tax free*—because the value of Trust B was "locked in" for estate tax purposes at the time of your death.

The assets that are placed in Trust A (the surviving spouse's Trust) will not be valued and taxed until his/her death, which could be many years later. So it would be smart, if possible, to place into Trust A those assets that will appreciate more slowly.

Now, under current law, remember, the amount of the estate tax exemption will increase over the next several years—to $1 million by 2006. So you *could* gamble that the surviving spouse will live long enough to get the $1 million exemption, and put appreciating assets in Trust A.

But you can't know for sure how much longer the surviving spouse will live. Plus, Congress can change the law any time it wants. (Frankly, we'll be surprised if we actually see a $1 million exemption.) In either case, the assets could appreciate to more than the surviving spouse's estate tax exemption, triggering estate taxes. That won't happen when appreciating assets are in Trust B.

Sometimes, with a common Trust, the division of assets between Trust A and Trust B is done on paper through bookkeeping. However, some attorneys prefer to actually change titles from the *old* common Trust to the *new* separate Trusts. They feel this more clearly defines which assets are in which Trust, in case they ever need to show the records to the IRS.

The surviving spouse doesn't have to worry about *how* to do this—your attorney, CPA or trust officer can help make sure everything is done properly and that your best tax planning options are used.

However, it *is* important that you and your spouse *both* realize what needs to happen when one of you dies so you don't lose the tax planning benefits. In Part Seven, we'll give you simple, step-by-step instructions for what needs to be done, when it needs to be done, and who needs to do it.

One Common Trust vs. Separate Trusts

As we mentioned earlier, regardless of whether you start out with one common Trust or two separate Trusts, the end results and benefits are the same.

Common A-B Living Trusts are routinely used in community property states. If you live in a non-community property state, your attorney may feel more comfortable with separate Trusts. But, common Trusts are becoming more "common," even in non-community property states. (The Bar Association in Missouri, a non-community state, has published a model common A-B Living Trust document that attorneys can use.)

For many long-married couples, common Trusts make a lot of sense. Those who have built their estates together over the years and are used to owning their assets together like the idea of having one Trust. It's easy for them to understand because it's similar to joint ownership (but without the risks). And one Trust is easier to manage than two Trusts—there is only one document and the assets do not have to be divided until one spouse dies.

However, there may be valid reasons why you may *not* want a common Trust. For example, you may not want to put all your assets in one Trust with your spouse's assets, especially if this is a new marriage and you have substantial assets of your own, or if you are expecting to receive a large inheritance. (Some couples have *three* Trusts—separate ones for property acquired *before* a marriage or for inheritances, and a common Trust for assets they want to own together or acquire *during* the marriage.)

If you live in a non-community property state and find the idea of a common Trust appealing, look for an experienced attorney who is familiar with the *drafting and funding* of common Trusts. Be prepared—your search may not be easy. And it simply may not be worth the time or trouble. (See Part Four for help in finding an attorney.)

Remember, ultimately it makes little difference whether you start out with one Trust or two. What's more important is that your Trust is done *correctly*. It is far better to have separate Trusts that are well drafted and properly funded than to have a common Trust that is not—or no Trust at all!

What's most important is that your Trust is done correctly

With a Will, you can save estate taxes—but you don't avoid probate

Note: The tax benefits are the same for both separate and common A-B Living Trusts. Some aggressive attorneys in non-community property states have attempted to use the common Trust as a way to get a stepped-up basis for *both* spouses' interests in Trust assets when one spouse dies, which is what happens in a community property state. But this is a benefit of community property *ownership*, not of a common Trust. In a non-community property state, *only the deceased spouse's interest* will receive a step-up in basis when one spouse dies. (An explanation of stepped-up basis can be found in Part One.)

Couldn't This Same Tax Planning Be Done In A Will?
Yes, but only if the Will includes a Trust in it. Remember, this is called a Testamentary Trust—and it does not *avoid probate*. A Testamentary Trust cannot go into effect until *after* the Will has been probated. With an A-B Living Trust, you save estate taxes *and* avoid probate.

Do You Have To Use An A-B Trust To Get Both Exemptions?
No. Any assets you leave to someone other than your spouse (say, to your kids) can be used to satisfy your exemption. But most married couples want all the money to be available to the surviving spouse. Then, whatever is left after he/she dies will go to the kids. The only way to provide for your spouse and use both exemptions is with an A-B Trust.

If Your Spouse Is Incapacitated
To make sure you and your spouse will be able to use both estate tax exemptions to which you are entitled and maximize your tax planning options, your A-B Living Trust must be set up while you are both alive and healthy. But if your spouse is incapacitated, you may still have some options.

In some states, you can place your spouse in a conservatorship and request permission from the court to sign estate planning documents for your spouse. (In California, the *doctrine of substituted judgment* is used to do this.) This would allow you to do estate planning for your spouse, including setting up a Living Trust for him/her (or even a common A-B Living Trust for both of you).

You can then transfer your spouse's assets (his/her share of any jointly owned assets and any separately owned assets) *out* of the conservatorship and *into* the Trust, and request that the conservatorship file be closed. The judge will often agree in order to reduce the court's work load and if he/she believes the Trustee will do a good job. (Having a Corporate Trustee involved, especially one the judge knows and has confidence in, will often help.)

Of course, you run the risk of the court not closing the file and staying involved—that decision will vary from judge to judge and from state to state. And you may run into some other problems. For example, if your spouse already has a Will, you would have to convince the court that if your spouse were competent today, he/she would now want a Living Trust instead.

Check with your attorney to see if this is possible in your state. But even if your state doesn't allow this, *you should still set up your own Living Trust* for your share of the estate.

In fact, depending on the size of your estate, it may be worthwhile to include an A-B provision. But you may only be able to use *both* estate tax exemptions if you die first. Here's why.

If you die first, Trust B (your Trust) would use your exemption. The remaining assets would go to your spouse's Trust using the marital deduction. So no estate taxes would be paid when you die. Your spouse's exemption would be used later when your spouse dies.

But if your spouse dies first (which may happen, since your spouse is already ill) and doesn't have a Trust, and everything is left to you, you would only be able to use *one* exemption—yours. If someone else (like your children) inherits some of your spouse's assets, some or all of your spouse's exemption could be used.

Of course, these options should *not* take the place of planning your estate while you and your spouse are both healthy. But if your spouse is *already* incapacitated, they may be worth investigating.

Will The Assets In Trust B Have To Be "Spent Down" If My Surviving Spouse Needs To Qualify For Medicaid?

Until a few years ago, the answer was "No." One of the benefits of an A-B Living Trust *was* that the assets in Trust B could be protected if the surviving spouse needed to qualify for Medicaid after the first spouse died.

To do this, the Trust document had to give the Trustee *discretion* over whether or not to distribute income and principal from Trust B to the surviving spouse. Then, if the surviving spouse needed to qualify for Medicaid, the Trustee would simply decide *not* to provide any income or principal to him/her. So the assets in the B Trust would be considered "unavailable" to the ill spouse—and could be preserved for the Beneficiaries of the deceased spouse.

However, the 1993 tax laws changed this. Medicaid now considers any assets that *could* be available to the surviving spouse *are* available. This means that if assets in Trust B *could* be used to provide for the surviving spouse, Medicaid says they *must* be used (spent down) before benefits will be available.

If you already have an A-B Living Trust and you are relying on this provision for Medicaid planning, you should contact an attorney immediately to find out about other options. Your best source for current information is an attorney who specializes in Elder Law. (See Part Five for help in finding an attorney.)

Of course, if you have a sizeable estate, you may be better off purchasing long term care insurance—or plan to pay for any long-term care expenses yourself.

> **Note:** Here's something you may find interesting. In 1996, Congress passed a law that made it a criminal act—*punishable by imprisonment*—to transfer assets if the intent was to qualify for Medicaid. (This became known as the "Send Granny to Jail" law.) You can imagine that many people were not happy about this. So, in 1997, Congress repealed this law. However, in its place, Congress made it a crime for an attorney (or other paid professional) to advise someone how to transfer assets in order to qualify for Medicaid.
>
> Now, pay attention here. Because it is no longer a crime to transfer your assets in order to qualify for Medicaid, it is now a crime to advise someone how to do something that is perfectly legal! Would someone please explain the logic in this? (And we let these people decide how to spend our money?!)

If You Are Married But Your Spouse Is Not A U.S. Citizen

If your spouse is not a U.S. citizen, he/she is not entitled to the marital deduction. So, if you die first and don't plan ahead, everything in your estate over the amount of the estate tax exemption at that time will be taxed. To prevent this, your attorney will use a *Qualified Domestic Trust* as part of your A-B Living Trust plan. (For an explanation of the Qualified Domestic Trust, see Part Nine.) If your spouse is not a U.S. citizen, make sure you tell your attorney at your first meeting, before any documents are prepared.

If You Are Not Married

If you are not married now (and that includes if you are divorced, widowed or have never been married) you cannot use the A-B Living Trust to save estate taxes. It is designed to use *both* spouses' estate tax exemptions. As a single person, you are entitled to just *one*.

You should still have a Living Trust for all the "non-tax" reasons we explained earlier. Then, if your estate is large enough to pay estate taxes, there *are* some other things you can do *in addition to* your Living Trust to reduce them. Some of these tax planning options are explained in Part Nine.

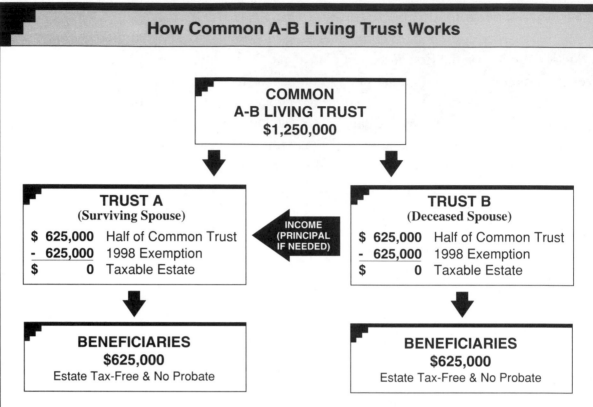

How Common A-B Living Trust Works

**COMMON
A-B LIVING TRUST
$1,250,000**

TRUST A
(Surviving Spouse)

$	**625,000**	Half of Common Trust
-	**625,000**	1998 Exemption
$	**0**	Taxable Estate

**INCOME
(PRINCIPAL
IF NEEDED)**

TRUST B
(Deceased Spouse)

$	**625,000**	Half of Common Trust
-	**625,000**	1998 Exemption
$	**0**	Taxable Estate

**BENEFICIARIES
$625,000**
Estate Tax-Free & No Probate

**BENEFICIARIES
$625,000**
Estate Tax-Free & No Probate

How It Works

1. While you are both living, you transfer your assets into one "common" Living Trust. Upon the death of one spouse, this common Living Trust automatically divides into two separate Trusts—Trust A for the surviving spouse and Trust B for the deceased spouse.

2. If the value of the common Trust is less than two federal estate tax exemptions ($1.25 million in 1998), half of the assets are placed in Trust A and half in Trust B. If the value of the common Trust is more than two exemptions, usually only an amount equal to one exemption ($625,000 in 1998) is placed in Trust B—the rest is transferred to Trust A using the marital deduction.

3. Trust B is taxed when the first spouse dies, but since its value usually does not exceed the amount of the estate tax exemption, no estate taxes are due. Trust A is taxed when the surviving spouse dies. In the meantime, the surviving spouse has complete control over Trust A, and can receive the income (and principal if needed for certain living expenses) from Trust B.

(1998 estate tax exemption used.)

How Common A-B Living Trust Works

4. When the surviving spouse dies, the assets in both Trusts are distributed to the Beneficiaries (which may be the same or different).

Benefits

■ **Reduce/Eliminate Estate Taxes**—With an A-B Living Trust, you and your spouse can both use your federal estate tax exemptions. In 1998, this lets you leave your Beneficiaries up to $1.25 million estate tax-free and with no probate—saving approximately $246,250 in federal estate taxes, plus probate fees.

■ **Provide for Surviving Spouse**—The surviving spouse has complete control over Trust A. In addition, he/she can receive the income (and principal, if needed for certain living expenses) from Trust B.

■ **Control for First to Die**—After the first spouse dies and the common Trust has been divided into Trust A and Trust B, no changes can be made to the provisions of Trust B—giving the first spouse to die complete control over who will eventually receive the assets in Trust B.

■ **Estate Tax-Free Appreciation of Trust B**—The assets placed in Trust B are valued and taxed only when the first spouse dies. There will be no re-valuation or estate taxes paid on any appreciation of these assets later when the surviving spouse dies and the assets in Trust B are distributed to the Beneficiaries.

■ **Estate Taxes Delayed Until Surviving Spouse Dies**—Since usually only an amount equal to the estate tax exemption is placed in Trust B, there are no estate taxes on Trust B when the first spouse dies. The rest of the assets are transferred to Trust A using the unlimited marital deduction. So no estate taxes will be due until after the surviving spouse dies. This leaves the estate intact until then, so the full amount is available to provide for the surviving spouse.

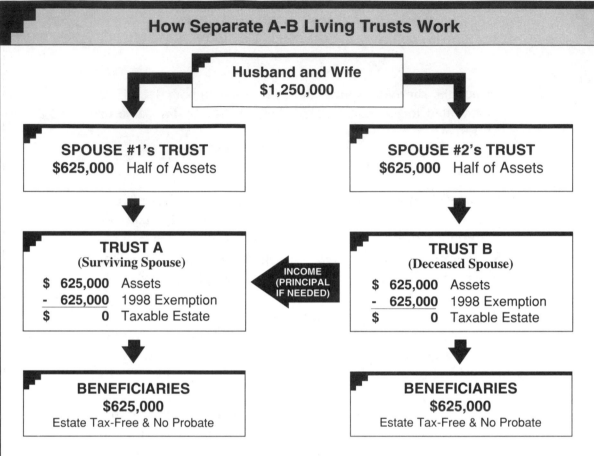

How Separate A-B Living Trusts Work

Husband and Wife
$1,250,000

SPOUSE #1's TRUST
$625,000   Half of Assets

SPOUSE #2's TRUST
$625,000   Half of Assets

TRUST A
(Surviving Spouse)

$	625,000	Assets
-	625,000	1998 Exemption
$	0	Taxable Estate

INCOME (PRINCIPAL IF NEEDED)

TRUST B
(Deceased Spouse)

$	625,000	Assets
-	625,000	1998 Exemption
$	0	Taxable Estate

BENEFICIARIES
$625,000
Estate Tax-Free & No Probate

BENEFICIARIES
$625,000
Estate Tax-Free & No Probate

How It Works

1. While you are living, you and your spouse divide your assets and transfer them into two separate Trusts. Periodically, you review the values of the assets in both Trusts and move assets between the Trusts to take full advantage of both exemptions.

2. When the first spouse dies, the deceased spouse's Trust becomes Trust B. If Trust B is more than the federal estate tax exemption ($625,000 in 1998), the excess is usually transferred to the surviving spouse's Trust (Trust A) using the marital deduction.

3. Trust B is taxed when the first spouse dies, but since its value usually does not exceed the amount of the estate tax exemption, no estate taxes are due. Trust A is taxed when the surviving spouse dies. In the meantime, the surviving spouse has complete control over Trust A, and can receive the income (and principal if needed for certain living expenses) from Trust B.

(1998 estate tax exemption used.)

How Separate A-B Living Trust Works

4. When the surviving spouse dies, the assets in both Trusts are distributed to the Beneficiaries (which may be the same or different).

Benefits

■ **Reduce/Eliminate Estate Taxes**—With separate A-B Living Trusts, you and your spouse can both use your federal estate tax exemptions. In 1998, this lets you leave your Beneficiaries up to $1.25 million estate tax-free and with no probate—saving approximately $246,250 in federal estate taxes, plus probate fees.

■ **Provide for Surviving Spouse**—The surviving spouse has complete control over his/her Trust (Trust A). In addition, he/she can receive the income (and principal, if needed for certain living expenses) from the deceased spouse's Trust (Trust B).

■ **Control for First to Die**—After the first spouse dies, no changes can be made to the provisions of Trust B—giving the first spouse to die complete control over who will eventually receive the assets in Trust B.

■ **Estate Tax-Free Appreciation of Trust B**—The assets in Trust B are valued and taxed only when the first spouse dies. There will be no re-valuation or estate taxes paid on any appreciation of these assets later when the surviving spouse dies and the assets in Trust B are distributed to the Beneficiaries.

■ **Estate Taxes Delayed Until Surviving Spouse Dies**—Since usually only an amount equal to the estate tax exemption is placed in Trust B, there are no estate taxes on Trust B when the first spouse dies. The rest of the assets are transferred to Trust A using the unlimited marital deduction. So no estate taxes will be due until after the surviving spouse dies. This leaves the estate intact until then, so the full amount is available to provide for the surviving spouse.

THE A-B…AND NOW C

If you are married and your combined net estate is *more* than two exemptions ($1.25 million in 1998), you should know about the A-B-C Living Trust. It works basically the same as the A-B Living Trust, but it adds another Trust— the "C" Trust.

This is *not* a way to avoid paying estate taxes if your estate is more than two exemptions. You are already using your two estate tax exemptions through the A-B part of your Living Trust.

Like the A-B Living Trust, the A-B-C Living Trust lets you *delay* payment of *any* estate taxes until the surviving spouse dies, so more will be available to provide for this spouse while he/she is living. It also lets the spouse who dies *first* keep control of more of the estate. Let's look at how it works.

Keep Control Over More Of Your Estate

This, too, is best explained with an example. And to keep things simple, let's again say you both die in 1998 when the estate tax exemption is $625,000.

If your estate is more than $1.25 million and you use an A-B Living Trust, the spouse who dies first will probably end up controlling only an amount equal to one estate tax exemption ($625,000). Usually that's all that's put in Trust B—the rest goes to the surviving spouse's Trust (Trust A) through the marital deduction to avoid paying any estate taxes when the first spouse dies.

So, for example, as the chart on the top of the next page shows, if your total estate is worth $1.5 million and you die first, you would probably only control $625,000 while your surviving spouse would control $875,000.

Maybe that's okay with you. But let's say you want things to be more equal. This could be important, as we mentioned before, if you have children from a previous marriage, or if you're concerned that if your spouse remarries, his/her new spouse could end up with everything except what's in Trust B.

Of course, *more* than the exempt amount can be placed in Trust B—giving you control over more of the estate. But then estate taxes would have to be paid on the excess when you die. And that would leave less to support your spouse.

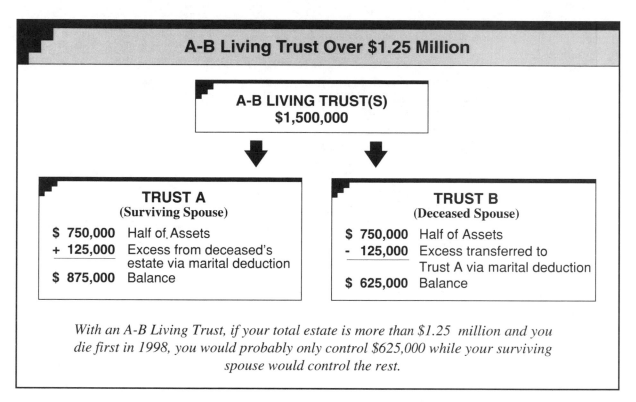

An A-B-C Living Trust would let you control more of the estate—*without* having to pay estate taxes when you die. Let's again say that your total estate is worth $1.5 million, and you die first in 1998.

As the chart on the following page shows, the estate is split *equally*—so that $750,000 goes into Trust A (your spouse's Trust) and $750,000 goes into Trust B (your Trust). Trust B is then *further divided.* An amount equal to the federal estate tax exemption ($625,000) stays in Trust B and the rest ($125,000) goes in Trust C.

Your surviving spouse controls Trust A, and you control Trust B *and* Trust C. When your spouse dies, the assets in all three Trusts will be distributed to the Beneficiaries you have each named—they could be the same or they could be different. So you each keep control over *half* of the estate.

Now, let's look at the benefits of not having to pay any estate taxes when the first spouse dies.

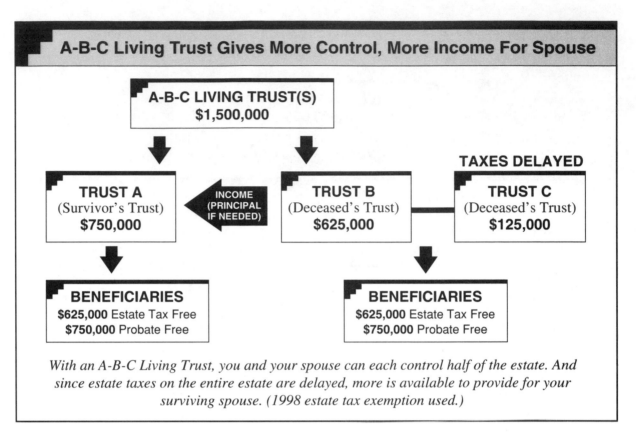

A-B-C Living Trust Gives More Control, More Income For Spouse

A-B-C LIVING TRUST(S)
$1,500,000

TAXES DELAYED

TRUST A
(Survivor's Trust)
$750,000

INCOME
(PRINCIPAL
IF NEEDED)

TRUST B
(Deceased's Trust)
$625,000

TRUST C
(Deceased's Trust)
$125,000

BENEFICIARIES
$625,000 Estate Tax Free
$750,000 Probate Free

BENEFICIARIES
$625,000 Estate Tax Free
$750,000 Probate Free

With an A-B-C Living Trust, you and your spouse can each control half of the estate. And since estate taxes on the entire estate are delayed, more is available to provide for your surviving spouse. (1998 estate tax exemption used.)

Delay Estate Taxes—Provide More For Surviving Spouse

Since, under current tax law, estate taxes on the assets in Trust C are *delayed* until the second spouse dies, this means *the entire estate* will be available to provide for your surviving spouse.

As we explained earlier with the A-B Trust (and as the chart above shows), your surviving spouse has complete control over the assets in Trust A, can receive income from Trust B and can also receive principal from Trust B, if needed, for health, education, maintenance and support.

Your spouse will also receive *all* the income from Trust C (under current law, the spouse *must* receive all the income from Trust C to qualify for this special tax treatment). Your spouse can also receive principal from Trust C, if needed, for health, education, maintenance and support.

Since the estate is not reduced by any estate taxes when you die, a larger amount will be available to invest and provide income to your spouse. And more money will be available in case your spouse needs it. Then, when your spouse dies, the assets in both Trust B and Trust C (50% of the estate at the time of your death) will go to the Beneficiaries *you* specify.

Now, remember, estate taxes on the assets placed in Trust C are not *eliminated*—they are just delayed until the surviving spouse dies. If the assets in Trust A and Trust C *together* are more than the federal estate tax exemption at that time, estate taxes will be due.

But, keep in mind that the estate tax exemption is gradually *increasing*. If your spouse dies in 2006 or later, under current law he or she would be entitled to a $1 million exemption. So the combined value of Trust A and Trust C could be as much as $1 million and no estate taxes would be due.

> **Note:** The "C" Trust as we've explained it here is technically called a "Q-TIP" Trust, which stands for "qualified terminable interest property." It sounds complicated, but it really isn't. The fact that the surviving spouse *must* receive the income from Trust C and may have access to the principal under certain conditions is his/her "qualified interest" in the property. It is "terminable" because this "interest" ends when the surviving spouse dies.

Dividing Assets Among Trust A, Trust B And Trust C

Just like the A-B Living Trust, when one spouse dies, the assets will need to be divided among the A Trust, the B Trust and the C Trust. As we mentioned earlier, it's not so important that the surviving spouse understands exactly *how* to do this because your attorney, CPA, or Trust officer will be able to help. However, it *is* important that *both* of you understand what needs to happen and when. If you are thinking about an A-B-C Living Trust, make sure you and your spouse read Part Seven.

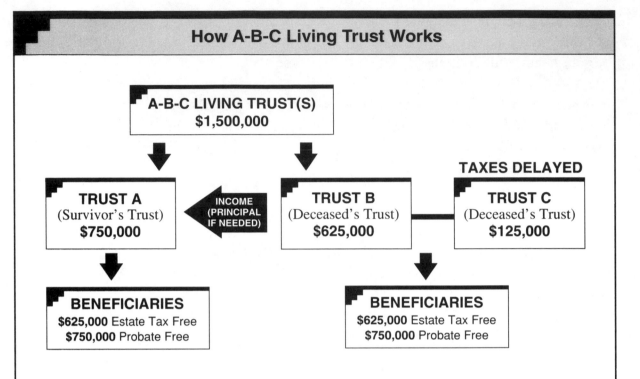

How A-B-C Living Trust Works

A-B-C LIVING TRUST(S)
$1,500,000

TRUST A
(Survivor's Trust)
$750,000

INCOME
(PRINCIPAL
IF NEEDED)

TRUST B
(Deceased's Trust)
$625,000

TAXES DELAYED

TRUST C
(Deceased's Trust)
$125,000

BENEFICIARIES
$625,000 Estate Tax Free
$750,000 Probate Free

BENEFICIARIES
$625,000 Estate Tax Free
$750,000 Probate Free

How It Works

1. While you are both living, you transfer your assets into one "common" Living Trust. Upon the death of one spouse, this Trust is divided equally. Half of the estate goes into Trust A for the surviving spouse. The other half (the deceased spouse's share) is divided between Trust B and Trust C. Usually only an amount equal to the federal estate tax exemption ($625,000 in 1998) is placed in Trust B; the excess is placed into Trust C.

   As an example, in the illustration above, the total estate of $1.5 million is divided so that $750,000 (half) is placed in Trust A, and the other half is divided between Trust B ($625,000) and Trust C ($125,000).

   If you and your spouse start out with separate Trusts, the assets will already be divided when one spouse dies. The assets in the deceased spouse's Trust are then divided between Trust B and Trust C as explained above.

2. Trust B is taxed when the first spouse dies. Trust A and Trust C are taxed when the surviving spouse dies. In the meantime, the surviv-

(1998 estate tax exemption used.)

How A-B-C Living Trust Works

ing spouse has complete control over Trust A, and can receive income (and principal, if needed, for certain living expenses) from Trust B. In addition, he/she will receive all the income from Trust C, and can receive principal, if needed, for certain living expenses.

3. When the surviving spouse dies, the assets in all three Trusts are distributed to the Beneficiaries.

Benefits

■ **Reduce/Eliminate Estate Taxes**—With an A-B-C Living Trust, you and your spouse can both use your federal estate tax exemptions. In 1998, this lets you leave your Beneficiaries up to $1.25 million estate tax free—saving approximately $246,250 in federal estate taxes, plus probate fees.

■ **Provide for Surviving Spouse**—The surviving spouse has complete control over Trust A and receives all income from Trust C. In addition, he/she can receive the income from Trust B and can have access to the principal of Trust B and Trust C, if needed, for certain living expenses.

■ **Control for First to Die**—When the first spouse dies and the common Trust is divided among Trusts A, B, and C, no changes can be made to the provisions of Trust B and Trust C—giving the first spouse to die complete control over who will eventually receive the assets in Trust B and Trust C (half of the common estate). (If you have separate Trusts, the spouse who dies first keeps control over the assets in his/her Trust, even after they are placed into Trust B and Trust C.)

■ **Estate Tax-Free Appreciation of Trust B**—The assets in Trust B are valued and taxed only when the first spouse dies. There will be no re-valuation or estate taxes paid on any appreciation when the surviving spouse dies and the assets in Trust B are distributed.

■ **Estate Taxes Delayed on Trust C**—The assets placed in Trust C are taxed only when the surviving spouse dies. This leaves the estate intact until then, so a larger amount is available to provide income (and principal, if needed) to the surviving spouse during his/her lifetime.

Summary

If you are interested in an A-B or an A-B-C Living Trust, be sure to mention it to your attorney. (You may want to discuss it with your personal tax advisor as well.) The ways in which we have explained them here are the ways in which they are most commonly used. However, depending on your situation, your attorney may recommend some variations of what we have explained here in order to set up your Living Trust to best meet your needs and objectives.

For example, the income from Trust B does not have to be paid just to your surviving spouse—it can also be paid to your children, grandchildren or others. And, as good as the Q-TIP sounds, it could limit future tax and other planning opportunities (because no one, including your surviving spouse, can make changes to it after you die). For more flexibility, you may want to give your spouse the ability to withdraw and distribute these assets after you die.

Also, if your estate is sizeable, you may need additional tax planning beyond an A-B or A-B-C Living Trust. If so, you may be interested in some of the tax-reducing strategies explained in Part Nine. Generally speaking, these would not *replace* your Living Trust—they would be *in addition to* it. Your Living Trust is the foundation of your *entire* estate plan.

Part Four

PLANNING FOR YOUR LIVING TRUST

Part Four—
PLANNING FOR YOUR LIVING TRUST

Now that you have a good understanding of what a Living Trust is, how it works, and the benefits of having one, let's start thinking about yours.

As you've seen, your Living Trust can be designed to include just about anything you want. But that also means you will need to make some important decisions.

In this section, we will prompt you to think about what you want to happen to you and your assets if you become incapacitated and when you die. We will give you information and examples so you can make sound, informed decisions about who will be your Trustee, Successor Trustee(s) and Beneficiaries, and when you want your Beneficiaries to receive their inheritances.

As you read this section, think about your situation and see which suggestions might be right for you and your family. Feel free to mark up the book and make notes in the margins as you read things you like, have questions about, or just want to think more about.

Later, in Part Ten, we'll help you organize your thoughts and decisions with our Personal and Financial Organizer.

Now, let's start planning for your Living Trust.

YOU MUST MAKE SOME BASIC DECISIONS

What *do* you want to happen to you and your assets if you become incapacitated and when you die? Here are some specific things you will need to think about and decide:

- If you become incapacitated, who do you want to take care of you? Who do you want to manage your financial affairs for you?
- Do you have specific requests about your medical care? Do you wish to receive care in a certain facility? Is there one you wish to avoid?
- Who do you want to receive your assets when you die? Are there any "special gifts" of sentimental value you want certain people to have?
- Do you want to leave something to your church or favorite charity?
- If you have minor children, who do you want to raise them if you (and your spouse) can't? Who do you want to manage their inheritance?
- When do you want your Beneficiaries to receive their inheritances?
- Do you have a child, spouse or other loved one who depends on you and will need special care?
- If there are stepchildren in your family, how do you want them to inherit from you (if at all)?
- Are there any persons you wish to disinherit?
- If your entire family dies before you, who would you want to have your assets?
- If you have a business, what do you want to happen to it?
- If you have pets, who do you want to care for them?

By the time you finish reading this section, you'll probably have the answers to a lot of these questions—and these may prompt you to think of others. Make some notes as things come to mind. Then, in Part Ten, we'll help you get everything organized.

Now, let's start finding some answers.

WHO WILL BE YOUR TRUSTEE?

What Does A Trustee Do?

A Trustee basically does what you do right now with your financial affairs—collect income, pay bills and taxes, save and invest your money for the future, buy and sell assets, provide for your loved ones, keep accurate records, and generally keep things organized and in good order.

Who Can Be Your Trustee?

As we mentioned earlier, you can be your own Trustee, which is what most people—especially those with smaller estates—choose to do. If you name yourself as Trustee, nothing changes after you set up your Living Trust—you continue to manage your assets and financial affairs just as you always have for as long as you are able.

If you are married, you and your spouse can be Co-Trustees. This way, if something happens to one of you, the other can continue to handle your financial affairs without interruption. Most married couples who own their assets together—especially those who have been married for some time—are usually Co-Trustees.

However, you don't have to be your own Trustee. You can name anyone you want as your Trustee or to be Co-Trustee with you. Some people choose an adult son or daughter, trusted friend or other relative. Some people like having the experience and investment management skills of a Corporate Trustee (a bank trust department or a trust company—more about them in a few pages).

Remember, naming someone else as your Trustee or Co-Trustee doesn't mean you lose control. The Trustee you name must follow the instructions in your Trust and report to you. Plus, you can always change your mind (and your Trustee) later.

One big advantage to having a Co-Trustee is that someone else would already be involved and familiar with your Trust if something happens to you. This would eliminate the time a Successor would have to spend to become knowledgeable about your Trust, your assets, your Beneficiaries and the personalities involved.

You can be your own Trustee or name someone else

If you do decide to name someone as your Co-Trustee (even your spouse), it might be a good idea to have your Trust require both signatures to buy or sell assets as long as both of you are alive and able (just like some bank accounts require both signatures). But if you are concerned that you can't trust this person, then he or she probably shouldn't be involved with your Trust.

Compensating A Trustee

All Trustees are entitled to receive reasonable compensation for their services. However, if you are your own Trustee, you probably won't pay yourself. And family members often don't think they should accept a fee. If you name a friend or family member as a Trustee or Successor Trustee, you may want to consider paying them anyway for their time and responsibilities.

Consider specifying the amount of compensation in your Trust document. This could go a long way toward preventing hurt feelings and future disagreements over how much your Successor Trustee will receive.

WHO WILL BE YOUR SUCCESSOR TRUSTEE(S)?

What Does A Successor Trustee Do?

Successor Trustees have a lot of responsibility and should be chosen carefully. Remember, if you (and your Co-Trustee) become incapacitated, your Successor Trustee will step in and take full control for you—paying bills, making financial decisions, even selling or refinancing assets. Your Successor will be able to do anything you could with your Trust assets—as long as it does not conflict with the instructions in your Trust document.

When you die, your Successor acts just like an Executor would—takes an inventory of your assets, pays your final bills, sells assets if necessary, has your final tax returns prepared, and distributes your assets according to the instructions in your Trust.

Remember that your Successor Trustee will be acting without court supervision—which is why your affairs can be handled more efficiently. But this also means it will be up to your Successor to get things started and keep them moving along. If needed, your attorney, trust officer, and/or CPA can help guide your Successor, so it isn't necessary for him/her to know exactly what to do and when. You just need to make sure you name someone who is responsible and conscientious.

Who Can Be Successor Trustees?

Successor Trustees can be your adult children, other relatives, a trusted friend, and/or a Corporate Trustee. If you choose an individual, you should name more than one in case your first choice is unable to act. They should be people you know and trust, people whose judgment you respect and who will also respect your wishes. They do not have to live in the same state you do (although it would be more convenient if they live close to you).

When choosing your Successors, keep in mind the type and amount of assets in your Trust, and the complexity of the provisions in your Trust document. For example, if you plan to keep assets in your Trust after you die for your Beneficiaries (if they are minors, have special needs, or will receive their inheritances in installments), your Successor would have more responsibilities for a longer period of time than if your assets will be distributed all at once.

Also keep in mind the qualifications of your "candidates." Consider personalities, financial/business experience, and time available due to their own family/career demands. Taking over as Trustee for someone can take a substantial amount of time and requires a certain amount of business sense.

■ When Considering Your Children

Many people name one or more of their adult children as Successor Trustee(s). Just be prepared for possible hurt feelings if you exclude any—children can be sensitive about these things.

As one solution, some people name all of their adult children to act together as *Co*-Successor Trustees. Depending on the number of children you have, where they live, and their personalities, this may or may not be a good idea.

If you have only two or three children who live in the same area as you (and they get along), then it could work out fine. But you don't want your affairs being run by a cumbersome committee that can't agree on anything. Also, keep in mind that all their signatures will be required for any transactions—and if they're spread out across the country, that could slow things down.

Choose your Successor Trustee(s) carefully

An alternative is to name all of your adult children as Successors, but instead of having them work together as Co-Trustees, list them *in order of who you think will do the best job*—and that may not necessarily be oldest to youngest (being older doesn't always make one wiser). So only your first choice would become your Successor, unless he/she is unable or unwilling to serve at that time, in which case the second would step in, and so on down your list.

If you decide to name an even number of your children (two or four) to act together, you could select just one of them to make decisions. Or you may want to add a Corporate Trustee as an impartial "third" to prevent any deadlocks in the event your children disagree. (Of course, if your children agree, they could not be overruled by the Corporate Trustee.)

■ Qualify Your Candidates

Make sure you ask the people you are considering if they want this responsibility. Don't put them on the spot and just assume they want to do this. It would probably be helpful for them (and you) to read Part Seven to see what needs to be done when someone becomes incapacitated and/or dies. You may also want to give each of them a copy of this book so they can become familiar with how a Living Trust works and understand the duties and responsibilities of a Trustee.

If you have any doubts about one of your candidates' abilities or desire to fulfill this responsibility—if you're not sure about his/her business sense or that he/she may not have the time and/or ability, or if you think this person may act emotionally rather than logically and rationally—you should probably name someone else or a Corporate Trustee as your Successor.

One final comment. As much as you love your children and would like to think they will be caring and unselfish once you're gone, *this* is the time to be realistic. If they really don't get along, or if there could be jealousies involved, you and your family will probably be much better off if you select a Corporate Trustee as your Successor Trustee. The fee a Corporate Trustee charges is a small price to pay if it keeps peace in your family.

SHOULD YOU CONSIDER A CORPORATE TRUSTEE?

What Is A Corporate Trustee And What Do They Do?

A Corporate Trustee is a bank trust department or a trust company that specializes in managing Trusts. They can manage your Trust for you now and/or after you die according to your instructions—they can buy and sell assets, handle required paperwork, maintain accurate records, and distribute income and assets as your Trust directs.

Why Would You Use A Corporate Trustee?

Family and friends are not always a good choice to be involved with your Trust—even if they do get along, they may be too busy with their own affairs, reside in a distant area or simply not be responsible or experienced enough to manage the Trust assets. You may also want professional help investing and managing your assets.

Do You Lose Control?

No—even if you name a Corporate Trustee as your Trustee or Co-Trustee, *you still keep control.* Until you become incapacitated or die, you can always change your Trustee if, for any reason, you become unhappy with your choice. And—this is very important—even after you become incapacitated or die, they *must* follow the instructions in your Trust. If they don't, they can be held legally liable.

When Would You Use A Corporate Trustee?

■ **There's No One You Can Trust**

You may have no one you can trust to take care of your financial affairs for you. You may be elderly, widowed, and/or in declining health, and have no children or other trusted relatives living nearby.

A Corporate Trustee can give you peace of mind, knowing a qualified professional you have personally selected will manage your financial affairs for you now and when you are no longer able to do so yourself. You won't have to worry about becoming a victim of an investment scam or a long-lost relative showing up to take control of your money.

Corporate Trustees are in the business of managing Trusts

■ You Want Help Managing Your Investments

You may not have the time, desire or experience to manage your investments by yourself. You may want to travel extensively, don't want to worry about your investments any more, or simply feel that a professional could do a better job than you. Maybe you have (or expect to) come into some money—from selling a business or other assets, or from an inheritance.

Good investment management is more important now than ever before. With people living longer and health care costs continuing to rise, our savings have to grow larger and last longer. Traditional investments like certificates of deposit used to work well—they were safe and their returns stayed ahead of inflation. But now we have to look at additional investment options to help our savings grow to the point where they can pay for our longer retirement years. And with so many options to choose from, this can be *very* confusing.

A Corporate Trustee has the experience, time and resources to manage your Trust and help you meet your investment goals. Many also have their own investment funds (you can evaluate them and compare their performance with other investments, including your own results).

You can still be as involved as you wish. You can have them make investment recommendations and present them to you for your decisions. Or you can authorize them to go ahead and make investment decisions *for* you based upon an already determined investment strategy, while you simply monitor their results through regular statements.

■ You Plan to Keep Assets in Trust for Your Beneficiaries

A Corporate Trustee can also be a good choice if you plan to keep assets in Trust for Beneficiaries who are minors or will receive their inheritances in installments—or if you have a child, spouse or other loved one who is disabled, or simply may need help managing his/her finances if something happens to you.

A Corporate Trustee will follow your Trust's instructions objectively and make sure your Beneficiaries' needs are taken care of for as long as your Trust specifies—even for life. You don't have to worry about a Corporate Trustee dying before a Beneficiary does.

■ Family May Need Help After You Die (Settling Your Estate)

The death of a loved one is a difficult time for a family. And an innocent error by a well-meaning but inexperienced relative or friend could negate your careful planning and cost your Beneficiaries thousands of dollars.

Many Corporate Trustees have experience with settling estates (preparing an inventory of assets, having appraisals done, preparing tax returns, making distributions, etc.) and can provide assistance and guidance to your surviving spouse and other family members when you die. Many are also familiar with various tax saving and estate planning strategies.

Benefits of a Corporate Trustee

- **Experience**—Managing Trusts is their business. They are familiar with all kinds of Trusts, tax and estate planning strategies, and legal responsibilities of Trustee.

- **Professional Asset Management**—Generally, a professional who has more time, resources, and experience can achieve better results than an individual.

- **Regulation**—They are regulated by both state and federal agencies. Also, most courts consider them to be "experts" and expect a higher degree of performance than from an individual.

- **Reliability**—They won't become ill or die, go on vacation, move away, or be distracted by personal concerns or emotions (as an individual might).

- **Objectivity**—They will follow your Trust instructions objectively and unemotionally. A family member may find this difficult—especially if he/she is also a Beneficiary of your Trust.

When Does A Corporate Trustee Start Managing Your Trust?

That's up to you. A Corporate Trustee can be your Trustee now (either acting alone or as a Co-Trustee with you) or a Successor Trustee.

Having a Corporate Trustee involved with your Trust now would let them become familiar with you, your Trust document, your assets, and your Beneficiaries' needs and personalities while you are still around to answer questions and provide direction. At the same time, you can see how the Corporate Trustee will perform in your absence, evaluate their investment performance and services, and see how comfortable you feel overall. Think of it as a kind of "Trustee test drive."

How Safe Are Trust Assets?

Trust assets are not insured by the FDIC. However, by law, trust assets must be kept separate from all other assets. For example, they cannot be loaned out or mixed with the Corporate Trustee's own assets. And they cannot be used to satisfy the Corporate Trustee's creditors. So even if a bank or Trust company fails, Trust assets are safe.

You are also protected against fraud, theft (for example, if an employee takes Trust assets and disappears), or if they make an error administering your Trust. And, in the unlikely event a Corporate Trustee did *not* follow your instructions or perform other duties as required by law, your Beneficiaries would have a much better chance of being compensated for any loss from a Corporate Trustee than they would from an individual.

Of course, there is no insurance or bond to protect you if your assets simply lose value due to a decline in market values.

How Much Does A Corporate Trustee Charge?

Their fees are usually based on the value and type of Trust assets they are managing and the services you want. Services and fees will vary. Some charge one fee that includes all their services. Others have "add-on fees" for certain services. Make sure you ask about them and compare.

Corporate Trustees begin charging a fee *only* when they start to act as Trustee. So if, for example, you name a Corporate Trustee as Successor Trustee, they won't charge you anything until they step in as your Trustee at your incapacity or death.

Are There Any Disadvantages Of A Corporate Trustee?

Because Corporate Trustees must objectively follow the instructions for the Trusts they manage, some Beneficiaries—especially those who want their money now instead of when the Trust states—have found them to be inflexible and a bit distant. Of course, in many cases, the reason the Trust was set up— and the Corporate Trustee chosen—was to keep the Beneficiary from getting the money until Mom and Dad (or whoever set up the Trust) says it's okay.

If, however, you are concerned about a Corporate Trustee being too "impersonal," you can always name a family member or close friend to act with them.

Also, with ongoing mergers and acquisitions, the Corporate Trustee you select now could become very different in the future. Trust officers also move from institution to institution. You may want to let your Beneficiaries be able to change to another Corporate Trustee if they *all* become dissatisfied.

How To Evaluate A Corporate Trustee

Corporate trustees are not all the same. They have different "personalities," fees, investment performances and services. For example, some do not manage real estate or settle estates. Most have minimum requirements on the amount of Trust assets they will accept, although at some it is as low as $50,000-$100,000—you may have that much in life insurance alone.

If you are considering a Corporate Trustee, talk to some. Visit them if you can. Ask how long their trust department has been in business. Compare their investment performances, fees, and services. Ask to see samples of statements or reports you would receive.

Facts and numbers are important—but so are the people. Do they seem to genuinely care about you and your family? Do they *listen* to you? Do they understand your concerns? Overall, how comfortable do you feel that they will be there for you and your family when you need them?

Should Everyone Use A Corporate Trustee?

No, of course not. If you have a modest estate and your Trust is fairly simple, you will probably be just fine being your own Trustee and having a capable family member step in for you when you are no longer able to manage your Trust yourself.

Corporate Trustees only charge a fee when they begin to act for you

But if your estate is larger, has a variety of assets, if your Trust includes tax planning, if assets will remain in your Trust for your Beneficiaries, or if you don't know who to name as your Successor Trustee, a Corporate Trustee can be a wise choice.

How to Provide for Your Beneficiaries

Remember, your Beneficiaries are the people and/or organizations who will receive your assets when you die. Although most people name family members as their Beneficiaries, you can leave your assets to any person(s) or organization(s) that you wish.

And as we mentioned earlier, one of the most powerful benefits of a Living Trust is that *you* keep control over who receives your assets and when they will receive them. Basically, you can do whatever you want.

In the next few pages, we'll give you some things to keep in mind as you decide how to provide for minor children, adult children, and other Beneficiaries, and Beneficiaries who may have special needs.

As you read this, think about your situation. But don't worry about all the little details. You just need to have a general idea of what you want. Remember, in Part Ten, we'll help you organize your thoughts and write them down.

Let's start first with "special gifts" you may want to make.

Special Gifts

You probably own some items of real or sentimental value—jewelry, antiques, or a collection (like coins, stamps, dolls, guns)—that you want a certain child, grandchild, other special relative, friend, or organization to have when you die. These are called "special gifts" or "special bequests."

In most states, making these gifts with a Living Trust is easy. All you have to do is make a list, on a separate sheet of paper, of your special gifts and who you want to have them. Then date the list, have it notarized, and keep it with your Living Trust.

If you change your mind, just make a new list and have it notarized. You don't have to go back to your attorney and change your Trust document—you can change your special gifts list at home. Your new notarized list is a legally recognized amendment to your Living Trust. So you can make changes as often as you like.

If your estate is sizeable, or if a gift is of substantial value, it would be a good idea to have your attorney review your list to avoid possible tax problems.

If your list starts getting long, you may want to break it down into smaller, separate lists, one for each person. This way, you won't have to re-do the entire list each time you make a change. Just make sure you date each list and always have new ones notarized.

To prevent possible family disagreements after you die, make your lists as specific as you can. It's much easier for you to do this now than to expect your children and other relatives to reach an agreement after you die that satisfies everyone. Otherwise, family disagreements could still prompt an estate sale.

Also, consider asking your children and other loved ones if there is something of yours they would like to have. There may be something that has a very special meaning to one of your children that you weren't even aware of—and wouldn't it be nice to know about that now?

Now, let's look at how to provide for your Beneficiaries with your other assets.

If You Have Minor Children

Remember, if you have minor children, your Living Trust should contain a Children's Trust to prevent the court from controlling the inheritance.

■ Naming a Guardian

You will need to name a Guardian for your minor children. This is a *very* important decision. The person you choose will be responsible for raising your children if both parents have died or are incapacitated. Guardians must be adults.

You will, of course, want to choose someone who respects your values and standards (moral and religious) and will raise your children the way you would want. If you want a couple to raise your children, it's a good idea to name one

You keep control over who receives your assets and when they receive them

121

You will need to name a Guardian and Trustee for your minor children

of them as your first choice and the other as your second choice—just in case they were to divorce later.

As we mentioned earlier in Part Two, the court must still officially approve your selection. In most cases, the court will go along with your choice. However, remember that if the other natural parent is still alive, he/she will usually be the court's preferred choice.

If you are a single parent with custody and really don't want your "ex" to be guardian, go ahead and name your preference anyway—your choice will, at the very least, receive careful consideration by the court. It's also possible that your "ex" may not be able to take the responsibility (or won't want it). Or the court could agree with you that he/she is not a suitable choice, and would want to know your choice as an alternative.

■ Naming a Trustee

Remember, the Guardian is only responsible for *raising* your children and does not control the inheritance. You also need to name a Trustee for your Children's Trust—someone who will be responsible for the safekeeping of the inheritance, and will provide the money for normal living expenses, education, medical care, and other needs from the assets in the Children's Trust.

The Trustee can be one or more individuals and/or a Corporate Trustee. (Depending on the size of the inheritance and type of assets, you may want the benefits of having a Corporate Trustee's experience along with the personal insight of a friend or relative.)

You can name the same person as Trustee and Guardian and, at first thought, it may seem more convenient to have just one person involved. But keep in mind that the person you want to raise your children may not be your best choice to handle the money—and vice versa.

■ One "Common" Trust vs. Separate Trusts

Like most parents, you will want the Trust assets to last long enough to provide for each of your children until they reach a certain age (for example, when the last one completes college).

Usually the best way to do this is to establish *one* Children's Trust and let the Trustee use his/her discretion to provide for each child's individual needs as they arise, just as you would. The remaining assets could be divided after your children are grown.

Of course, you could have separate Trusts for each child with the inheritance split equally among the Trusts, but this is less flexible. And although this would, on the surface, appear to treat each child equally, it could result in *unequal* treatment.

First of all, your children are different ages and their needs will last for different lengths of time. For example, the youngest will need to be provided for several years longer than the oldest, and his/her funds could be depleted even before reaching college age—while the oldest one may be able to finish college and have money left over.

Also consider if one child became ill or injured and needed special medical treatment. If you were alive, you wouldn't stop providing for this child's care after you had spent a certain amount of money—you and your other children would probably sacrifice to make sure this child received the treatment he/she needed. But if you create separate Trusts for each child, your Trustee won't have that option.

■ Give Your Children's Trustee Flexibility

You may want to give your Trustee some flexibility in how to use the Trust assets. For example, the Guardian may need some extra assistance in providing for your children. Put yourself in the shoes of your children's Guardian for a moment—suddenly you have additional children to raise. Is there enough room for everyone in your home, or do you need to add on an extra bedroom? Can you handle the extra work load yourself or do you need to hire a part-time helper? You might even need a larger car.

Caring for your children should not be a financial burden on the person(s) you have asked to be Guardian—as long as you have planned and left enough assets to provide for them adequately. And if you trust your Trustee to manage the inheritance, he/she should be able to use good judgment to provide for the necessary comfort and well-being of your children.

Note: This is a good time to review your assets and insurance with your insurance agent or financial advisor. Do you realistically have enough assets to provide for your children and/or spouse the way you would want if something happened to you today? Or what if something happened to your spouse—would you have enough to manage without him or her? If you don't have enough assets to provide for your family as you would like to, you may want to increase your life insurance.

■ Allowing for Loans/Advances for Your Older Children

To make sure the Trust assets provide for all your children, you probably will want to keep the Trust intact until the youngest has reached an appropriate age.

But, at the same time, you may not want to penalize your older children who may need funds to help purchase a home, pay for a wedding, start a business, etc. while they are waiting for the youngest to "grow up."

You might consider allowing for an advance or loan from their inheritance, which would be subtracted later when the Trust assets are distributed. Your Trustee should, of course, make sure the advance is appropriate and justified (both in amount and purpose), so that the amount withdrawn from the Trust does not adversely affect the other children. You may want to give your Trustee some guidelines—such as specifying a limit on the amount of the advance to be considered.

If You Have Minor Grandchildren

Your Living Trust can also include a Children's Trust for your grandchildren. You will need to name a Trustee (perhaps a parent and/or a Corporate Trustee) to manage the assets until each child reaches the age(s) at which you want him/her to receive the inheritance.

If your estate is sizeable, you may want to consider transferring some of your assets to a separate Trust for your grandchildren *now,* while you are living, to reduce your estate tax liability. Just make sure you don't leave anything *directly* to your minor grandchildren—you don't want to cause a guardianship.

Note: If the inheritance to your grandchildren is substantial, a generation skipping transfer tax may be involved. (See Part Nine for more information.)

If You Have Adult Children

Once your children (and other Beneficiaries) are adults, you have many options for giving them their inheritances. You'll first need to decide how much you want each one to receive, and then when you want them to receive it. Keep in mind that your Beneficiaries and their circumstances are different—and what may be right for one is not necessarily right for another.

■ **How Much Do You Want Each to Receive?**

As we mentioned earlier, most parents want to treat their children fairly. This may mean giving each an equal share *or* it may mean giving more to one child than to another. For example, you may want to give more to a son who is a teacher than to a daughter who is a doctor. Or you may want to "compensate" a son or daughter who takes care of you during an illness or your last years.

Some parents worry about leaving their children with too much money. They want their children to have enough money that they can do anything they want, but not so much that they will do nothing! If this concerns you, just remember that no one said you have to give *everything* you own to your children. In fact, it may be better not to give them anything *at all*—and keep the assets in Trust for your grandchildren and future generations, and/or make a generous contribution to a favorite charity.

■ **When Do You Want Them to Receive Their Inheritances?**

Next, you need to decide *when* you want them to receive their inheritances. Let's look at some commonly used options.

Distribution Option 1: Give Some Now

If you can afford it, you may want to consider giving your Beneficiaries some of their inheritance now, while you are living. Of course, you must take care of yourself first. Most people want to make sure they first have enough to last for as long as they live. And if they are married, they want to make sure there is enough to provide for the surviving spouse. As a result, most people typically hold onto *all* their assets until the second spouse dies.

But with people living longer, this approach doesn't work as well as it used to. It's not unusual for parents to be in their 80's or even in their 90's when they die—meaning their children may be in their 60's or 70's when they receive their inheritances. If the surviving spouse is much younger (for example, if this is a second marriage), the kids may *never* see their inheritances.

Treating your children fairly may mean giving more to one than to another

If you can afford to give your Beneficiaries some of their inheritances *now*, you will experience the joy of *seeing* the results—of seeing your children buy a home, start a new business, or seeing your grandchildren go to college—and knowing it may not have happened without your help.

You may also have a child who wants to do worthwhile, but low-paying (or non-paying) work—like teach, be a full-time volunteer, or even be able to stay at home to raise your grandchildren. You could provide them with additional income now so they could afford to do it.

Giving now can also reduce your estate taxes. For more information on gifting, see Part Nine. Just remember, *never* give away more than you can afford.

Distribution Option 2: Lump Sum
You could have your Trust distribute all of your assets to your Beneficiaries in one lump sum as soon as possible after you die. This is a very common method of distribution. If your Beneficiaries are responsible adults, this may be a good choice, especially if they are older and you are concerned that they may not have many years left to enjoy the inheritance.

However, keep in mind that once a Beneficiary has possession of the assets, he/she could lose them. For example, a creditor could seize the assets for payment of debts or settlement of a lawsuit. An ex-spouse could end up with a good portion (or even all) of the inheritance through a divorce settlement. Even a current spouse can have access to assets that are placed in a joint account or if your Beneficiary later adds his/her spouse as a co-owner.

So, if it bothers you that a son- or daughter-in-law could end up with your assets—or that a creditor could seize them—a lump sum distribution may *not* be the right option. If you want to be sure your assets "stay in the family," you may want to consider installments or even keeping the assets in your Trust.

Distribution Option 3: Installments
Many people prefer to give their Beneficiaries more than one opportunity to invest or use their inheritances wisely—which doesn't always happen the first time around. So, instead of giving their Beneficiaries their inheritances all at one time, they give it to them in installments.

Using the "installment method" also provides some protection against creditors (even an ex-spouse). They can only have access to assets that the Beneficiary has actually received. So, in most cases, they would *not* be able to get the assets that are still in the Trust. (However, if your Beneficiary is not paying child support or spousal support as ordered by a court, in some states Trust assets can be used to pay these obligations.)

Installments can be done just about any way you wish. Here are some you may want to consider.

At Certain Intervals

One way is to have your Trust distribute portions of the inheritance at certain intervals after you die. For example, one-third when you die; another third, five years later; and the final third, five years after that. (If you are married, you may want distributions to begin after both you and your spouse die.)

Just make sure you review this part of your Trust from time to time to see if it still works for your situation. Depending on how old your children are at any given time—and how much longer you live—you may not want to make them wait for years after you die before they receive the full inheritance. There's the chance they may not live long enough to receive all of it.

At Certain Ages

As an alternative, installments could be distributed after you die as a Beneficiary reaches certain ages—for example, the first installment at age 25, a second at age 30, a third at age 35, etc.

Again, if you choose this option, make sure you review your Trust periodically. Otherwise, your Beneficiaries could have already passed those ages by the time you die and would receive their inheritances in one lump sum—defeating your intention of distributing it in installments. To prevent this, your Trust can specify that if your Beneficiaries have passed these ages when you die, the inheritance would then be paid in installments every so many years (as above).

Installments give your Beneficiaries more than one chance to act wisely

At Certain Occasions

Be careful about linking the distributions to certain milestones like marriage, birth of a child, etc. It could be that your Beneficiary doesn't marry or have children. (This could also encourage an insincere marriage, and part of the inheritance could end up outside the family.)

Using graduation from college as a distribution time can also present some potential problems. For example, how would you define "college"—two-year, four-year, trade school? And what if a Beneficiary decides to pursue a career (music, dance, acting, art, etc.) for which a college degree isn't necessary?

Distribution Option 4: Keep Assets in Trust

You may decide to keep assets in the Trust and *provide* for a Beneficiary, but not actually give the assets to him or her. Here are some situations with which you may be able to identify.

An Irresponsible Beneficiary

If you feel a Beneficiary is too irresponsible to receive outright control of his/her inheritance (or has a problem with drugs, alcohol, gambling, etc.), you can specify that the inheritance remain "in Trust" for his/her lifetime or until he/she reaches a more mature age.

The Trustee will manage and invest the inheritance, and provide for the Beneficiary's basic needs as you instruct. (If you don't think your Beneficiary is responsible enough to receive a regular income from the Trust, the Trustee can pay rent and other expenses directly so the Beneficiary never actually has the money.)

Give some thought to your choice as Trustee. A family member acting alone may be too sympathetic and easily swayed—or just the opposite. You may want to have a Corporate Trustee be a Co-Trustee to add some objectivity and share the responsibility. You'll also need to specify who will receive any remaining inheritance if the Beneficiary dies before receiving the full amount of the inheritance.

You may also want the Trust to include a *Spendthrift Clause* to protect the Trust assets from creditors. Generally, this says that the Beneficiary cannot voluntarily spend any Trust assets or income before they are paid to him/

her. So if, for example, your irresponsible son or daughter buys an expensive sports car, the Trust cannot be held responsible for payment.

Protection from Creditors/Spouse

As we mentioned earlier, if you are concerned that a son- or daughter-in-law—or a creditor—could have access to the inheritance, you may want to keep the assets in Trust and just provide periodic income to your Beneficiary.

Incentive to Work

Maybe you want to give a Beneficiary a little extra incentive to work and lead a productive life. For example, one father was concerned that his beach-loving son would continue to simply "ride the waves" while he waited around for Dad to die. The son saw no reason to seek regular employment—he knew he would receive a sizeable inheritance when Dad died. To encourage his son to be more productive, Dad arranged for the inheritance to *stay* in Trust. And for every dollar the son earned on his own, the Trust would match it.

> **Note:** If you decide to "income-match," make sure your Trust will provide for your Beneficiary if he/she is unable to work due to illness or injury. And don't forget about retirement—do you want your Beneficiary to work *for as long as he/she lives* in order to receive an income from the Trust?

Beneficiary Doesn't Need the Money

You may have a child who is already financially secure and doesn't really need the money. Instead of giving the inheritance to this child, you could keep the assets in Trust for your grandchildren and future generations. You can still provide periodic income to your child and have the assets available as a kind of "safety net" if circumstances change and he/she needs some money.

Loved One with Special Needs

You may have a spouse, child, sibling, parent, or other loved one who is disabled or may simply not be able to handle an inheritance by him/herself after you die. This is a perfect time to keep the inheritance in Trust, and have the Trustee provide for this person as you would (another good time to consider a Corporate Trustee).

You may decide to keep the assets in Trust

If this person is receiving government benefits, the next two sections will be of particular interest to you. The first one explains how a *Special Needs Trust* lets you provide for a Beneficiary without jeopardizing valuable government benefits. The second section explains some recent changes in the law you need to know about if your spouse is currently eligible for or may require Medicaid.

Providing For Disabled Dependents (Special Needs Trust)

If you have a spouse, child, sibling, parent, or other loved one who is physically, mentally or developmentally disabled—from birth, illness, injury or drug abuse—he/she may be entitled to government benefits (Supplemental Security Income and/or Medicaid) now or in the future. However, most of these benefits are available only to those with very minimal assets.

Like many others, you may find yourself faced with a difficult choice—if you leave a substantial inheritance to this person, he/she will be disqualified from receiving the government benefits which may be crucial for his/her care. On the other hand, you may not want to have to disinherit this person in order to preserve these benefits.

There is a third option. With a *Special Needs Trust* within your Living Trust, you can provide for a disabled child or other loved one without interfering with his/her benefits.

The Special Needs Trust should be very specific in stating that its purpose is to *supplement* government benefits—that is, to provide only benefits or luxuries *above and beyond* the benefits the Beneficiary (the disabled person) receives from any local, state, federal or private agencies.

It is extremely important that the Special Needs Trust not duplicate any government-provided services and that the Beneficiary not have any resemblance of ownership of the Trust assets. Otherwise, it is very possible that the government would attempt to seize the Trust assets for repayment of services provided or determine that the Beneficiary does not qualify for future benefits because he/she has ample assets and income to provide for adequate care.

To make sure the Beneficiary does not have any implied ownership in the Trust assets, the Special Needs Trust should give the Trustee complete control over the distribution of the assets and any income they generate—the Beneficiary should not be able to demand any principal or interest from the Trust.

You should also instruct the Trustee to purchase only goods and services that government benefits do not provide—such as airline tickets to visit relatives, furniture, stereo, etc. (The Trustee should make the purchase directly, instead of giving the money to the Beneficiary and letting him/her make the purchase.) A spendthrift clause is also a good idea for extra protection.

Providing for a loved one with special needs takes special planning

■ Who Should Be Trustee?

Of course, you (and your spouse, if you are married) will continue to provide for this person while you are alive and able. But someone will need to assume this responsibility after your death (or incompetency), so you will need to name a Trustee.

The most obvious choice is another family member or close personal friend who has a deep concern for this person's welfare. This may be one or more of your healthy adult children.

As with any Trustee, be sure to discuss this with the person(s) you have in mind. Make sure they have the time, ability, and desire to take on this responsibility. Also, be aware of a possible conflict of interest, especially if your other children will inherit the Trust assets after your disabled child has died—they may be more interested in preserving the Trust assets than in putting the disabled child's needs first.

A Corporate Trustee can be a good choice, especially if you do not want to burden other family members with this responsibility or don't want to worry about a possible conflict of interest. And, of course, you don't have to worry about your Beneficiary outliving the Corporate Trustee—they'll be around to provide for your Beneficiary for as long as he/she lives.

You may want to consider using both. For example, the Corporate Trustee can manage the assets and a relative can be responsible for determining and purchasing the goods and services which will make your Beneficiary more comfortable. You may also want to consider having a Corporate Trustee work with you now—to take advantage of their investment skills and to have them become familiar with your Beneficiary and his/her needs.

■ How Much Should You Put Into the Trust?

Among other things, you will want to take into consideration how long you expect this person to live, the kind of care he/she will need, the benefits available (now and projected), how much income the assets can be expected to generate, how much you can afford to put into the Trust, and how much you want to give to other Beneficiaries.

■ Seek Professional Assistance

As you can see, providing for someone with special needs takes more thought and is more complicated than providing for your other Beneficiaries. Also, the laws vary from state to state. *Make sure* you use a local attorney who has experience in setting up Special Needs Trusts—standard Beneficiary wording just will not do.

Special Needs Trust For Your Spouse

If your spouse is receiving (or may need to qualify for) Medicaid benefits, you may want to set up a Special Needs Trust to provide your spouse with some extra services and benefits that are not covered by Medicaid. It would work like a Special Needs Trust for any other Beneficiary. But, because of a recent change in the law, it would have to be set up a little differently.

For now, at least, to preserve Medicaid eligibility, a Special Needs Trust for your spouse must be created *by a Will* after you die. To set it up now, your attorney will write a brief Will, the only purpose of which is to create this Special Needs Trust when you die. Then you designate which assets you want to go into this Trust. (Your other assets stay in your Living Trust.) The downside is the assets that will go into this Special Needs Trust will probably have to go through probate.

Now, remember, laws can change. In fact, several attorneys have been working to have the wording changed so a Special Needs Trust for your spouse can be set up through your Living Trust—*without* a special Will and probate. An attorney who specializes in Elder Law can help keep you informed.

Remember, you only need a Special Needs Trust if your spouse is currently eligible for or is likely to require Medicaid—and Medicaid is only available to those who have very little assets. If you have long term care insurance or you pay for medical expenses yourself, you don't need a Special Needs Trust. Your

Living Trust will let you provide for your surviving spouse—just as you wish—for the rest of his/her life.

Disinheriting

Are there any relatives you specifically do not want to inherit from you? This could be a touchy subject, but if you have strong feelings about this and it's important to you, it should be included in your Living Trust. Otherwise, they may think you just forgot them and may try to contest your Trust.

If Your Beneficiaries Die Before Receiving Their Inheritances

As we've said before, most people leave their assets to family members. And if a Beneficiary dies before receiving the inheritance, you basically have two choices to determine how this Beneficiary's share will be distributed.

The legal phrases in your Trust document that specify how this is done are *per capita* and *per stirpes*. This may seem confusing at first—especially if you have trouble following family trees. But it is important for you to understand how these provisions work because they distribute the assets very differently. The flow charts on the following pages should help you understand them.

You should also think about who you would want to have your assets if *all* of your Beneficiaries die before you. Many people specify their church, a favorite charity, or foundation.

Charities, Churches And Foundations As Beneficiaries

As you think about who will be your Beneficiaries, consider including a favorite charity or foundation. Take a few minutes to think about organizations or causes that are special to you—some national, perhaps international, and some local. There are many excellent ones, and they are all in need of funding to continue their work. There is sure to be one or more that you would like to help. In addition to the tax benefits of charitable donations, you have the power to do something good, to express yourself—to put something of value back into the world.

For example, you may have been very active in your church, synagogue, or other religious, fraternal or charitable organization—perhaps it provided support to you at a critical time in your life—and you would like to return the support. Maybe someone very close to you died from cancer, Alzheimer's or

Giving to a charity lets you give something back to the world

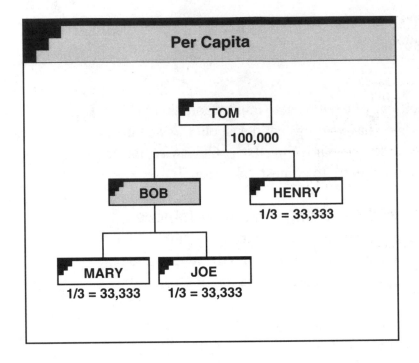

Per Capita

TOM
100,000

BOB

HENRY
1/3 = 33,333

MARY
1/3 = 33,333

JOE
1/3 = 33,333

Distribution per capita (or *by pro rata* or *share and share alike*) means that the surviving descendents will receive equal shares of the inheritance, regardless of generation. Let's say Tom, a widower, has two grown sons—Bob and Henry. Bob dies before his father Tom. Henry and his brother's two children (Tom's grandchildren—Mary and Joe) will each receive one-third of Tom's estate.

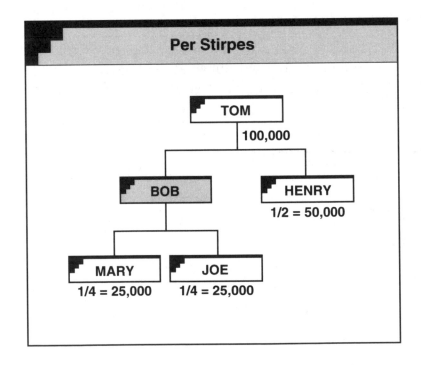

Per Stirpes

TOM
100,000

BOB

HENRY
1/2 = 50,000

MARY
1/4 = 25,000

JOE
1/4 = 25,000

Distribution per stirpes (or *by representation*) means that your surviving descendents will only receive what their immediate ancestor would receive. Using the same example, Henry will receive 50% of his father's estate. Bob's children (Mary and Joe) will each receive 25% of their grandfather's estate, splitting the 50% their father would have received.

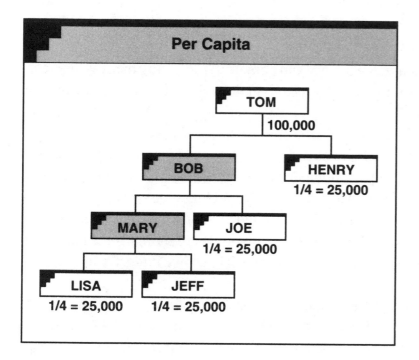

Now let's carry this a generation further. Let's say that Bob's daughter Mary, who had two children (Lisa and Jeff), also dies before her grandfather. When Tom dies, under the *per capita* instructions his four beneficiaries—son Henry, grandson Joe and great-grandchildren Lisa and Jeff—will each receive one-fourth of his estate.

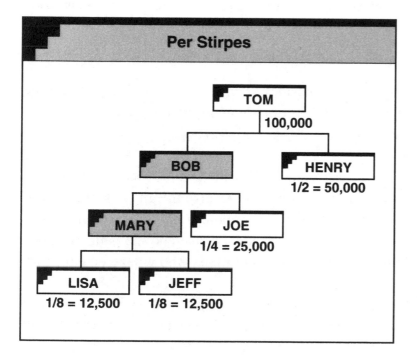

However, under *per stirpes* instructions, Mary's children would split the inheritance their mother would have received. Henry receives 50%, Mary's brother Joe receives 25% and Mary's two children will each receive 12.5% (splitting Mary's share).

With a Living Trust, the charity gets the maximum benefit of your gift

another disease, and you would like to help fund research to find a cure. Many people give in the memory of a loved one. You may feel very strongly about education, child abuse, the hungry and homeless, protecting the environment, world peace, animal rights, the arts, organ donation—the list of worthwhile causes is endless.

Your gift can be as specific or as general, as large or as small, as you want to make it. You could set up a scholarship program for underprivileged children, buy new chairs or religious textbooks for your church or synagogue, or help fund a building project. The charity or foundation of your choice will be glad to make suggestions and help you set up your gift program. (Some may even be able to recommend an attorney who specializes in Living Trusts.)

Including a charity as a Beneficiary of your Living Trust lets the charity get the maximum benefit of your gift. It will not be reduced or delayed by the probate process (as would happen if you made the gift through a Will). And as we explained in Part Two, because a Living Trust is more private, because distributions can usually be made more quickly, and because a Living Trust can be more difficult to contest, there is less chance your gift will be contested (as frequently happens when charitable gifts are made through Wills).

Some people have told us that, when they set up a Living Trust, they take some or all of the money they will save by not going through probate and give it to a charity.

> **Note:** Make sure you specify the legal name and the location (including address) of the organization you want to receive the gift. For example, if you want the local office of a national organization to have it, make sure you clearly state so—otherwise, the local office and the national office could end up fighting each other in court to see who will receive the gift.

Also, if you are unsure whether or not the organization will be around to receive the gift, list an alternate charitable Beneficiary. Otherwise, the gift will probably end up in court, and the court will have to decide who will ultimately receive it.

In Part Nine, we explain some of the ways you can give to a charity or foundation so you (or your estate) will receive special tax advantages.

IF YOU NEED MORE HELP MAKING DECISIONS

By now, you probably have a pretty good idea of who you want to be your Trustee, Successor Trustee(s) and Beneficiaries, and how (and when) you want your Beneficiaries to receive their inheritances.

But if you are still unsure about something, here are some things you can do:

■ First, re-read the appropriate section(s) a couple of times. Make notes in the margins of things you don't understand, want to know more about, or want to think about some more. Then…

■ Discuss it with your spouse (if you are married), close friends, and professionals like your attorney, trust officer, CPA, or financial advisor. Talk to as many people as you feel comfortable discussing these matters with. Ask what they have done, and what they might do if they were in your shoes.

■ Sometimes just talking out loud with someone helps you make a decision—or makes you feel better about one you've already made.

■ Take a sheet of paper, write down your options and list the advantages and disadvantages of each one.

■ Write your questions/concerns on the Organizer and ask your attorney.

If you're having trouble with a decision, try not to worry about it too much. Sometimes you just have to clear your head and come back to it later. You'll eventually make a decision that feels right for you.

Now, let's look at how you can find the right attorney to prepare your Trust document, and the steps you will need to take to set up your Living Trust.

Part Five

SETTING UP YOUR
LIVING TRUST

Part Five—
SETTING UP YOUR LIVING TRUST

Now that you have a general idea of who you want to be your Trustee, Successor Trustee(s), and Beneficiaries (and how you want them to inherit), let's go through the process—step-by-step—of setting up your Living Trust.

In this section, we'll help you find the right attorney to prepare your Trust document—we'll even give you specific questions to ask as you interview attorneys. Then we'll explain what information your attorney will need, what you can expect when you meet with your attorney and some other documents your attorney should prepare that will give you extra protection.

HOW TO FIND THE RIGHT ATTORNEY

You have to be careful (and even a bit skeptical) as you search for the attorney who will prepare your Living Trust for you. You'll want to make sure the attorney has experience *specifically* with Living Trusts. Just having "a lot of experience in estate planning" isn't enough—that usually means Wills and probate.

Your attorney should also be someone with whom you feel comfortable sharing your personal and financial situation—and will charge you a fair price. In the next few pages, we'll help you find such an attorney.

Before you actually start your search, it would be a good idea to complete the Organizer in the back of this book. This will encourage you to actually *write down* your decisions about your Trust, questions you want to ask your attorney, information about your assets, and the size of your net estate.

The more you know about what you want your Trust to do, the size of your estate, and the type of assets you have, the easier it will be for you to evaluate attorneys and select one who is right for you. You'll feel much more confident as you interview them, you'll save a lot of time—and you'll save money.

Get Referrals
■ People You Know
The first step in locating your attorney is to get referrals from people you know and trust. Ask your friends and associates if they have Living Trusts and, if so, who prepared them. Are they satisfied? Are they aware of other attorneys you should consider?

You can also ask other professionals who work with estate planning attorneys—your banker, trust officer, CPA, life insurance agent, and financial planner are usually good sources. Your investment broker, family or business attorney, church/synagogue, or a charity may also be able to make some recommendations.

Here's a question to ask professionals: "If your mother needed a Living Trust, who would you recommend to set it up for her?"

■ SPARRS: New "How-to-Find-An-Attorney" Service For Our Readers
We are well aware that finding the right attorney is no simple task. In fact, "How do I find an attorney?" is still the number one question we get from readers all over the country. In this section, we give you some help on how to interview and select an attorney. But many of our readers have asked if we can do more—by helping them find attorneys in their areas.

SPARRS (Schumacher Publishing's Attorney Rating and Review Site) is our solution. SPARRS is an exclusive, on-line database of estate planning attorneys—unique because it contains ratings and reviews from actual clients. It's accessible through our Web Site on the Internet: **www.estateplanning.com**. And it's FREE.

On SPARRS, you can search by state—even by zip code—to get information about attorneys in your area. You can find out about their practice, areas of expertise and read what their clients have to say about them. *Only SPARRS has unedited reviews and ratings of attorneys by their actual clients.* Wouldn't *you* like to know what an attorney's clients have to say about his/her services before you hire one?

If you're not on the Internet (yet), ask your kids or grandkids to help you. Or go to a local school or public library—most have Internet access. This could be a great excuse for you to find out what the "world wide web" is all about. (You can also call our SPARRS hotline: 1-800-260-0789, but it will take you longer to get the information.)

■ Certified Estate Planning Attorneys

The bar associations in some states have certification programs for attorneys who specialize in estate planning. Requirements vary, but usually the attorney must devote a certain amount of his/her practice to estate planning, complete a certain number of hours of continuing education courses each year, and may have to pass periodic exams.

It would be a good idea to call your local bar association (it should be in your phone book, or call directory assistance) to find out if your state has a similar program, what the requirements are, and to see if you can get a current list of attorneys in your area who meet them. At the least, the information will help you better qualify the attorneys you interview. (However, as we explain on the next page, you should be cautious about attorney referrals from your local bar.)

■ Living Trust Seminars

With the growing popularity of Living Trusts, some attorneys present free seminars. This is an excellent way to observe and evaluate the attorney from a distance. (After reading this book, you'll know more about Living Trusts than some seminar presenters.) It's also a good opportunity to ask questions (and hear other people's questions).

Does the attorney speak in plain English that you can understand? Is the presentation organized and well done? How well does the attorney answer questions? Does the attorney give you something to take home and read?

Usually, the attorney will stay after the seminar to meet the attendees, answer individual questions, and schedule appointments. Many offer a free consulta-

Start with referrals from people you know and trust

tion. Some even give attendees a discount off the usual cost of the Trust. This can be good for both of you—the attorney saves time by explaining the basics to several people at one time and you save money on your Trust.

If you are interested in attending one of these seminars, check your local newspaper for advertisements or listen to a local talk radio station. If you do attend, remember that the quality of the seminar is only part of it. In the end, what counts is the quality of the documents the attorney prepares for you. You will still want to interview and evaluate the attorney.

■ Prepaid Legal Services Plans

Many employers, associations and unions offer prepaid legal services plans to employees and members. Several are also being offered directly to the public through credit cards.

Under these plans, some legal services—such as review of legal documents and consultations—are free. Other services are offered at discounts, and the attorney's normal hourly rate may be reduced. Most of these plans use local attorneys to provide the services.

If you belong to or qualify for membership in one of these plans, this may be a way to have your Trust done at a lower cost. However, a referral from the plan does not guarantee an attorney has experience in Living Trusts. You will still need to personally interview the plan's attorneys. Just remember—a lower cost is no bargain if your document is not properly prepared.

■ Local Bar Association

Your local bar association can also give you names of some estate planning attorneys. But that's about all they can do—they cannot recommend one attorney over another. Attorneys often pay a fee to be on the referral list. And the bar just rotates down the list—usually with no knowledge of the attorney's experience or qualifications. Some bars charge for this "referral." In many cases, you might as well use the yellow pages—at least they're free.

■ Avoid "Scams" and Rip Offs

Watch out for all kinds of scams and rip offs—they are out there. It was probably inevitable that some unethical people would find ways to make some quick money by capitalizing on the growing popularity of Living Trusts and taking advantage of other people.

The most publicized scams, of course, are non-attorneys, using high pressure tactics, selling "cookie cutter" Living Trusts in seminars and door-to-door. But you could also be taken advantage of by an attorney. Some routinely draft Living Trusts and don't fund them. Others write Testamentary Trusts in Wills when their clients really wanted Revocable Living Trusts.

How can you make sure you find the right attorney and not become a victim of one of these scams or rip offs? Your best protection is to become an informed and educated consumer—which you are doing now—and use common sense. The next section on how to evaluate an attorney will be especially helpful.

How To Evaluate An Attorney

Once you have several attorneys to consider, you will need to start narrowing your list down. First, look to see if any attorneys have been recommended to you by more than one source—and see who recommended them. If you keep hearing some of the same names from people you respect and trust, that's probably a pretty good sign.

Next, find out where the attorney is located. You might as well start with those closest to you. But, while convenience is a consideration, the right attorney may be worth a little *in*convenience.

Keep in mind that you are looking for an attorney who has experience, has the right personality for you, and whose fees, services, and qualifications match your needs.

■ Telephone Interview—An Eleven-Point Checklist

The next step is to call the attorneys on your list. You don't need to have a lengthy conversation at this point—try to keep it to about five minutes. That's plenty of time to find out whether or not this attorney may be right for you.

If the attorney can't speak with you when you call, leave a message with your name and who referred you. Then see how long it takes before the attorney calls you back.

Keep in mind that *you are the customer*. Don't be intimidated or afraid to ask questions.

Become an informed consumer and use common sense

145

Here are specific questions you will want to ask.

1. Tell the attorney you want a Living Trust document that will avoid probate when you die and a conservatorship (guardianship) if you become incapacitated. Then ask the attorney if he/she does Revocable Living Trusts.

If the attorney tries to talk you out of a Living Trust, suggests a Will or joint ownership, or tries to convince you that a Living Trust is complicated and expensive—or that most people don't "own enough" to need a Living Trust (that they're only for the wealthy)—ask him or her to explain why. If you are not satisfied with the explanation, find another attorney.

2. Ask the attorney how many years he/she has been doing Living Trusts and about how many he/she has done. Ask what percentage of his/her practice is devoted to Living Trusts.

If the attorney has done hundreds of Living Trusts but only started doing them a year ago, that tells you the attorney has done a lot of them—but it may not tell you the quality of the documents. On the other hand, if the attorney has been doing Living Trusts for ten years but has only done 12, that may not be enough experience.

Ideally, you will find someone who specializes in Living Trusts and has done a lot of them over a long period of time. This is not a *guarantee* that the attorney knows what he/she is doing, but it's a good indicator.

Here's the point. If you needed a triple bypass operation, would you choose a doctor who has only done a few or would you choose the specialist who devotes most of his/her time to this very operation? It's essentially the same thing—with the doctor, we're talking about your health, and with the attorney, we're talking about your wealth.

Now, this is not to say that a less experienced attorney couldn't do a great job, especially for a smaller estate. It's not uncommon for less experienced attorneys to work with more seasoned "mentors." Find out who the newer attorney goes to for advice and who reviews his/her work. Common sense will take you a long way here.

3. If your estate is more than the federal estate tax exemption ($625,000 in 1998), ask how many Living Trusts with A-B and A-B-C provisions the attorney has done and over how many years. (After you complete the Organizer, you'll know how much your estate is worth and if you need these provisions.)

Again, the more of these the attorney has done and the longer he/she has been doing them, the better off you will probably be.

4. Ask who will actually write your Trust document.

In larger firms, it would not be unusual for the attorney you meet with to collect your information, instruct an associate to draft the document, then review it to make sure it is accurate. This is perfectly acceptable—and will be less costly than if a senior attorney did the actual writing.

What you want to avoid is an attorney who knows little (if anything) about Living Trusts, who just collects your information and then sends it to an attorney in another state who prepares a "cookie cutter" Trust document.

5. Ask how many Living Trusts the attorney has administered (or settled) when clients became incapacitated or died.

Some attorneys have written a lot of Living Trusts, but—either by choice or lack of experience—have little or no experience administering them. An attorney who has "hands-on" experience administering Living Trusts at incapacity and death—and has seen his/her Trust documents work— could be very helpful to your family later on if they have questions or need assistance with your Trust.

6. Ask how much the attorney charges for Living Trusts. Many attorneys charge a flat fee if your estate is less than the federal estate tax exemption ($625,000 in 1998), and another flat fee if you are married and your combined estate is less than two exemptions ($1.25 million in 1998). (See Part Three for a discussion of the federal estate tax exemption.) Be sure to ask if there are any charges that are in addition to this fee, such as for transferring assets into your Trust.

Remember, you are the customer

If the attorney charges by the hour, it will be harder to get an estimate over the phone. Tell the attorney how much your estate is worth, and ask if he/she can give you a "ballpark" estimate—or what the cost has been for similar size estates.

In either case, be wary if the attorney is reluctant to talk about pricing.

7. Ask how long it will take, and decide if that is acceptable to you.

Since you will be prepared and organized, usually the attorney will be able to provide you with a first draft of the documents within a couple of weeks. It may take another couple of weeks for you to review them and have any corrections made. However, if you or the person who is getting the Trust (for example, a parent) is ill, that may be too long. If you need the Trust done sooner for a valid reason, ask if the attorney will accommodate you. Remember, *you're* the customer.

8. Ask the attorney to send you a biography. (Most will be happy to do so.)

When you receive it, look to see where the attorney went to school. Does he/she have any advanced degrees or professional designations? Does the attorney take continuing education courses? Does he/she teach or write on topics for other attorneys?

9. Ask how much malpractice insurance the attorney has.

If your assets are worth $1 million, would you want to go to an attorney who only has $100,000 of malpractice insurance?

10. Can you come in for a free consultation?

Many attorneys are willing to spend 15-20 minutes with you at no charge to answer your general questions. But if the attorney charges a reasonable fee for this meeting, it still may be worth it—depending on the size of your estate, the qualifications of the attorney, and the strength of the referral.

11. Evaluate the conversation.

What do you think? Were you comfortable with the attorney? Did the attorney seem willing to answer your questions, or did you feel you were only taking up his/her time? Could you understand him/her?

Did the price estimate seem reasonable? (Remember, you're comparing the cost of a Living Trust to the potential costs and inconveniences of probate *and* a possible conservatorship.) Don't be afraid or embarrassed to shop around and to compare prices. But, at the same time, be careful not to sacrifice quality for price. You want the best *value*—not the cheapest price.

You want the best value— not the cheapest price

■ Personal Interview—A Ten-Point Checklist

The next step is to schedule a personal meeting with the attorneys who are at the top of your list. Be considerate and keep your time limit in mind. If your meeting is for 20 minutes, take no more than 20 minutes.

Again, remember that *you* are the customer. *You* are interviewing the attorney. Most attorneys will want your business—and *you* will decide who gets it.

Here are some things to look for and ask.

1. Is the attorney prompt? Is the staff courteous? Is the attorney's office neat and clean? Does the attorney appear to be well-organized?

2. Show this book and your completed Organizer to the attorney.

If the attorney tries to downplay the information and discourage you from wanting to avoid probate, keep looking. The attorney you want to deal with should endorse any information that correctly explains Living Trusts.

3. Confirm the price estimate.

The attorney should be able to look quickly at your completed Organizer and give you a pretty good estimate.

4. What documents are included in this cost?

Most attorneys will prepare the following documents *in addition to* your Living Trust document. (These are explained at the end of this section.)
- Pour Over Will;
- Durable Power of Attorney for Property Management;
- Living Will and/or Durable Power of Attorney for Health Care.

5. How much assistance does the attorney provide you with changing titles and beneficiary designations? Does the attorney do any for you? Is there an additional charge? If you have a problem, will the attorney call on your behalf? Is there an additional charge for this? Or does the attorney just do the documents and leave this part of the process completely up to you?

Many attorneys also include pre-written letters you can send to your bank, savings and loan, etc. with instructions for changing titles (these are very helpful). How much assistance the attorney gives you is usually another good indication of the quality of work he/she does.

6. Ask if the attorney minds if you get a second opinion of his/her recommendations or if you have the documents reviewed by another attorney after they are done.

If the attorney is confident in his/her work, not only should he/she *not* mind, he/she should *encourage* you to do this. (By the way, it should only cost you $100-$200 for the review—and that's money well-spent for the peace of mind you will have when you know your Trust is done properly.)

7. Ask if the attorney will notify you of any changes in the law that might affect your Living Trust.

The more conscientious attorneys think of you as a lifelong client, and want to make sure your Trust does not go out of date. Other attorneys don't feel they have any responsibility to you once your Trust is done.

8. Ask if there are any clients you can call for a referral. (If clients have given their permission, this is perfectly okay.)

9. Ask to see a sample of the documents you will receive. (If there is not enough time during your meeting, you can look at these in the reception area or another office afterwards.)

Look for the Living Trust document, then the additional documents mentioned above in Question #4.

The documents should be well organized and easy to follow. Some attorneys put the documents in a binder, with a table of contents, divided sections, and a summary of each document in simple English.

While the way the documents are written and organized can be a good reflection of the type of work the attorney does, keep in mind that a pretty package does not necessarily mean that the documents are well written. It still could be a good idea to have the attorney's work reviewed by another attorney.

10. Evaluate the meeting.

How do you feel now that you have met the attorney? Do you feel confident in his/her abilities? Does he/she speak in plain English that you can understand? Did the attorney seem to be genuinely interested in you and your family's welfare? Did the attorney seem willing to answer your questions and encourage you to voice your concerns—or did you feel you were only taking up his/her time?

Trust your instincts. If you feel good about the meeting, this may be the right attorney for you. But if something doesn't feel right, then it probably isn't—and you'll want to keep looking.

Meeting With Your Attorney

Once you've selected the attorney to prepare your Living Trust, here's how the process should go.

1. Call the attorney's office to schedule an appointment to have your Living Trust prepared. Ask what information you should bring with you. Many attorneys can mail you a list of the documents they will need. Here are some your attorney may want to see:

A pretty "package" doesn't mean the documents are well written

- Copies of deeds;
- Existing Wills or Trusts;
- Pre-marital and/or divorce agreements;
- Most recent statements from accounts (checking, saving, brokerage, money market, etc.);
- Copies of stock certificates and bonds you have in your possession; Insurance policies;
- Plan documents for company retirement/saving plans; Certificates of ownership for vehicles (especially if they are valuable);
- If you are owner of a sole proprietorship: balance sheet, list of assets, Schedule C of latest income tax return, fictitious business name statement, list of licenses or permits;
- If you are owner of a closely-held corporation: articles of incorporation, bylaws, minutes, most recent corporate income tax returns, annual statement, balance sheet, buy-sell agreements, voting trust agreement, stock certificate;
- If you are a partner in a partnership: the partnership agreement, buy-sell agreement, amendments, most recent partnership income tax returns, balance sheet, annual statement.

Your attorney isn't asking to see all this just because he/she is nosey—it's just that *your attorney can only help you create a plan that is as good as the information you provide.* If, for example, you underestimate the value of your assets, the attorney won't be able to help you plan properly and you could end up paying too much in taxes.

The information you share with your attorney is confidential—you've probably heard of the term "attorney/client privilege." By law, your attorney cannot reveal any of this information. You should feel comfortable enough with your attorney that you can be completely honest—if not, maybe you should look for another attorney.

2. Mail a copy of your completed Organizer to your attorney in advance, so he/she will have time to review it *before* your meeting.

3. At your first meeting, the attorney should review your information, ask you some questions, answer your questions, and will probably make some suggestions for you to consider. Just like a doctor, your attorney needs to "examine" you (your information and needs) before administering the treatment (preparing your Trust).

If your attorney charges by the hour, you should be able to get a definite cost now that he/she has seen all your information and knows what you want.

4. Your attorney will then prepare a draft of the documents for you to review and approve. As we mentioned earlier, in most cases, this will only take two or three weeks, but if your plan is complicated it may take a little longer. (It could also happen more quickly, depending on your needs.)

5. When you receive the drafts, make sure you read them carefully. Be sure you understand everything. Don't be afraid to ask questions.

6. After you have approved the drafts, the final documents will be prepared. You (and your spouse) will sign them, and usually they will be notarized. There often are two original documents—so if by some chance you misplace one, you will have another original.

7. Some attorneys will prepare a Schedule of Assets and attach it to the Trust document. This is a list of all the assets that will be transferred to the Trust. Often, there are three schedules—one for each spouse's separate assets, and one for jointly owned assets.

Listing assets on a schedule *does not mean they are in your Trust*—you still have to change titles and beneficiary designations to do that. The main purpose of this is for convenience—it will give you a checklist of assets that are to be transferred, and it will be helpful for your Successor Trustee as a guide to what the Trust assets are.

8. Titles and appropriate beneficiary designations will then need to be changed—otherwise, you've just wasted your time and money. *Remember, your Living Trust can only protect the assets you transfer into it.* This "funding" process is explained thoroughly in Part Six.

Your attorney can only create a plan that is as good as the information you provide

Other Documents Your Attorney Should Prepare

As we mentioned earlier, there are some other documents your attorney should prepare in addition to your Living Trust to give you extra protection, convenience, and control.

Some will act as a kind of "safety net" for assets inadvertently left out of your Trust. For example, something may happen to prevent you from changing all the titles and beneficiary designations, or you could receive an inheritance or win the lottery and not have time to put the assets in your Trust. Or you could just forget an asset.

Other documents will give you control over decisions that may need to be made about your medical care when you are not able to make them.

Let's look at what these documents are and what they can do for you.

For Control Over Assets Left Out Of Your Living Trust
■ **Pour Over Will**

A Pour Over Will is a very short Will that acts as a safety net. It states that if an asset is discovered after you die that was inadvertently left *out* of your Living Trust, the asset is to go *into* your Trust. The "forgotten" asset will probably have to go through probate, but at least your Pour Over Will "catches" the asset and sends it back (pours it over) into your Living Trust so it can be distributed as part of your overall Living Trust plan.

There is another reason you may need a Pour Over Will. In some states, the Guardian for minor children must be named in a Will. So if you have a Children's Trust in your Living Trust, your attorney will also name the Guardian in your Pour Over Will to satisfy this requirement. This also keeps your Living Trust private, because only the Pour Over Will would have to be admitted to court when the Guardian is appointed. (Even in states that do not require this, many attorneys will go ahead and name the Guardian in the Pour Over Will anyway—so your Living Trust would not have to be admitted to the court and made public.)

■ Durable Power of Attorney for Asset Management

Your Living Trust document can only give your Successor Trustee (or Co-Trustee) the authority to manage *the assets you put in your Trust*. A Durable Power of Attorney for Asset Management gives your Successor limited authority to manage assets that are *not* in your Trust.

For example, if you are incapacitated and your Successor Trustee finds that you forgot to put an asset into your Trust—or you receive an inheritance or win the lottery in your personal name—this document, when properly written, can give your Successor the authority to change the title and put the asset into your Trust for you. Your Successor will also be able to do this for you if you are well and simply out of the country or otherwise unavailable.

Another benefit of this document is simply convenience. Although your Living Trust gives authority to your Successor Trustee (or to your Co-Trustee) to act for you, some people and institutions (like hospitals and nursing homes) still may not be that familiar with Living Trusts. Instead of trying to educate them in an emergency, your Successor can show them the Durable Power of Attorney document, which is readily recognized by just about everyone. (Besides, you will probably consider your Living Trust plan to be private, and you may not want it shown to strangers.)

A Durable Power of Attorney can also give your Successor Trustee the power to sign your tax returns (which cannot be done in a Living Trust).

It is important that these powers are given only to the same people you name as your Successor Trustees (and Co-Trustee, if you have one) and in the same order as you have listed them. In other words, the powers should be given to the Trustee who steps in for you—they should go to the Trustee position, rather than to a specific individual. So, if your first choice for Successor Trustee is unable to act, your second choice (or third, if necessary) will have this authority.

■ These Are Only Extra Precautions

These extra safety nets *should never take the place of changing titles and beneficiary designations to your Trust while you are alive and able.* Don't put off completing your Trust thinking that these provisions will do it for you.

A Pour Over Will sends a "forgotten asset" back into your Trust

Certificate Of Trust—For Convenience

As you begin changing titles, some institutions may insist upon having a copy of or reviewing your Trust. For example, your bank will probably want to see your Trust before changing your accounts, safe deposit box, etc. Your bank is not being nosey, and you shouldn't think of this request as a nuisance or invasion of your privacy. Because it's for their protection—*and yours*.

Before they change the titles on your accounts, they need to see the name of your Trust, who is authorized to be Trustee and Successor Trustee, if the Trustee has the necessary powers to transact business for the Trust, that you have signed your Trust, and that it is notarized. The reason is they do not want the liability of giving control of your assets to someone *unless they are sure* you want this person to have control—and you wouldn't want that, either.

However, they do not need to see a listing of your Trust assets, who the Beneficiaries of your Trust are, and how you will provide for them.

So that you do not have to show them your entire Trust document, your attorney can prepare a *Certificate of Trust* or a *certified copy of your Trust*. This is a shortened version of your Trust that will usually satisfy these requests. It verifies the existence of your Trust, explains the powers given to the Trustee, identifies the Successor Trustees, etc., but it does not reveal any of your confidential information (like your assets, your Beneficiaries, and their inheritances).

Your attorney may call this document by another name, but he/she will probably know what needs to be prepared.

For Control Over Decisions About Your Medical Care

Throughout this book, we have been discussing how to keep control of your *assets* if you become incapacitated and when you die. When your attorney prepares your Living Trust document, he/she will also probably prepare one or both of the following documents to give you control over *medical* decisions that may need to be made when you are not able to make them yourself. This can be very important for both you and those who will care for you.

By completing one or both of the following documents, your family will know what kind of treatment you want (and don't want) and who you want to make medical decisions for you when you can't.

■ Living Will

Many people think a Living Trust and a Living Will do the same things because the names are so similar. But they do very *different* things.

A Living Trust, as you have learned in this book, is for your *financial* affairs. It lets you keep control over your assets if you become incapacitated and after you die.

A Living Will is for *medical* affairs. It is a simple document that lets your physician know the kind of life support treatment you would want in case of terminal illness or injury. The wording for a Living Will is short and standard. You can get a copy of one from your attorney, doctor, hospital, or nursing/medical association.

Living Wills became popular after Karen Ann Quinlan fell into an irreversible coma in the 1970's. You may recall that, because she was legally an adult and had left no written instructions regarding what she would have wanted in this situation, her family was forced to wage a lengthy court battle to have her removed from life support.

Limitations of Living Wills

You should be aware that a Living Will may or may not do what you expect it to do. In some states, for example, a Living Will is binding—if a doctor or hospital refuses to honor it, they must withdraw from the case.

But in other states, it is not legally binding on anyone—it is simply a "directive" to your physician. Many doctors and hospitals are reluctant to discontinue any life sustaining treatment (remember, they have been trained to *save* lives). And if a family member objects to your wishes as expressed in your Living Will, it's almost certain the doctor and hospital will not follow through as you have requested—most just don't want to be held liable.

Also, a Living Will is very limited. It addresses the use of life support only in very specific *terminal* situations (where death is imminent). So it would not be of any use to someone who may exist for years in a coma or a vegetative state. (Since death is not "imminent," this would not be considered a terminal situation.) In Karen Quinlan's situation, for example, a Living Will would not have been enough. She was in a lingering coma, so death was not imminent.

Living Wills and Living Trusts do different things

Also, in most states, a Living Will does not allow for nutrition (food and water) to be discontinued. And because a Living Will is a *statutory* document, the wording can't be altered or personalized.

■ Durable Power of Attorney for Health Care

This document gives you more control than a Living Will. It lets you give legal authority to another person (called your agent or surrogate) to make *any* health care decisions for you if you are unable to make these decisions for yourself. And, unlike a Living Will, a Durable Power of Attorney for Health Care *is* legally binding and enforceable.

Your agent would be able to make decisions regarding the use of life support not only if your condition is terminal, but also if you are in a coma or vegetative state—and, in many cases, your agent would be able to order nutrition (food and water) stopped.

A Durable Power of Attorney for Health Care is also very valuable if you need surgery or medical treatment of *any* kind and there is the possibility you will not be able to make medical decisions for even a short length of time.

This document is now available in most states, although the name may vary slightly. Florida, for example, has a Health Care Proxy; some states call it a Medical Power of Attorney.

It would be a good idea to share your thoughts and wishes about this subject with your family and loved ones. You should also talk with your doctor. Find out how he/she feels about a Durable Power of Attorney for Health Care and Living Wills, explain your opinions, and confirm that your doctor will honor your wishes. (If your doctor is not supportive of your position, you may want to find one who is.)

Also, if you live part of each year in two states, consider having documents prepared in both states. That way, you won't have to worry about whether or not your doctors will accept documents that don't look like the ones they are used to seeing.

. . . .

Now that you have found the right attorney and had your documents prepared, let's look at what's involved in putting assets in your Living Trust.

Part Six

....

FUNDING YOUR LIVING TRUST

Part Six—
FUNDING YOUR LIVING TRUST

Once you have signed your Living Trust document, the next step is to change titles and beneficiary designations to your Trust. This is called "funding" your Living Trust.

This is probably the most important part of getting a Living Trust. If you have signed your Living Trust document but haven't changed titles and beneficiary designations, you've simply wasted your money. You may have a great Trust, but until you fund it, it doesn't control anything—because your Living Trust can only control the assets you put into it.

Remember, when you put assets in your Living Trust, you do not lose control of them. You can continue to buy and sell assets just as you did before. And anything you put into your Living Trust can always be taken out later.

In this section, we'll discuss who is responsible for funding your Trust, how difficult this process is, and then explain the general procedures for changing titles and beneficiary designations for the most common types of assets people own. We suggest that you look for the ones you own and skip over the others. If you own something that is not included here, your attorney can tell you how to put it into your Trust.

WHO WILL FUND YOUR TRUST?
You should know, before your Trust is set up, how much of the funding process the attorney will do. The most conscientious attorneys we know will do *all* the

Your Living Trust can only control the assets you put into it

funding. They want their clients' Trusts to be as effective as possible—so they personally make sure everything is put into the Trust properly.

Usually, however, it is a combination of the attorney doing some and you doing some. Ideally, your attorney should review each asset with you, explain the procedure to you, and together you should decide who will be responsible for each asset. Many attorneys will put your home in your Trust for you at no additional cost. Some also have legal assistants who can put other assets in your Trust for you at a lower hourly rate than if the attorney does it.

Depending on how much the attorney charges, how comfortable you are with the process, how much time you have, and how interested you are in keeping your costs down, you may want to do many of them yourself.

Most attorneys have pre-written letters you can send to your bank, investment broker, insurance company, etc. that tell them how your assets should now be titled. At the least, your attorney should give you very specific instructions and the exact wording to use for titles and beneficiary designations. The wording will include the name(s) of the Trustee(s), the name of your Trust, and the date you sign the Trust document. So it will be something like this: " John Doe and Mary Doe, Trustees of the Doe Family Trust, dated month/day/year."

How DIFFICULT IS THE FUNDING PROCESS?

As you will see in the next few pages, most titles and beneficiary designations are not difficult to change. Some are done by using an Assignment—a short (usually one-page) document your attorney will prepare that identifies the asset and states that you are transferring its ownership to your Living Trust.

Others will require written instructions from you, giving the institutions the exact wording to use on the titles and beneficiary designations (usually the pre-written letters from your attorney will be all you need). Some institutions have their own forms that you will need to complete (for example, life insurance companies have standard forms to change the Beneficiary on policies).

Most changes can be handled through the mail and by telephone. Some will require your signature to be notarized or guaranteed (we'll explain who can do this for you).

Even though the process itself is not really difficult, it will take some time. How *much* time will depend on how many titles and beneficiary designations you have to change and how quickly the institutions respond. Most will be cooperative. However, you *may* encounter a few people who are still unfamiliar with Living Trusts. (Since Living Trusts have become so popular, this doesn't happen as often as it used to.) If you do have any difficulties, usually a quick call from your attorney will clear things up.

If you decide to do most of the funding yourself, we suggest that you make it a priority and keep going until you're finished. Start with your assets that have the largest values, then work down to the smaller ones. Remind yourself *why* you are doing this—and look forward to the peace of mind you'll have when your Living Trust is complete.

Now let's look at how titles and beneficiary designations are changed.

HOW TO CHANGE TITLES AND BENEFICIARY DESIGNATIONS

If You Live In a Community Property State
If you live in one of the eight community property states, your attorney may suggest that jointly-owned assets—especially real estate—be retitled as community property *before* they are put in your Trust.

As we explained in Part One, when one spouse dies, community property assets receive a *full* step-up in basis. This reduces the capital gains tax that would be due when the assets are eventually sold. With joint ownership, *only the deceased's share* would receive a step-up in basis—so you would have a bigger gain (profit) when the assets are sold, and would pay more in capital gains tax.

Community property status can be retained when the assets are put in your Living Trust. So, by retitling jointly owned assets as community property *first*, you will get the full step-up in basis when one spouse dies.

If You Live in a Noncommunity Property State
If you live in a noncommunity property state and have owned an asset jointly with your spouse since before 1976, the asset may be entitled to a full step-up

in basis when one spouse dies. If you change the title on it now (even to your Living Trust), you could lose the full step-up—the deceased spouse's share would still get a step-up, but the surviving spouse's share would not. This could cause your surviving spouse to pay more in capital gains tax if he/she decides to sell the asset after you die.

If the asset is your personal residence, losing the full step-up will not be a problem unless the gain is more than $500,000. (If you are married, up to $500,000 of the gain on the sale of your personal residence is now exempt from capital gains tax. See page 167.) But it could be a problem for other assets like farmland, commercial real estate or stocks.

If this sounds like it could apply to your situation, check with your tax advisor *before* you change the title. (For more information, see *Gallenstein v. United States*, a 1992 Sixth Circuit Court of Appeals case. Other circuit courts have followed this ruling in similar cases.)

Your Home, Real Estate, Land, Condominium, Etc.

Depending on the state in which the property is located, a correction deed, grant deed, warranty deed, assignment, or quitclaim deed will be used to change the titles of real estate to your Living Trust.

The new deed will include how the property is titled now (before you put it into the Trust), what the new title should be (to put it into your Trust) and the legal description of the property. The deed for each property will be signed by you, witnessed, notarized, and recorded in the county where the property is located.

Again, your attorney will probably put your home in your Living Trust for you at no extra cost. This is usually a good idea since the home is the most valuable asset most people own, and the legal description and titles must be exact.

■ Out of State Property

If you own property in another state, you will want to transfer it to your Living Trust to prevent a conservatorship and/or probate there. Your attorney can contact a title company or an attorney in that state to handle the transfer for you.

You may also be able to do part (or all) of it yourself. First find out what is involved—check with an attorney or escrow office in that state to find out the proper form to use, to verify the process, and to get the name and address of the recording office. In some states, your Trust may have to be recorded—if so, a Certificate of Trust should be all that is needed. However, it may be more convenient (and wise) to have the local attorney or escrow office handle the transfer for you.

■ Current Mortgage

Putting real estate—especially your home—into your Living Trust should not disturb your current mortgage in any way. Even if the mortgage contains a "due on sale or transfer" clause, retitling your home in the name of your Living Trust should not activate the clause. (It would still be a good idea to contact the lender *before* you transfer the property so you don't inadvertently activate the clause, especially if you own rental property or commercial real estate. The lender may charge a small fee to approve the transfer.)

In the past, some people who wanted to put their homes into their Living Trusts were met with resistance. Many banks, savings and loans, and mortgage companies (called primary lenders) who write home mortgages simply did not understand Living Trusts. Many were also afraid the *secondary* lenders—institutions who buy home mortgages from these primary lenders, providing them with more money to loan out—would not buy mortgages if the borrower was a Living Trust instead of an individual.

But things have changed as Living Trusts have become so popular. Fannie Mae, Freddie Mac and Ginnie Mae (which buys FHA home mortgages)—the major secondary lenders—all now consider a Revocable Living Trust to be an "eligible borrower" as long as normal guidelines are met (for example, the property must be owner-occupied, they want to make sure the Trustee is authorized to borrow against the property, and they usually want the owner to be a Trustee, which most people are anyway).

These recently published guidelines will make it much easier to transfer your home into your Living Trust, to refinance your home after it is in your Living Trust (without having to temporarily remove it from the Trust), and even to purchase new real estate in the name of your Living Trust.

If you do run into resistance, it will probably be from a lender who has not informed its loan officers about Living Trusts or simply doesn't want to change the way it does business. If this happens to you, you can always take out the mortgage in your personal name and then transfer the property to your Living Trust after the closing—or you may want to find another lender.

Putting your home into your Living Trust should not disturb your mortgage

■ **Homeowner's, Liability, and Title Insurance**

Your homeowner's and liability insurance should be changed to reflect your Living Trust on the title and the Trustees as additional insureds. (If you are your own Trustee, it will show you as Trustee instead of you as an individual.) Your agent will be able to make this change for you (probably at no charge). Usually all the insurance company will need is a letter of instruction from you and a copy of the new deed.

Title insurance should also be changed. Check to make sure your title insurance company will still insure title when your Living Trust is the owner of the property. Most will. In fact, one of the largest title insurance companies routinely issues title insurance when the property is in a Living Trust. (And they do not require a separate title search.)

■ **Property Taxes**

Most owners of real estate pay a property tax every year based on the appraised value of the property. Transferring real estate to a Living Trust should not cause your property to be reappraised because the underlying ownership is the same (remember, it's *your* Trust) and because the Trust is revocable (remember, you can take the property *out* of your Trust and put it back into your individual name at any time).

Even so, you may need to notify the tax assessor's office. In California, for example, a "Preliminary Change of Ownership Report" must be filed. This is a simple form (with check boxes) that the attorney usually completes at the same time the new deed is prepared.

■ **Transfer Tax**

Generally, a transfer tax is charged whenever property is sold. Putting real estate into a Living Trust does not constitute a sale, because you can take the property out of the Trust at any time. So, in most states, there will be *no* transfer tax when you transfer property to your Living Trust.

However, a few states and counties are looking for creative ways to raise revenue and they may charge a transfer tax anyway. For example, Pennsylvania *used* to charge a transfer tax when real estate was transferred into a Living Trust and *any* Beneficiary was someone other than a spouse, grandparent, parent, child, grandchild (and spouse) or sibling (and spouse). So if you named a friend or a charity as a Beneficiary of your Living Trust (even as an Alternate Beneficiary), you had to pay a transfer tax on real estate you put into your Living Trust. This tax was recently repealed, specifically for Living Trusts.

■ Exemption From Capital Gains Tax When Residence Sold

Previously, if you were over age 55, you were allowed a one-time $125,000 exemption of the gain (profit) on the sale of your home. Also, if you sold your home and bought a new one for at least the same price within two years, the profit from the sale of your previous residence was exempt from capital gains tax, providing you had owned and made this house your principal residence for at least three of the previous five years. Putting your home in a Living Trust had no effect on either of these exemptions.

Thanks to *The Taxpayer Relief Act of 1997*, we have a *new* capital gains tax exemption that *replaces* these two previous ones. Now, under current tax law, if you sell your home and you are single, up to $250,000 of your gain (profit) will be exempt from capital gains tax—providing you have owned and made the house your principal residence for at least two of the past five years. (If you are married, up to $500,000 will be exempt.) You can use this exemption only once every two years. Having your home in a Living Trust will have no effect on you getting this new capital gains tax exemption.

■ Homestead Exemption From Creditors

As we explained in Part Two, part or all of the value of your home may be protected from creditors' claims under your state's homestead laws. Putting your home in a Living Trust should not cause you to lose this protection.

■ Rental Real Estate

Under current tax law, the expenses you have from rental real estate (including mortgage interest, property taxes, insurance, repairs, depreciation and other operating expenses) can usually be deducted *only* from rental income.

If you don't have enough rental income (called "passive income") to offset your expenses (called "passive losses") in the year they are incurred, you can carry the excess losses ("net losses") forward and deduct them from rental income in subsequent tax years. If you have not been able to deduct all of your losses by the time you sell the property, you can write them off then.

As usual, there are exceptions:

Putting your home in your Living Trust has no effect on the new capital gains exemption

1. If you earn your living mainly in the real estate business (for example, you are a contractor, builder or broker), you may not be affected by these "passive loss" rules.

2. If your Adjusted Gross Income (as defined on IRS Form 1040) is less than $150,000 and you actively participate in the management of the property (approve repairs and new tenants, write checks, make management decisions, etc.), you can deduct up to $25,000 in net losses each year from your *ordinary* income (wages, tips, etc. as defined by the IRS on Form 1040). (If your AGI is more than $100,000, the $25,000 is gradually phased out so that, by the time the AGI is $150,000, the amount of passive net losses that can be deducted from ordinary income is reduced to "0.")

Transferring rental real estate to your Living Trust does *not* affect the way you handle these losses while you are living. However, if you are currently allowed to deduct up to $25,000 in net losses from your ordinary income, these losses may be handled differently *after* you (and your spouse) die. For a full explanation, see Part Eight.

■ If You Suspect the Property is Contaminated

You can still put contaminated property in your Living Trust but the Trustee can personally be responsible for any clean up. As we explained in Part Two, if you are your own Trustee, this won't affect you because you are *already* responsible. But, remember, if the clean up is not complete by the time your Successor Trustee steps in, he/she (and, ultimately, your Beneficiaries) can also be liable. If you suspect that property you own may be contaminated, be sure to read the discussion of this in Part Two. And make sure you tell your attorney *before* you transfer the property to your Trust.

Credit Cards, Notes You Owe

Setting up a Living Trust should not affect any credit cards, loans or notes you owe. These are not assets, so you don't need to do anything with them. You just continue making your required payments as usual.

Mortgages, Loans, And Notes Owed To You

If you have "owner-financed" any assets (for example, you "took back" a note on a house you sold), loaned someone money or have any other notes payable to you, you will need to *assign* these mortgages/loans to your Living Trust.

This is done by an Assignment (as we explained earlier). It is signed by you only (not the other party), notarized and attached to the original document. If the original mortgage was recorded, some attorneys will also record the assignment.

If you have loaned someone money without documenting the loan, this would be a good time to put it in writing to prevent disputes over the terms and nature of the loan. Write up the terms of the loan and have it signed by the other party. An Assignment can then be prepared to transfer the loan to the Trust.

Checking, Saving, And Pay-on-Death Accounts

You will need to change the ownership of your checking and saving accounts to your Living Trust. New signature cards will then need to be signed by the Trustee(s). If you are your own Trustee, you can sign the signature cards with just your usual signature.

You may need to sign new account agreements. Some institutions will require a new account, with a new account number and new checks. If you are your own Trustee, the information on your checks does not need to change—they can still be printed with just your name, address, and telephone number on them—and you continue to sign checks the same way you always have.

If you have named Beneficiaries on any accounts, you'll want to change them to your Living Trust. For example, you may have established an account and named your spouse, child or grandchild as the Beneficiary. These are called "Totten Trusts." The account title probably includes the words "in trust for" (or "ITF"), "as trustee for" (or "ATF"), "payable-on-death" (or "POD"), or "transfer on death" (or "TOD").

Remember, by changing the Beneficiary on these to your Living Trust, you prevent the possibility of the court taking control of the funds if your Beneficiary is a minor or incapacitated when you die, or dies before (or at the same time as) you. The institution will probably have its own form to change the Beneficiary.

To change the ownership or Beneficiary of an account, the institution will probably ask to see a copy of your Trust document. Remember, this is for your protection and, as we explained in Part Five, a Certificate of Trust should satisfy their requirements.

Change Beneficiary of pay-on-death accounts to your Living Trust

Certificates Of Deposit

These should be retitled in the name of your Trust. Some let you name a Beneficiary—if yours does, the Beneficiary should also be your Trust. You do not need to cash these in to do this.

Some institutions will retitle the certificates immediately with no penalties. If yours requires you to wait until the certificate matures, you can go ahead and change the Beneficiary and use an Assignment to transfer your ownership interest to your Trust. Then, when the certificate matures, you can change the title to your Trust before you renew it.

> **Note:** This process does not apply to IRAs that are invested in CDs. We discuss IRAs and your Living Trust later in this section.

What About FDIC Insurance?

The Federal Deposit Insurance Corporation (FDIC) insures deposits at banks and savings associations that are FDIC members for up to $100,000 per account category per institution. "Deposits" include checking and saving accounts, retirement accounts (including IRAs and Keoghs), NOW accounts, and CDs. Securities, mutual funds and other such investments are not considered "deposits" and therefore are not covered by the FDIC.

When you retitle FDIC-insured accounts in the name of your Living Trust, the insurance coverage may change. In fact, your Living Trust accounts may qualify for *much more* FDIC insurance.

The general formula the FDIC uses when determining insurance for Living Trust accounts is: (the number of Grantors living at the time the FDIC-insured institution fails) times (the number of qualifying Beneficiaries living at the time the institution fails) times $100,000.

So, for example, if you and your spouse have one Living Trust together (you are Co-Grantors) and have named your three children and five grandchildren as the Beneficiaries—and certain conditions, explained below, are met—your Trust would be insured for up to $1,600,000 while everyone is living. (Two Grantors times eight qualifying Beneficiaries times $100,000 = $1,600,000.) By contrast, if you and your spouse had a joint account instead, it would only be insured for up to $100,000.

For your Living Trust to be eligible for this additional coverage, it must meet certain conditions, which include:

The title of the account must indicate that a Trust is involved. For example, " John Doe and Mary Doe, Trustees of the Doe Family Trust, dated month/day/year," "Doe Family Trust," and "Doe Family Revocable Trust," would all be acceptable titles.

A qualifying Beneficiary can only be a spouse, child or grandchild of the Grantor (a parent, sibling, niece, nephew or non-relative does not qualify) and must be listed *by name* in the "deposit account records" of the institution (for example, on the signature card).

There can be no conditions in the Trust that would prevent a qualifying Beneficiary from eventually receiving his/her share of the Trust after you (and your spouse) die. For example, it is not okay to say that "my daughter will receive her inheritance *only* when she removes that ring from her nose" or "my son will receive his inheritance when he graduates from medical school"—because if these events never happen, the Beneficiary would not receive his/her share.

Credit Union Accounts

Most credit union accounts can easily be transferred to your Living Trust. To do this, you will need to set up a new account titled in your Trust's name and transfer your existing account(s) to it.

Of course, to have an account at a credit union, you must be a member. And in order for your Trust to qualify, all "parties" of your Living Trust—the Grantor(s), Trustees, *and* Beneficiaries—must be eligible for membership. Since most Living Trusts only include family members (who are usually eligible to join anyway), this is not a problem for most people.

If you have named a Corporate Trustee as a Successor Trustee (which some people do), this may still be okay—because when a Corporate Trustee steps in, they will usually close the credit union account anyway and transfer it to an account they manage.

If your Living Trust does not qualify as a member, there are still some things you can do. You can name your Living Trust as the "pay on death" Beneficiary

Accounts titled in the name of your Living Trust may qualify for more FDIC insurance

on the account or add your Living Trust as a "joint owner with right of survivorship" (joint owners do *not* have to be members). Then, when you die, your credit union accounts will automatically be owned by your Trust.

No special membership card or agreement is usually required when you open the new account for your Living Trust. The credit union will probably ask to see your Trust document to make sure it qualifies for membership, what the Trustee's powers are, who the Successor Trustees are, and when they are authorized to step in. (Although they may need to see who your Beneficiaries are, they do not need to know how you will provide for them.)

Your Trust, just like any other member, will be entitled to vote at annual meetings. However, since the Trust is not a person, someone (usually the Trustee) will need to be given the authority to vote for the Trust.

These rules apply to federal credit unions (more than half of the 14,000 credit unions are federally regulated), but even those that are state regulated will often follow these guidelines.

> **Note:** If you think you may want to take out a loan at some point, you should probably keep an individual account with the minimum required balance. That's because your Trust would only be allowed to borrow an amount equal to its own value.

Safe Deposit Box

You will need to change the box authorization card to your Trust and the Trustee(s) will need to sign the card. This will allow your Successor Trustee to have ready access at your death or incapacity. Your bank or savings and loan officer can help you do this.

Stocks/Bonds/Mutual Funds

■ Street Accounts

If you maintain an account in the name of your bank or brokerage company (called a "street account") or invest in a mutual fund, they will need written instructions from you to change the name on your account to your Trust.

Call them first to see if you should send a letter of instruction (remember, your attorney will probably include sample letters with your Trust) or if they have their own form they can send you—or if they have their own procedures you will need to follow.

They may request that your signature be guaranteed. Your local banker or broker can probably do this for you (just call ahead and make sure). You will sign the form or your letter in your banker's or broker's presence, and he/she will affix a stamp that "guarantees" your signature.

They may also ask to see a copy of your Trust document (again, the Certificate of Trust should be all they need).

■ If You Possess Certificates

If you have possession of actual stock and securities certificates, you can set up an account at a brokerage house or other financial institution. They will transfer the titles to the name of your Trust for you and keep the certificates for you. This way you do not have to worry about misplacing them, losing them in a fire, or making frequent trips to your safe deposit box.

If you are more comfortable keeping the actual certificates yourself, you will need to have new certificates issued in the name of your Trust. (Never write or mark on an original stock or bond certificate.) Your broker or banker can have them reissued for you (they may charge a small fee).

You can also do this yourself. Your attorney can prepare a "stock power," a short document that assigns the securities to the Trust, identifies what is being transferred (for example, 50 shares of General Electric stock), the certificate numbers, and the name(s) of the Trustees. You'll sign the stock power and have your signature guaranteed (as above).

You'll then need to locate the stock transfer agent. This is the organization that is authorized to transfer title on stocks and bonds. For bonds, the transfer agent is usually the institution from which you receive payments on the bond. If you have stock certificates, don't rely on the name of the transfer agent on the certificate—it may be outdated. Call a brokerage house and ask them. Your attorney may also be able to find out the transfer agent for you.

Send the transfer agent—by certified mail—a letter, instructing them to issue new certificates in the name of your Trust; a Certificate of Trust; and the certificates. Send the stock power separately, also by certified mail. (Do not send the stock power and the certificates together in the same envelope—if someone intercepts them, they would be able to negotiate them.) Make sure you keep copies. And check the new certificates as soon as you receive them.

If you have lost a certificate, contact the transfer agent and request an "Affidavit of Lost Certificate and Indemnity Agreement." Complete and sign the affidavit, and follow the instructions to furnish bond.

Savings Bonds

Series E, EE, H and HH bonds can be transferred to your Living Trust with no adverse tax consequences. You will continue to receive current income from Series H and HH bonds. Accrued interest on Series E and EE bonds can continue to be deferred until the bond matures.

To have savings bonds re-issued in the name of your Living Trust, you'll need form PD-1851. If you have named a Beneficiary on a savings bond, you can also change it to your Trust using form PD-4000. (If you are changing a Beneficiary on a Series E bond, the current Beneficiary will need to sign the form; if this person is deceased, you will need to send along a death certificate.)

You can call the Federal Reserve Bank yourself to order forms or if you have questions (since forms change, make sure you verify which one(s) you need and the procedure). If you live in the mid-west or western U.S., you can call their customer service number in Kansas City: 1-800-333-2919. If you live in the eastern part of the country, call the customer service number in Pittsburgh: 1-800-245-2804. (By the way, the representative we spoke with was very knowledgeable and helpful—and said they get a lot of calls from people who want to re-issue their savings bonds in the names of their Living Trusts.)

Automobiles/Boats/Other Vehicles

Most states will permit a vehicle title to be re-issued in the name of your Trust. Also, some states now allow you to name a Beneficiary for your vehicle. If yours does, your Trust should be the Beneficiary. In some states, however, this will require the payment of an excise (transfer) tax, just as if the Trust had purchased the vehicle.

Take Florida, for example. Currently, Florida has a $100 "new wheels tax" (in addition to other registration fees). This fee does not apply if you trade in your existing car for a new one. But it does apply if you buy an additional car or if you have never owned a car before. So, because your Trust has not owned a car before, you will have to pay the "new wheels tax" when you transfer it into your Trust. But you will only have to pay it once; you won't have to pay it again if you replace that car with another one.

However, a car is considered "exempt" property in Florida. So, if you plan to leave your car to your spouse or an heir, you don't need to transfer it to your Trust and spend the $100. Your spouse or heir can transfer the car title after you die for less than $100. But if you plan to leave your car to someone else, then it is probably worth putting it into the Trust and paying the $100 fee. (Don't you just love finding out what's going on in Florida?!)

You may want to call your state's license bureau to find out the process where you live. Depending on the costs involved and the value of the vehicle, you may want to wait until you purchase your next one and title it in the name of your Trust.

If the value of the vehicle is within the amount your state allows to transfer without probate, your attorney may even suggest that you leave your vehicle out of your Trust. (As we explained in Part One, most states allow very small estates—some as low as $15,000—to transfer without probate.) Also, if you are using a Corporate Trustee, they may not want to manage your car—unless, of course, it is of considerable value.

If you do title a vehicle in the name of your Trust, notify your insurance company so they can change your policy to reflect the change of ownership and list the Trustee as an additional insured (if you are your own Trustee, it will show you as Trustee instead of you as an individual). They may request a copy of the new registration and a letter of instruction from you. They will probably make the change for you at no charge.

Personal Untitled Property

Many attorneys will probably prepare either a Bill of Sale or an Assignment to transfer personal property (like your furniture, artwork, clothing, jewelry, cameras, sporting equipment, books, etc.) to your Trust. If these articles are of substantial value, you would want them in your Trust.

However, if the value of these articles is low enough that a probate would not

Some states let you name your Living Trust as Beneficiary for your car

Your Living Trust can be owner and Beneficiary of your insurance policies

be required in your state (as we explained above), your attorney may recommend leaving these out of your Trust. They could also be intentionally left out if there was a desire to cut off creditor's claims in probate (as we explained in Part Two).

Life Insurance

In many cases, you will want your Living Trust to be both the Beneficiary and the owner of your insurance policies.

Naming your Trust as the Beneficiary gives you maximum control over the proceeds. It keeps the courts from getting involved if your loved ones are incapacitated, die before you (or at the same time as you), or are minor children. You can keep the proceeds in Trust until you want your loved ones to receive the money. You can be sure the money is used to pay your final expenses. And by naming your Trust instead of your spouse as the Beneficiary, you can even keep control of the funds if your spouse should remarry.

> **Note:** If you live in a community property state and the insurance was purchased with community property funds, your spouse is entitled to half of the proceeds—and may need to sign a consent form if you want to name your Living Trust as Beneficiary.

Naming your Trust as the owner of your policies gives you maximum control over the policies and more flexibility. For example, if you name your spouse or someone else as the owner, you might worry that they will cancel the policy or change the Beneficiary.

If you have a policy that has a cash value and you name your Trust as the owner, your Successor Trustee would be able to borrow on the policy at your incapacity to help pay for your care. And if you suffer from a terminal illness, your Successor could apply for a "Living Benefit" currently offered by many insurance companies. (Under this program, the "death benefit" is paid to you *before* you die—instead of to your Beneficiary *after* you die—so the cash is available to help meet expenses while you are living.)

However, if your estate is large enough that it would have to pay estate taxes, you should probably consider having a Life Insurance Trust (or other arrangement, like a Family Limited Partnership) to save estate taxes. We explain how they work in Part Nine.

Employer-Provided Insurance

These would include life insurance (including split dollar insurance), accident insurance and disability insurance your employer provides for you. Your Living Trust should be the Beneficiary when you have the option. Your employee benefits or personnel department will have the appropriate forms and can help you complete them.

Sole Proprietorship

Business licenses and DBAs (doing business as) should be changed to show your Living Trust as the owner. An Assignment is used to transfer business property to your Trust.

Closely-Held Corporation

First check to make sure that transferring your interests to a Living Trust will not trigger an event covered by a buy-sell agreement. (If it does, you can request that the document be changed.) The appropriate corporate records will then need to be prepared to transfer title. Share certificates will also need to be re-registered in the name of your Trust. To do this, a Stock Power (prepared by your attorney) and the certificates will need to be sent to the attorney or officer who handles the transfers.

Subchapter S Corporation

With a subchapter S corporation, both the earnings and any losses of the corporation are passed through to the owners personally. Earnings are taxed only once at the personal level and any losses can be deducted from ordinary income. (With a "C" corporation, earnings are taxed twice—once at the corporate level, and again at the personal level when the earnings are distributed. And, until the corporation is sold or liquidated, losses can only be deducted from corporate earnings.)

Transferring subchapter S corporation stock to your Living Trust does not cause any change or any problem while you are living. After you die, however, the stock can only stay in your Living Trust for up to two years—after that, it would lose its "S" status and become a "C" corporation.

But this rarely happens—because two years is usually *plenty* of time to distribute the stock to the Beneficiaries so the "S" status can be retained. If you don't want your Beneficiaries to receive the stock outright, the IRS also allows

*Business
interests can be
transferred
to your
Living Trust*

it to be transferred to other Trusts that meet its qualifications to retain the "S" status. The IRS creatively calls one of these "qualified subchapter S Trusts" (QSST).

Your attorney should plan for the distribution of subchapter S stock when he/she prepares your Living Trust document.

Limited Partnerships/Corporations/Limited Liability Companies

If you are involved in any real estate (or other) partnerships, corporations or limited liability companies, your interest should be assigned to your Trust. This probably will not disturb the existing agreement or affect your partners in any way, but you should check the agreement or corporate by-laws just to be sure.

The general partner may already have a form to assign your interest to your Trust. If not, your attorney can prepare one. The Assignment should identify your interest that is being transferred, how the interest should be titled, and that the Trustee accepts any liabilities as well as benefits.

Send the Assignment to the general partner with a letter instructing him/her to make the transfer. Since other documents may need to be prepared to complete the transfer, you may want to give the general partner a limited power of attorney to sign the other documents for you. (The general partner may charge a fee to do this.)

General Partnership Interests

This transfer is handled in the same way as a limited partnership. However, your signature will probably need to be notarized, and the Assignment should include a provision for the other partners to consent to it. The partnership agreement may also require you to send the Assignment to the other partners or general partner to sign—as verification of their acceptance—and return the Assignment to you.

If you are using a Corporate Trustee with your Trust, they may not be able to serve as a general partner. A special Trustee may have to be appointed instead.

Copyrights, Patents, And Royalties

"Intellectual properties" such as these can usually be transferred to your Living Trust with an Assignment drafted by your attorney. (Make sure your attorney is familiar with these.)

Oil And Gas Interests

Transferring proven oil and gas interests—mineral leases, overriding royalty interests, production payments, and working and operating interests—can all be transferred to your Living Trust without losing the percentage cost depletion deduction (similar to depreciation). Your Trust and/or Beneficiaries can continue to claim the deduction after you die.

The process to put these interests into your Trust will vary, depending on the state in which the property is located. You may want to have your attorney do these transfers for you. They can be tedious—the legal descriptions and depletion allowances must be exact, and you want to be sure everything is done properly.

Club Memberships

As long as the membership agreement does not prohibit it, a club membership can be assigned to your Trust. Some membership agreements allow you to name a Beneficiary—if yours does, it should be your Living Trust.

Foreign Assets

Foreign assets can be transferred to a Living Trust if Revocable Living Trusts are recognized in that country. You or your attorney will need to contact an attorney in the country where the assets are located to find out if there are any specific advantages—or disadvantages—to putting these assets in your Trust and the process that should be followed.

Assets Requiring Special Consideration

While you should start with the general premise that *all* titles and beneficiary designations should be changed to your Living Trust, there are a few assets that you may not want in—or cannot be placed into—your Living Trust. Here are some you may own.

IRA, 401(k), 403(b), Pension, Profit Sharing, Keogh And Other Tax-Deferred Plans

These are all plans that were created to encourage you to save for your retirement. They are called *tax-deferred* plans because you did not pay income taxes on this money when the contributions were made. The income taxes are *deferred* until you withdraw the money at a later time—ideally, at your retirement when your income (and tax bracket) is lower.

You can't leave your money in these accounts forever. At a certain point, usually age 70 1/2, Uncle Sam says you must start taking it out. The amount you are required to withdraw each year (your required minimum distribution) is determined by dividing the value of your tax-deferred accounts by the life expectancy of you and your Beneficiary. (The intent is that, by the time you and your Beneficiary are both expected to die, your tax-deferred savings will be fully withdrawn.)

Of course, you can withdraw *more* than your required minimum distribution at any time. But if you don't need it all (or if you die before you use it all up), you'd probably like to let this money continue to grow tax-deferred for as long as you can—with as much as possible going to your spouse and/or children, and as little as possible going to taxes.

Uncle Sam doesn't make this easy—the rules are complicated and loaded with tax traps and penalties. And expensive mistakes are easy to make by both you *and* your Beneficiaries.

You will not be able to change the ownership of these plans to your Living Trust. You *can* name your Living Trust as the Beneficiary. But before you do, you should consider some other options. As you will see in the next few pages, who you name as Beneficiary will have a significant impact on how much of your tax-deferred savings will go to Uncle Sam—in income and estate taxes.

■ Who Should Be Your Beneficiary—If You Are Married
Option 1: Spouse as Beneficiary

Most married couples, especially those who have been married for some time, name their spouses as Beneficiary. The two main reasons are that 1) most couples want this money to be available to provide for the surviving spouse, and 2) depending on which spouse dies first, the money can continue to grow tax-deferred well beyond both spouses' lifetimes. Here's how it would work.

If you die first, your surviving spouse can "roll over" your tax-deferred account into his/her own IRA, further delaying income taxes until he/she must start taking required minimum distributions at age 70 1/2. When your spouse does the rollover, he/she names a new Beneficiary—preferably a much younger one (as your children and grandchildren would be).

While your spouse is living, the Beneficiary is assumed (by the IRS) to be no more than ten years younger than your spouse. But after your spouse dies, the Beneficiary's *actual life expectancy* will be used for the remaining required minimum distributions.

Now, here's what this can mean. Let's say, for example, that when you die, your 70-year-old spouse rolls over your tax-deferred account into an IRA and names your 25-year-old grandson as Beneficiary. According to the IRS, their combined life expectancy—used to determine your spouse's required minimum distributions while your spouse is living—is about 26 years. Let's say your spouse dies two years later. Now, the required minimum distributions are calculated using your now 27-year-old grandson's actual life expectancy of 55 years! That's a lot of years of continued tax-deferred growth!

By the way, under current IRS policy, your spouse can do this rollover and stretch out the IRA even if you had started taking required minimum distributions before you died.

Of course, naming your spouse as Beneficiary means that your spouse will have full control of this money after you die, which may not be what you want. For example, you may have children from a previous marriage or feel that your spouse may be too easily influenced by others after you're gone. (Your spouse doesn't *have* to do a rollover, you know. A total lump-sum distribution could be very tempting—even if all the income taxes would have to be paid at once!)

Choose the Beneficiary for your tax-deferred plans carefully

Naming your spouse as Beneficiary could also cause you to pay too much in *estate* taxes. Remember, in Part Three, we explained how you can waste your estate tax exemption if you leave everything to your spouse. If your estate is large enough to pay estate taxes and most of your estate is made up of your tax-deferred savings, naming your spouse as the Beneficiary could cause you to waste some or all of your exemption. (If you have other assets that can be applied to your exemption, this would not be a problem.)

Also, we're assuming here that you will die first. If your spouse dies before you, you can name another Beneficiary. But, if you have already started taking your required minimum distributions when your spouse dies, you will not be able to use the new Beneficiary's life expectancy. That means no "stretch out" over your children's or grandchildren's life expectancies.

If any of these "disadvantages" fit your situation, you may want to consider naming a Trust (but not necessarily your Living Trust) or your children or grandchildren as Beneficiary of some or all of your tax-deferred savings.

Option 2: Trust as Beneficiary
With a Trust as Beneficiary, you can provide for your surviving spouse for as long as he or she lives, yet keep control over who receives the money after your spouse dies. Plus the proceeds can be used to satisfy your estate tax exemption and save estate taxes. (See Part Three for an explanation of estate taxes.)

The income tax benefits are not *as* good as when the spouse is the Beneficiary. That's because *only a spouse* is entitled to the rollover option. So, while this money can provide for your spouse and save estate taxes, you will not be able to "stretch out" the tax-deferred growth beyond your spouse's life expectancy. Here's why.

With a Trust as Beneficiary, the distributions can be paid over your life expectancy and the life expectancy of *the oldest Beneficiary of the Trust*. If you are married and your spouse is a Beneficiary of the Trust, your spouse will probably be the oldest Beneficiary. So, after you die, the distributions can be paid to the Trust over *no longer than* your spouse's life expectancy.

If your spouse is not a Beneficiary of this Trust, then the oldest Beneficiary may be one of your children. That would let you extend the tax deferral over your child's life expectancy. But then the money would not be available to your spouse unless your child wants to be generous.

IMPORTANT: To be able to use your life expectancy and the life expectancy of the oldest Beneficiary of the Trust, the IRS says the Trust must meet the following five requirements:
1) All Beneficiaries of the Trust must be individuals.
2) The Beneficiaries must be "identifiable" from the Trust document.
3) A copy of the Trust document must be provided to the plan.
4) The Trust must be valid under state law.
5) The Trust must be irrevocable when you die or when you become age 70 1/2 —*whichever occurs earlier*. (The actual date is April 1 of the year following the year in which you reach age 70 1/2.)

If the Trust does not meet all five requirements, you will only be able to use *your* life expectancy. That will cause your required minimum distributions to be higher while you are living. But, more importantly, it could cause the entire balance to be paid to the Trust within one year after you die.

For most people, the first four requirements are easy to meet. The last one is not especially difficult—it just takes some planning.

While you are *under age 70 1/2*, a Revocable Living Trust can be the Beneficiary because *it becomes irrevocable* when you die. But once you *reach age 70 1/2* and start taking required minimum distributions, the Trust must be *irrevocable*. So, you have a couple of choices.

1) If you are under age 70 1/2 (and have a great memory), you can name your Revocable Living Trust as Beneficiary. Then, at age 70 1/2, set up a separate irrevocable Trust just for these proceeds. But this means you *must remember* to set up the new Trust and change the beneficiary designation. Of course, there is the chance that you could become incapacitated before then, and would not be able to set up the irrevocable Trust. So, in your Durable Power of Attorney for Asset Management (see Part Five), you may want to give your Agent (Successor Trustee) the ability to do this if you can't do it yourself.

2) If you don't have such a great memory, set up a separate irrevocable Trust now. Remember, nothing will be in this Trust until after you die and the

Your Living Trust can be Beneficiary until you are age 70 1/2

distributions are paid to it each year. Even though the *Trust* is irrevocable, you still have total flexibility. That's because, until you die, *you can change the Beneficiary of your IRA or tax-deferred plan* at any time and as often as you wish. You could even set up a *new* irrevocable Trust if you want to change your instructions or Trust Beneficiaries.

Caution: Some Revocable Living Trusts are being written so they automatically become *irrevocable* when the Grantor becomes age 70 1/2. That takes care of the irrevocable Trust requirement. But it also means you won't be able to make any changes to your Living Trust after you become age 70 1/2. That may not be what you want.

Note: If your tax-deferred money is in a company-sponsored plan (like a pension or profit sharing plan), you may be able to delay the irrevocable Trust requirement (and your required minimum distributions) beyond age 70 1/2 as long as you continue working (and own no more than 5% of the company). But if your money is in an IRA, you're stuck with 70 1/2.

Option 3: Children, Other Individuals as Beneficiary

If your spouse will have plenty of assets—or if you have reason to believe your spouse will die before you—you could name your children, grandchildren or other individuals as Beneficiary.

The tax benefits can be great. Since you are not leaving this money to your spouse, your estate tax exemption can be applied to it—that saves estate taxes. And if your Beneficiary is much younger than you (like your children and grandchildren would be), you can get maximum "stretch out" on the income tax deferral.

In fact, if your objective is to have this money grow beyond your and your spouse's lifetimes, naming your children/grandchildren as Beneficiary instead of your spouse is the only way to *ensure* that. (Remember, if your spouse dies before you—or chooses not to do the rollover after you die—there will be no stretch out.)

While you are living, your Beneficiary will be assumed to be no more than ten years younger than you. But after you die, your Beneficiary's actual life expectancy can be used for the remaining distributions. That could stretch out the tax-deferred growth for many more years.

But, as we explained in Part Two, any time you name an individual as a Beneficiary, you lose control. After you die, your Beneficiary can do whatever he/she wants with this money—including cashing out the full balance of the account and destroying your careful plans for long-term, tax-deferred growth. Money that has been withdrawn would also be available to the Beneficiary's creditors, spouses and ex-spouses. And if you leave a substantial amount to a grandchild, it could be subject to the Generation Skipping Transfer Tax—a 55% tax, which is *in addition to* estate and income taxes. (See Part Nine for a full explanation.)

For maximum control (especially with a minor or irresponsible individual), set up a Trust for this person and name the Trust as the Beneficiary as explained earlier in Option 2. You can still get the stretch out—remember, the distributions can be paid out over the life expectancy of the oldest Beneficiary of the Trust. Just make sure the Trust meets all five requirements.

Option 4: Charity/Foundation as Beneficiary

If you are planning to leave an asset to charity anyway after you die, a tax-deferred account can be an excellent asset to use. That's because when you name a charity as the Beneficiary, there will be *no income or estate taxes* on this money after you die.

If you name a Charitable Remainder Trust (explained in Part Nine) as Beneficiary, your spouse, children or others can receive an income for a set number of years or for as long as they live—and you will still save income and estate taxes. You can also set up your own charitable foundation and have the foundation pay your kids a salary to run it. (See Part Nine.)

The main disadvantage with naming a charity as Beneficiary is that it has no life expectancy. So, during your lifetime, your required minimum distributions will be higher than with another Beneficiary.

Option 5: Some or All of the Above as Beneficiary

You don't have to choose just *one* of these options. You can split a large IRA into several smaller ones and name a different Beneficiary for each one. (If you name several Beneficiaries for one IRA, just the *oldest* Beneficiary's life expectancy will be used. But with a separate IRA for each Beneficiary, you can get the maximum stretch out over *all* their ages.) If your money is in a company plan, you can roll it into an IRA and then split it.

You can split a large IRA into smaller ones

Your spouse may need to sign a consent form

This will make things a little more complicated when figuring your distribution each year (since one will have to be figured for each IRA). But getting the maximum stretch out can be well worth it. Just make sure you do the split *before* you start taking your required minimum distributions. (Another time to split one IRA into several is when a surviving spouse does a rollover and names new Beneficiaries.)

> **Note:** Any time you name someone other than your spouse as the Beneficiary, you need expert advice. You'll need to find an attorney who is experienced in this area, especially if you have large amounts in these plans. Also, your spouse may need to sign a consent form—even in noncommunity property states, spouses now have rights to retirement plan and other benefits.

■ Who Should Be Your Beneficiary—If You Are Not Married

If you are not married, your decision will be less complicated. You can name any individual, a Trust, or a charity as the Beneficiary.

If you want an individual to receive this money after you die, consider setting up a Trust for that person and *naming the Trust as the Beneficiary* to keep more control. Just remember that the Trust must meet the five requirements listed in Option 2.

Before you make a decision, read Options 2-5 above carefully. And make sure your attorney has experience in this area—especially if you have a sizeable amount in your tax-deferred plans.

■ How to Change the Beneficiary Designation for Your Tax-Deferred Plans

You can change your Beneficiary at any time, but it's much better to finalize it *before* you start taking your required minimum distributions. That's because a change in Beneficiary after this time will not change the amount of your distribution—unless the new Beneficiary has a *shorter* life expectancy, which would cause the money to be paid out faster. (Sorry—after you start taking your distributions, Uncle Sam will not let you name a younger Beneficiary to stretch out the income tax deferral.)

To change the Beneficiary of employer-sponsored plans (such as a 401(k), pension, or profit sharing plan), contact your employee benefits or personnel department for the proper form. To change the Beneficiary of your IRA or Keogh, you will need to contact the institution where your account is located.

Some plans have restrictions on what you can do on the beneficiary designations. Be sure to read the document carefully. If the plan will not let you do what you want to do, consider rolling your money into an IRA as soon as you can. If your money is already in an IRA and the institution will not agree to what you want, consider moving your IRA to another institution.

■ Roth IRA

You may also want to consider rolling your tax-deferred money into a new Roth IRA. You have to pay ordinary income taxes on the full amount when you roll it over. But there's a special exception—if you do the rollover in 1998, you have four years to pay the taxes. Then, once your money is in a Roth IRA, you can leave it there *for as long as you wish,* because there are *no* required minimum distributions. And, as a general rule, after five years or age 59 1/2 (whichever is later), *all withdrawals from a Roth IRA will be tax-free.* So you would be able to ignore everything you've just read in this section! Your tax advisor can help you determine if this would be a good move for you.

■ SPECIAL REPORT: *Are You Saving Your IRA For The IRS?*

We have just given you a very general overview of these options. This is, undeniably, a very complicated area of estate planning—frustrating for consumers and professionals alike. Many of the existing laws are unclear, and the laws are constantly changing. And, unless you plan ahead, the IRS could take up to 80% or more of your tax-deferred money—in estate taxes, income taxes and penalties—before it ever reaches your Beneficiaries.

Because there is so much interest and confusion, new developments and, for many people, a lot of money at stake, we are preparing a *new* Special Report entitled, *Are You Saving Your IRA For The IRS?* For information, call us (1-800-728-2665), send us an e-mail (ira@www.estateplanning.com) or write us.

Tax-Deferred Annuities

Tax-deferred annuities sold by insurance companies are not IRAs or qualified plans. As a result, they are not governed by the same IRS rules as the plans listed above and the preceding discussion does not apply to them.

Before you name a Beneficiary, read your contract carefully. There may be some restrictions or income tax issues you need to be aware of when making this decision.

For example, if you are married, naming your spouse as Beneficiary may allow the tax-deferred payments to continue over your spouse's lifetime after you die—while naming someone other than your spouse (like your Living Trust) could cause the balance to be paid out all at once after you die. (One solution may be to name your spouse as first Beneficiary and your Living Trust as second Beneficiary.)

Incentive Stock Options

Stock options are often used as a form of compensation for valued employees, who are given the right to buy company stock at some point in the future at a predetermined (and usually very favorable) price.

Usually, you have to wait until a certain amount of time has passed before you can "exercise" the option (buy the stock). You do not pay income taxes until the stock is later "disposed of"—which, according to the IRS, is a "sale, exchange, gift or transfer of legal title."

The laws are not clear about whether putting stock options into your Living Trust would cause you to violate the "waiting time" or if this would be considered a "transfer of legal title," which then would cause you to pay income taxes at that time.

However, we are aware of at least one company that has written to the IRS, asking for an opinion on whether transferring incentive stock options to a Revocable Living Trust would be considered a "disposition." The response from the IRS (called a "Private Letter Ruling") states that it would not be.

You or your attorney will probably want to read the plan document to see if there are any restrictions on transferring these options to your Living Trust. You may also want to write the plan administrator for approval. Depending on how long you have before an option expires, you may want to just wait until *after* you exercise the option and then transfer the stock to your Living Trust.

Section 1244 Stock

Business owners know that many new businesses fail, so they often incorporate under Section 1244 of the Internal Revenue Code. If the business is later sold or liquidated at a loss, this allows the stockholders (the owners) to take the loss on the stock as an *ordinary* loss instead of a *capital* loss.

Normally, when you sell stock (and other investments) and have a loss, it is considered a *capital loss* and can only be used to offset *capital gains* (your profits when investments are sold). If your capital losses exceed your capital gains for that year, under current tax law you are only allowed to deduct $3,000 of the excess loss per year from your ordinary income (wages, tips, etc. as defined by the IRS on Form 1040).

But with 1244 stock, the stockholders can deduct the loss from *ordinary* income instead of from just capital gains. Individuals can currently deduct up to $50,000 in these losses per year; married couples filing jointly can deduct up to $100,000 in losses per year. Any excess loss can be rolled forward to subsequent tax years.

Under current tax law, transferring Section 1244 stock to a Living Trust would cause you to lose this tax benefit. Whether or not you will want to put this stock in your Living Trust will probably depend on how long you have been in business and how profitable the business is.

If you think the business may have to be sold or liquidated at a loss, you probably do not want to put Section 1244 stock in your Living Trust. However, if the corporation is successful and there is little chance of a loss, you may want to go ahead and do so. We suggest you discuss this with your attorney and accountant before you decide.

Professional Corporations

State laws require shareholders of professional corporations (like doctors and dentists) to be licensed members of their professions. Since a Living Trust is revocable and you keep control of the assets you put in it, some attorneys feel that transferring a professional corporation to a Living Trust would not be a problem. But because the laws do not specifically mention Living Trusts, many attorneys suggest that you leave these out of your Trust for now—at least until the laws are changed to include Living Trusts.

Part Seven

. . . .

THE FINAL STEPS TO YOUR PEACE OF MIND

Part Seven—
THE FINAL STEPS TO YOUR PEACE OF MIND

Now that you have your Living Trust and you have funded it with your assets, you may be wondering what you need to do now. Actually, you don't *have* to do anything else for your Trust to work—except, of course, to remember that any assets you acquire from now on need to be titled in the name of your Trust.

However, there are some things you can do now that will make things much easier for your family when something happens to you. For example, when you funded your Trust, you had to locate title documents and find out exactly what assets you own. Instead of just dumping all that information back into a drawer (or several drawers), we'll show you how to organize this information so it will actually *mean* something to your spouse, children, and/or Successor Trustee when it is needed.

Also, as your personal, family and financial situations change, you may need to change your Trust. In this section, we'll give you some examples of changes in your life that may affect your Trust—and we'll explain what you need to do to change it.

And, finally, we'll explain step-by-step what your surviving spouse (or Successor Trustee) needs to do if you become incapacitated and when you die.

Once you understand what will need to happen and the information your family will need, you'll be able to organize things and prepare them. Then you'll know you've done *the best you can do* for your family—and that will give *you* great peace of mind.

ORGANIZE INFORMATION FOR YOUR FAMILY

Think for a few moments about what would happen if you became incapacitated or died today. Would your spouse, family and/or Successor Trustee know what to do?

Would they know where to find your Trust document and the health care documents you signed? Do they know who should be notified? Do they know what insurance you have and what benefits they can apply for? Do they know what assets you own and where they are located? Do they know who your attorney and accountant are? If you own a business, do they know what to do to keep it operating? Do they know who to call if they need help?

Maybe you don't want them to know everything about your assets right now. That's okay—you don't have to *tell* them. But, as you will see as you read this section, it's very important that they know where to find this information *when they need it.*

Here is a checklist of things you can do now that will make things much easier for your family later.

■ Read the Rest of this Section Carefully.
When you understand what your spouse, family and/or Successor Trustee will need to do when something happens to you, you'll want to make things as easy for them as possible—and you'll be motivated to organize things for them.

■ Inform Others.
Give copies of your health care documents (Durable Power of Attorney, Health Care Proxy, Living Will) to your physician and designated agent.

You may want to purchase additional copies of this book for your Successor Trustee(s) and Beneficiaries so they will understand what a Living Trust does, why you have chosen to have one, and what they may need to do.

■ Store Original Documents in Safe Place.
Keep originals of all your documents (titles, Living Trust, health care documents) in one safe place—like a fire-proof safe or a safe deposit box. Make copies for the notebook described next.

■ **Create a Notebook of Financial and Personal Information.**
Buy one or two three-ring binders to hold this information. You can enter this information by hand, typewriter, or computer—the main thing is to *do* it and keep it current. Here are some things to include:

A copy of this book.

A copy of your Living Trust document.

A copy of your health care documents.

A listing of your assets, where they are located, current values, account numbers, date of purchase, purchase price, date transferred to your Trust, name of contact person. (The Organizer in the back of this book will be helpful.)

A copy of year-end bank and investment account statements.

Safe deposit box location, a list of its contents, and location of the key.

A listing of your creditors (people to whom *you owe* money, like mortgages, credit cards, etc.). Include names, addresses, phone numbers, and amount owed.

A listing of people who *owe you* money. Include names, addresses, phone numbers, and the amount owed.

A listing of your insurance policies and other benefits to which your family may be entitled when you die. Include policy numbers, company, location, amount of benefit, phone numbers, contact person.

Names, addresses and telephone numbers of your personal advisors (attorney, banker and/or trust officer, insurance agent, financial advisor/broker, physicians, etc.).

A calendar marked with important financial dates that occur regularly—when certain bills are paid (including insurance), when property taxes are due, when to meet with the accountant to prepare income taxes, etc.

Does your family know where to find the information they will need?

Review your Trust and other information annually

- A list of medications you are taking and when.

- At least two letters of instruction, one to be opened if you become incapacitated and the other when you die. (You could also make an audio or video tape.)

  At incapacity: Include any special instructions or wishes regarding your care, the care of others who depend on you (minors, parents, pets, etc.), people to notify (include address/phone), continuation or sale of a business.

  At your death: Include people to notify (and their addresses/phone numbers), instructions for funeral/burial/cremation (and organ donation), the care of others who depend on you (minors, parents, pets, etc.), continuation or sale of a business.

- If you have minor children or other dependents who rely on you, you may want to do separate instructions (letter, video or audio) to the person who will care for them. You may want to include particular likes, dislikes, places to go, foods to eat, friends, etc. This can give you peace of mind, knowing that you will be able to pass this information on if something should happen to you unexpectedly.

- You may also want to write letters (or make an audio or video tape) to your spouse, children, grandchildren, and other loved ones. You may want to tell them of special memories you have and how much they mean to you. Perhaps you want to make amends. You may also want to tell your family why you are taking the time now to put everything in order for them—and encourage them to do the same for their families. These "letters" can give you tremendous peace of mind, and can be a source of great comfort to your loved ones for years to come.

- **Show Your Spouse, Family Member and/or Successor Trustee Where This Information is Located.**
Remember, you don't have to show them all the details yet if you don't want to. But you should at least let one or two people know that you have organized this information and where they can find it when something happens to you.

■ Review Your Notebook Annually.

Once a year, pull your notebook out, read through it (and this section of the book) and see if anything needs to be updated. Just like an annual physical, think of this as your annual *Trust* checkup. Link this review to an annual occasion—a holiday, your birthday, beginning of the year, after tax time—so it just becomes something you do every year.

Have you bought or sold any assets? Did you remember to title the new ones in the name of your Trust? Do you need to make any adjustments to take full advantage of the increasing estate tax exemption (explained in Part Three)? Do your instruction letters still say what you want them to say? Do you need to make any changes to your Trust document? (See the next page for situations that could create a need to change your Trust document and how to change it.)

■ Have a Trial Run.

Tell your spouse and/or Successor Trustee to pretend that you have just become incapacitated. Have them go through the checklists on the following pages and see if they can find the information they will need. Then, have them repeat the process as if you have just died.

Will this take some time? Yes. But it's a very *unselfish* use of your time. Remember, you don't have to do all this—once you set up your Trust and transfer your assets to it, the Trust will work.

So, what do *you* get out of this? The satisfaction of knowing you have done everything you can to make things easier on your family. You do it out of love—it's your final gift to them. You are also setting an example for your family, and perhaps they'll do the same for theirs.

CHANGING YOUR LIVING TRUST

Your Living Trust is a snapshot of you, your family, and your assets right now, at this point in time. But people and situations change—and your Trust may need to change, too.

Basically, you should change your Trust any time it no longer does what you want. If you review your Trust every year as we suggest, you will become very familiar with it—and you will be able to keep it current with your situation.

Here's a checklist of events that could prompt a change in your Trust. We suggest that you review this list each year when you review your Trust.

Changes in Your Family Situation

You and Your Spouse
- You marry, divorce or separate;
- Your health (or your spouse's health) declines;
- Your spouse dies.

Your Children, Grandchildren, Parents, and Other Beneficiaries
- Birth or adoption;
- Marriage, divorce or separation;
- Finances change (good or bad);
- Parent or other relative becomes dependent on you;
- Minor becomes an adult;
- Attitude toward you changes;
- Health declines;
- A child, grandchild or other Beneficiary dies.

Changes in Your Economic Situation

- Value of assets changes dramatically (up or down);
- Change in business interests (new partnership or corporation, you plan to sell a business, etc.);
- You buy real estate in another state;
- You are planning to retire and need to designate a final Beneficiary for tax-deferred plans before distributions start.

Outside Changes

- Changes in the laws, state or federal (for example, the increase in the federal estate tax exemption). Be sure to find out if your attorney will keep you informed when changes occur that would affect your Trust.)
- You plan to move to a different state;
- Successor Trustee (or Guardian for minor children) moves away, becomes ill, dies, or changes his/her mind about accepting the responsibility.
- You change your mind about a Successor Trustee or Guardian for your minor children.

Remember, you do *not* need to change your Trust when you buy and sell assets. But you *do* need to title newly acquired assets in the name of your Trust.

How to Change Your Trust

If you decide you want to make a change, don't write on your Trust document. Once you have signed the Trust document, it must not be altered.

If you want to change something that is in the Trust document itself, your attorney will prepare an amendment to your Trust (which you will sign), and it will probably be notarized (just like your Trust document). Amendments are usually pretty simple, and it should not take your attorney very long to do one (nor should it cost you very much). You do not need to do anything to your assets—they are already in your Trust. Your attorney will just change the Trust document that *controls* your assets.

Remember, in most states, if you keep a separate list of your Special Gifts (specific items that you want to go to certain people or organizations), you do not need to make any changes to your Trust. You just need to update the list and have it notarized.

. . . .

On the following pages, you will find checklists for your surviving spouse and for your Successor Trustee so they will know what needs to be done when something happens to you. As you will see, some of the steps are the same. But we felt that having separate checklists would make it easier on them.

MY SPOUSE IS INCAPACITATED. WHAT DO I NEED TO DO?

If you and your spouse have transferred your assets to your Living Trust, you will be able to continue to manage your financial affairs without court interference. Even if the incapacity is not expected to be lengthy (for example, if your spouse has had a stroke or heart attack and is expected to recover), not having to deal with the courts will be a great relief.

Here's a checklist that will help you get started when you may not know where to begin. Since many married couples have one Living Trust together—they are Co-Grantors and Co-Trustees—that is how this checklist is written.

Your Living Trust can change with you

If you and your spouse have separate Trusts and you are Successor Trustee of your spouse's Trust, this list will still be helpful. But you should also read the checklist for the Successor Trustee which follows.

■ **Take Care of Your Spouse First.**

Make sure your spouse is receiving quality care in a supportive environment—and that you are comfortable with the hospital or nursing home, doctors, and staff.

■ **Notify Insurance Company, Spouse's Employer, and Others.**

Be sure your insurance company has been notified, and that the physician has a copy of the health care documents (Durable Power of Attorney for Health Care, Health Care Proxy, Living Will) you and your spouse signed when your Trust was prepared.

Notify your spouse's employer, friends, and relatives. (You may want to have a family member or friend help you with this.) If your spouse wrote you a letter (as explained earlier in this Section) explaining what you should do at his/her incapacity, it may be very helpful.

■ **Find the Trust Document.**

Hopefully, you already know where it is. See if you are able to write checks and sell assets with just your signature. Many Trust documents are written so that one spouse can act alone after the other becomes incapacitated. However, some documents name a Co-Trustee (like a son or daughter, or a Corporate Trustee) to act with the well spouse. If a Co-Trustee is required, notify him/her as soon as possible.

■ **Notify Your Attorney.**

Notify the attorney who prepared the Trust document. He/she should be aware of the incapacity in case you have questions. Remember, you've never done this before, and it may be comforting for you to know there is someone you can call.

■ **Find Out What Your Insurance Covers.**

If you don't already know what your insurance covers, you will need to find out now. Assuming your insurance will cover a certain procedure or facility could be a very costly mistake. Find out your alternatives *before* making a major decision. (If you need help understanding your coverage, your insurance agent or your spouse's personnel/benefits department may be able to help you. Most insurance companies also have a toll free telephone number you can call 24-hours a day if you have questions.) If you have long term care insurance, make sure you are familiar with the coverage if it turns out the incapacity will be lengthy.

■ Have Doctor(s) Document Spouse's Condition.

It may be necessary to have the appropriate physician write a letter documenting your spouse's condition. (Some Trust documents will only require a letter from an M.D., some from one or two specialists, others require none.) You will probably need to show this letter to the bank and others so you can sign checks and sell assets (if necessary).

■ Apply for Benefits.

Apply for any disability benefits to which your spouse may be entitled—through your spouse's employer, private insurance, Veteran's benefits, Social Security, etc.

■ Become Familiar with Your Finances.

You need to know what assets you have, where they are located, and what your income sources are. You may need to put together a budget. Familiarize yourself with any business dealings your spouse was involved with. If you own real estate, make sure you have keys, take care of any utilities, etc. If your spouse has a business, you will probably need to make arrangements for its continuation.

Hopefully, you and your spouse organized this information as we suggested. (You can see now how much easier things will be if you did.)

If you find any assets that were left out of the Trust, use the Durable Power of Attorney to transfer them into the Trust as soon as possible so they will not have to go through probate when your spouse dies. However, it's possible that an asset was *intentionally* left out of the Trust for creditor protection (see Part Two). You may want to check with your attorney *first*.

■ Put Together Team of Advisors.

Depending on the size of your assets and the expected length and severity of your spouse's incapacity, you may want to put together a team of professional advisors—like your attorney, accountant, banker and/or trust officer, financial advisor, and insurance advisor—to help you. You may also want to include an adult son or daughter or a close friend.

Be sure to consult your advisors *before* you sell *any* assets, especially stocks, real estate or a business. There could be serious tax consequences, and they may be able to suggest some better alternatives. If your spouse has a business, your advisors can help with decisions about its continuation.

■ Keep Records, Take Care of Taxes and Accountings.
Keep careful record of medical expenses and file claims promptly. Keep records of the bills you have paid and any income received. And don't forget that income tax returns must be filed by April 15 each year. Contact your accountant early to find out what information he/she will need so you will have plenty of time to locate statements, etc.

■ Keep Successor Trustee(s) Informed.
It may be appropriate, depending on the Trust document, to keep your Successor Trustee(s) informed in case something happens to you.

Above all, try to keep a balanced perspective. Nothing should be more important right now than spending time with your spouse. If you find that managing your financial affairs and caring for your spouse is becoming too much for you to handle, consider having someone you trust help you with the finances—like an accountant, capable son or daughter, or even a Corporate Trustee (they can manage your investments *and* do the bookkeeping for you). You can always resume more of the responsibilities later.

My Spouse Is Incapacitated. What Do I Need To Do?

☐ **Take Care of Your Spouse First.**

☐ **Notify Insurance Company, Spouse's Employer, and Others.**

☐ **Find the Trust Document.**

☐ **Notify Your Attorney.**

☐ **Find Out What Your Insurance Covers.**

☐ **Have Doctor(s) Document Spouse's Condition.**

☐ **Apply for Benefits.**

☐ **Become Familiar with Your Finances.**

☐ **Put Together Team of Advisors.**

☐ **Keep Records, Take Care of Taxes and Accountings.**

☐ **Keep Successor Trustee(s) Informed.**

MY SPOUSE HAS DIED. WHAT DO I NEED TO DO?

When your spouse dies, there are some things you need to do to "settle" your spouse's estate and plan for your future. This will be especially important if your Trust has tax planning (A-B or A-B-C provisions).

If you and your spouse have changed titles and beneficiary designations to your Living Trust, this will be much easier for you. Since there will be no probate, you will be able to do things on your own schedule (instead of the court's), and in private.

You may be able to handle much of this yourself. But it would be wise to get some guidance from your professional advisors (attorney, bank/trust officer, accountant, financial advisor, etc.). You may also want to ask some family members to help you.

Here's a checklist to help you get started. Since many married couples have one Living Trust together—they are Co-Grantors and Co-Trustees—that is how this checklist is written.

If you and your spouse have separate Trusts and you are Successor Trustee of your spouse's Trust, this list will still be helpful. But you should also read the checklist for the Successor Trustee which follows.

■ Take Care of the Funeral.

Enlist a family member to help with funeral arrangements, flowers, cemetery marker, announcement in paper, special wishes for service, notifying friends, relatives, employer, etc. If your spouse left you some written instructions regarding the service, burial, people to notify, etc. (as we suggested earlier), this will be much easier on everyone involved.

■ Find the Trust Document.

Hopefully, you already know where the Trust document is. See if you will be able to act alone or if a Co-Trustee has been named to act with you. If a Co-Trustee is required, notify him/her as soon as possible.

■ Contact Attorney to Review Trust Document/Process.

It would be wise to schedule an appointment with an attorney (or a Corporate Trustee, especially if named as Co-Trustee) as soon as possible to review your Trust document, your assets, your responsibilities, and to develop a schedule. You may want to have a family member or friend go with you.

Even if you have a modest estate, an hour or so with an attorney can be worth the time and expense to confirm what you need to do. It's also comforting to know there is someone you can call if you have a question.

If your estate is larger, if there are assets (like an IRA) of sizeable value, if your Trust has tax planning or complicated provisions, or if you're just not sure about what needs to be done, this meeting will more than pay for itself.

You don't have to go back to the attorney who prepared your Trust—although he/she would be more familiar with the document. You can go to another attorney (see Part Five if you need to find one). A Corporate Trustee experienced with Trust administration can also help you.

■ Order Death Certificates.

Order at least 12 certified death certificates (you can usually get these from the funeral home). You will need these to collect benefits and conduct other business. Multiple copies will help speed things up, since you won't have to wait to get copies back before you can give them to someone else.

■ Take Care of Ongoing Bills, Final Expenses.

You can continue to pay your regular on-going bills (utilities, telephone, etc.). However, if your estate is larger (more than the federal estate tax exemption), there may be some tax reasons why you should not pay the mortgage on your home and other real estate. Notify the lender of your spouse's death and that the next mortgage payment may be delayed a few days (just until you are able to meet with your attorney to start settling the estate).

Keep careful records of final medical bills and funeral expenses—they may be deductible. Submit medical claims promptly.

■ Put Together a Team of Advisors.

It's very important for you to realize that you are not alone—and that no one expects you to be able to do everything all by yourself. Nor should you. This is a very emotional time, and even routine tasks may seem overwhelming. An innocent error could turn out to be an expensive mistake.

Depending on the size of your estate, you may want to put together a team of professionals to advise and/or help you—like your attorney, accountant, banker and/or trust officer, financial advisor, and/or insurance advisor. You may also want to include an adult son or daughter or a close friend as a sounding board.

Before you sell any assets, apply for any benefits (especially your spouse's IRA and other retirement plans), or change any investments, talk to your professional advisors about your options—they may be able to recommend choices that will provide you with maximum income and save substantial amounts in taxes. *Don't rush these decisions*—they usually do not have to be made right away.

Also, if your spouse had a business, your advisors will be able to help you make arrangements for its continuation or sale.

■ Inventory Assets/Determine Current Values.

Before you meet with your attorney, it would be a good idea to put together a preliminary list of all your assets and their estimated values. Later on, you'll need to determine the exact values for accounting and tax purposes.

This information is very important for several reasons:

1. You need to know exactly what assets you have and what your income sources are. You and your advisors will need to plan for your future.

2. Your attorney, accountant and/or trust officer need to know this information so they can suggest ways to save taxes, help you settle the estate, file tax returns (remember, a federal estate tax return is required if the gross value of the estate is more than the estate tax exemption at that time) and advise you.

3. Documenting the value of assets when your spouse dies can save a considerable amount in capital gains tax when the assets are sold.

Remember, when an asset is sold, capital gains tax will be due on the profit—the difference between the cost *basis* (what you paid for it) and the selling price. The death of a spouse changes the basis of your assets.

If you live in a non-community property state, only your deceased spouse's interest in the assets in your common Trust will receive a new basis equal to the value as of his/her death. If your spouse owned an asset separately (either in a separate Trust or identified as separate property in your common Trust), the entire asset will receive a new basis equal to its value. (Also, as discussed in Part Six, if you and your spouse jointly owned an asset since before 1976, *both* interests may get a new basis.)

If you live in a community property state, both your spouse's interest and your interest in each community asset will receive a new basis. If the assets have appreciated *over* their cost, the new basis will be a *stepped-up* basis. (See Part One for an explanation of stepped-up basis.) If the value of the assets is *below* their cost, the new basis will be a *stepped-down* basis.

4.   If your Trust has tax planning (A-B or A-B-C provisions), your attorney, accountant or trust officer will need this information to help you decide which assets should go into each Trust to maximize the tax planning.

If you find that an asset is still in your spouse's name and was not transferred to your Living Trust, it may have to be probated. Depending on the value and type of asset, you may be able to do this yourself, or your attorney can help you.

How to Determine Values

It is important that current values are appropriately determined—otherwise the IRS will not accept them. The IRS has specific rules that must be followed in establishing "fair market value" when an estate tax return is required or when calculating basis for income tax purposes. In other words, a "ballpark" estimate by a neighbor who happens to be a real estate agent—or your best guess—usually will not do.

Your banker and broker can provide you with the values of accounts on the day your spouse died. *The Wall Street Journal* for that day can also be a good source for values of stocks and mutual funds. Some items (especially real estate and collectibles) will need to be appraised—this should be done as soon as possible. Your attorney or trust officer can recommend a reputable appraiser. There are also companies that do estate valuations—your attorney or trust officer will know about them, too.

■ Do Tax Planning.

You will need to consider the income tax consequences before you apply for benefits or sell any assets. For example, you may have several choices for how your spouse's IRA and other retirement benefits can be paid to you (including rolling over the proceeds into your IRA, a lump sum, payments over your lifetime and perhaps someone else's lifetime)—and you should know the tax implications of each *before* selecting one. Your advisors will be able to help you and determine a payout option that is best for your situation.

Also, don't forget that income tax returns must be filed by April 15 each year. Contact your accountant early to find out what information he/she will need so you will have plenty of time to locate statements, etc. A state inheritance tax return may also need to be filed.

> **Note:** If the gross value of the estate is more than the federal estate tax exemption, or if there is an A-B or A-B-C provision in your Trust, there are other steps that need to be taken. A full explanation follows.

■ Apply for Benefits.

After consulting with your advisors, you will know which payout (distribution) option to choose when applying for benefits from life insurance companies, retirement plans, your spouse's employer, Veteran's benefits, Social Security, associations, and any others that might pay a death benefit.

■ Pay Bills.

Verify and pay all bills and taxes. Make a final accounting record of all assets and bills paid, and keep it with your records. (A bookkeeper, accountant or Corporate Trustee can show you how to do this or do it for you.)

■ Make Special Gifts.

If your spouse had a list of items he/she wanted certain people or organizations to have, you can go ahead and make them.

■ Keep Things Organized for Your Successor Trustee(s).

Keeping good records from now on will be very helpful for your Successor Trustee(s). You may also want to keep your Successors informed so they will know what to do if you become incapacitated and when you die.

Tax Planning if the Estate is More Than the Federal Estate Tax Exemption (or the Trust Contains an A-B or A-B-C Provision)

In addition to a final income tax return, if the gross value of the estate is more than the estate tax exemption in effect at that time, a federal *estate tax return* will need to be filed within nine months of the death—even if no estate taxes are due. Also, a state inheritance or estate tax return will probably need to be filed (even if no tax is due).

■ If The Trust Does Not Have Tax Planning

If the value of all the assets is more than the estate tax exemption and your Living Trust did not include any tax planning (the A-B or A-B-C) provisions, your attorney will probably use the marital deduction to transfer all the assets to you so no estate taxes will be due now. (But remember, estate taxes *will* be due when *you* die if your estate is more than the exemption at that time.)

Disclaiming

Your attorney may suggest that you *disclaim* some of the assets to reduce estate taxes when you die. Instead of going to you, these assets would go to the Beneficiary(ies) who would receive them if you were not living. Your deceased spouse's estate tax exemption could be applied to these assets, so no estate taxes would be paid on them now *or* when you die.

This can save your family a lot in estate taxes—if you don't need some of the assets *and* you are willing to give them up. However, to be able to disclaim an asset, you must not have received any benefit from it. So if your quick estimate shows that your assets are more than the estate tax exemption in effect at that time, it would be wise to wait until you meet with your attorney before you sell any assets, change any titles, or apply for any benefits.

■ If Your Trust Has Tax Planning

If you have an A-B or an A-B-C provision in your Living Trust, your attorney will help you put into place the provisions that you and your spouse wanted in your Trust to save estate taxes and/or provide additional control.

This planning process should be begun as soon as possible. Since the assets will be divided, it's important not to sell or retitle any assets, or apply for any benefits, until after you meet with your attorney. In preparation for this meeting, it would be a good idea for you to review Part Three (where we explain the A-B and the A-B-C provisions) and the following pages.

Since the surviving spouse is often named as the Trustee of Trust B (and Trust C), this section has been written with that in mind.

Assets Will Be Divided

You and your attorney (and trust officer when there is a Corporate Trustee involved) will decide how to divide the assets between Trust A and Trust B (and Trust C). Sometimes this is done by placing specific assets in each Trust, sometimes by putting a percentage of each asset in each Trust.

A listing of the assets that are placed in each Trust will be prepared, including their estate tax values and their values at the time the division is made.

Remember, the assets in Trust A are *yours*. You can sell, spend or invest them however you wish. You can change any provisions in Trust A, including the Beneficiaries if you wish. As long as you are a Trustee of your Trust, you continue to file your regular income tax return using your social security number.

However, the assets in Trust B (and Trust C) are *not* yours. They belong to the Beneficiaries your spouse named. The assets will stay in Trust B (and Trust C) so they can be used to help support you for as long as you live. In the meantime, as the Trustee, *you are safeguarding* the assets for the Beneficiaries.

> **Note:** As we explained in Part Three, depending on the provisions in the Trust document, you may be entitled to receive the income earned by the assets in Trust B (and principal, under certain conditions). The Beneficiaries of Trust B may also be allowed to receive some benefits while you are living.

If there is also a C Trust (QTIP), you will receive *all* the income the assets in Trust C earn. You may also be able to receive principal from Trust C—again, depending on the provisions in the Trust. The Beneficiaries of Trust C will not receive its assets until after you die.

Investing

You will probably want to have some professional help investing the assets, especially the assets in Trust B (and Trust C). Since you will probably be receiving all the income, you will want investments that produce income. At the same time, the Beneficiaries would like to see their assets increase in value—or at least not lose value. Your broker, financial advisor or a Corporate Trustee can help you decide how to invest them and avoid a conflict of interest.

Recordkeeping

Certain bookkeeping procedures must be followed for Trust B and Trust C. These are not especially difficult, and you will probably be able to handle them yourself after they are set up and explained to you. (If you don't want to do the accounting, you can have a bookkeeper, accountant, or Corporate Trustee do it for you.) For example:

You cannot mix your assets in Trust A with any of the assets in Trust B or Trust C—so Trust B and Trust C will have their own separate bank accounts. All income and expenses must be applied to the appropriate Trust. For example, if you receive a check for income that was generated by the assets in Trust B, it must be deposited in Trust B first—even though you will eventually receive the income. You can then write yourself a check for that amount.

Trust B and Trust C will have their own separate tax identification numbers and separate tax returns will be filed for them each year. (Your accountant can do this—or if you use a Corporate Trustee, they will do this for you.)

Keeping the assets separate is not really that difficult. You just have to understand that there are now two (or three) Trusts and *only one is yours*—the other Trust(s) belonged to your spouse, and you are taking care of the assets until you die.

It may help to remember *why* you are doing this—and that is primarily to save taxes. Remember, having an A Trust and a B Trust could save *hundreds of thousands of dollars* in estate taxes. Instead of supporting Uncle Sam, this money will help support *you* and the other Beneficiaries. And that's probably worth a little extra paperwork.

Keeping the Trust assets separate and the bookkeeping up to date will be *tremendously* helpful when your Successor Trustee(s) steps in if you become incapacitated and when you die. If you don't do this, your Successor Trustee, your accountant and your attorney might be able to re-create the records—but just think how time consuming and expensive that would be. And if they *can't* recreate the records, your Beneficiaries could lose a good part of their inheritance to Uncle Sam in *unnecessary* taxes.

By the way, this recordkeeping is required because of the tax planning—*not* because you have a Living Trust. If your tax planning had been done in a Will, you would have to do it then, too—*and* you would have had to go through probate.

My Spouse Has Died.
What Do I Need To Do?

☐ **Take Care of the Funeral.**

☐ **Find the Trust Document.**

☐ **Contact Attorney to Review Trust Document/Process.**

☐ **Order Death Certificates.**

☐ **Take Care of Ongoing Bills, Final Expenses.**

☐ **Put Together a Team of Advisors.**

☐ **Inventory Assets/Determine Current Values.**

☐ **Do Tax Planning.**

☐ **Apply for Benefits.**

☐ **Pay Bills.**

☐ **Make Special Gifts.**

☐ **Keep Things Organized for Your Successor Trustee(s).**

I'M THE SUCCESSOR TRUSTEE. WHAT ARE MY RESPONSIBILITIES?

If you have been named as Successor Trustee for someone—perhaps your spouse, parents or a good friend—you don't do *anything* until this person becomes incapacitated or dies. But you may be wondering what you need to do then.

You may not know very much about the Trust—why it was set up, what it does, what your responsibilities will be. As a start, we suggest that you read this book to get an overview of the benefits of a Living Trust and how it works. The checklists which start on the next page will also be helpful.

The most important thing for you to remember as Trustee is that *these assets are not yours.* You are safeguarding them for others—for your incapacitated spouse, parent(s) or good friend while they are living and later, until the assets are distributed after this person dies, for the Beneficiaries. When you sign your name and conduct business, it will be as the Trustee—not as you, personally.

As a Trustee, you have certain responsibilities. For example:
- You must follow the instructions in the Trust document.
- You cannot mix Trust assets with your own. So you will need to keep separate checking accounts and investments.
- You cannot use the Trust assets for your own benefit.
- You must treat all Beneficiaries the same—you cannot favor one over another.
- The Trust assets must be invested in a "prudent" (conservative) manner, in a way that will result in reasonable growth with minimum risk.
- You are responsible for keeping accurate records, filing tax returns, and reporting to the Beneficiaries as the Trust requires.

As you can see, these responsibilities are pretty much based on common sense—especially when you keep in mind that a Trustee is safekeeping assets for others. You are not required to do all of the accounting and investing yourself—you can have professionals help you if you wish.

The following checklists will help give you some direction at a time when you may not know where to begin.

I'M THE SUCCESSOR TRUSTEE. WHAT DO I DO AT THE GRANTOR'S INCAPACITY?

■ **Oversee Care of Ill Person.**

Make sure this person is receiving quality care in a supportive environment—that the hospital or nursing home, physician(s) and staff are qualified. Check to make sure the insurance company has been notified.

Make sure the attending physician has a copy of the health care documents (Durable Power of Attorney for Health Care, Health Care Proxy, Living Will). If someone has been appointed to make health care decisions (Agent), check to make sure he/she has been notified. If not, find the health care documents (they should be with the Trust document) and give copies to the doctor and Agent.

Offer to help notify this person's employer, friends and relatives. If the person wrote a letter explaining what you should do at his/her incapacity (as we suggest), it may be very helpful.

■ **Find the Trust Document.**

Hopefully, you already know where it is. See if you will be able to write checks and sell assets with just your signature or if someone will be a Co-Trustee with you. If you have a Co-Trustee, notify him/her as soon as possible.

■ **Notify Attorney.**

Notify the attorney who prepared the Trust document. He/she should be aware of the incapacity in case you have any questions. You may also want to schedule an appointment to go over the Trust and your responsibilities. Remember, you've probably never done this before, so you are bound to have some questions along the way. And it will be comforting for you to know there is someone you can call.

■ **Find Out What the Insurance Covers.**

Assuming the insurance will cover a certain procedure or facility could be a very costly mistake. Find out the alternatives before a major decision is made. (If you need help understanding the coverage, the insurance agent or the person's personnel/benefits department may be able to help you. Most insurance companies also have a toll free telephone number you can call 24-

hours a day if you have questions.) If the person has long term care insurance, make sure you are familiar with the coverage if it turns out the incapacity will be lengthy.

■ Have Doctor(s) Document the Incapacity.

It may be necessary to have the appropriate physician(s) write a letter documenting the person's condition. (Some Trust documents will only require a letter from an M.D., some from one or two specialists, others require none.) You will probably need to show this letter to the bank and others so you can sign checks and conduct business as Trustee.

■ Look After Minors.

If there are any minor children, read the Trust document for instructions for their care. (If the incapacity is expected to be lengthy, a Guardianship hearing will probably be required to officially appoint the Guardian. The attorney can help you with this.)

■ Become Familiar with the Finances.

You need to know what the assets are, where they are located, and their current values. You also need to know where the income comes from, how much it is, and when it is paid—as well as regular, ongoing expenses. You may need to put together a budget.

Familiarize yourself with any business dealings this person was involved with. If there is real estate, make sure you have keys, take care of utilities, etc. If this person owns a business, you will probably need to make arrangements for its continuation.

Hopefully, the person organized this information as we suggested. But if not, you'll need to start a list of the assets, where they are located, account numbers, current values, phone numbers, and your contact persons. The Organizer in the back of this book will be very helpful in this process.

If you don't know what assets this person has, the accountant, banker, broker, employer, adult children, and close friends may know. Look for bank and brokerage account statements. Is there a safe deposit box or a safe? Last year's income tax return may also be helpful.

If you find any assets that were not transferred to the Trust, use the Durable Power of Attorney to transfer them into the Trust as soon as possible so they will not have to go through probate when this person dies. If you have any problems, contact the attorney who prepared the Trust. Usually a phone call from the attorney will be all that is needed. (Keep in mind, however, that an asset may have been intentionally left out of the Trust. You might want to check with the attorney before you transfer the asset.)

■ Apply for Benefits.

Apply for any disability benefits—through the employer, private insurance, Veteran's benefits, Social Security, etc.

■ Put Together Team of Advisors.

Depending on the values of the assets and the expected length and severity of the incapacity, you may want to put together a team of professional advisors to help you—like the attorney, accountant, banker and/or trust officer, financial advisor, and insurance advisor. Be sure to talk to them *before* you sell *any* assets. There could be some tax consequences, and they may be able to suggest better alternatives.

■ Notify Bank, Broker, Etc.

Notify the bank and others that you are now the Trustee for this person. They will probably want to see a copy of the doctor's letter, Trust document, and your personal identification.

Transact any necessary business for the incapacitated person. You can receive and deposit funds, pay bills (including mortgage and other obligations) and, in general, use the person's assets to take care of him/her until recovery or death. (If you have any problems, a quick phone call from the attorney should straighten things out.)

■ Take Care of Recordkeeping and Accounting.

Keep careful records of medical expenses and file claims promptly. Keep a ledger of the bills you have paid and any income received. An accountant or bookkeeper can show you how to set up these records properly. (The Trust document may require you to send accountings to the Beneficiaries.)

Don't forget that income tax returns must be filed by April 15 each year. Contact the accountant early to find out what information he/she will need so you will have plenty of time to locate statements, etc. Also, find out when property taxes are due.

If, for whatever reason, these responsibilities prove to be too much, consider having a bookkeeper, accountant or a Corporate Trustee help you. A Corporate Trustee can manage the investments and do the recordkeeping for you.

If you feel you simply cannot handle any of the responsibilities due to work or family demands—or for any other reason—you can resign and let the next Successor Trustee step in. If no other Successor Trustee has been named, or none are willing or able to serve, a Corporate Trustee can usually be named.

I'm The Successor Trustee. What Do I Do at the Grantor's Incapacity?

- [ ] **Oversee Care of Ill Person.**
- [ ] **Find the Trust Document.**
- [ ] **Notify Attorney.**
- [ ] **Find Out What the Insurance Covers.**
- [ ] **Have Doctor(s) Document the Incapacity.**
- [ ] **Look After Minors.**
- [ ] **Become Familiar with the Finances.**
- [ ] **Apply for Benefits.**
- [ ] **Put Together Team of Advisors.**
- [ ] **Notify Bank, Broker, Etc.**
- [ ] **Take Care of Recordkeeping and Accounting.**

I'M THE SUCCESSOR TRUSTEE. WHAT DO I DO AT THE GRANTOR'S DEATH?

The Successor Trustee has essentially the same duties as an Executor named in a Will. But if the titles and beneficiary designations have been changed to the Trust, the probate court will not be involved. This means you will be able to act on *your* schedule (instead of the court's).

The Trustee is responsible for seeing that everything is done properly and in a timely manner. You may be able to do much of this yourself, but an attorney, Corporate Trustee and/or accountant can give you valuable guidance and assistance. The following checklist will give you an overview of what needs to be done.

■ Assist with the Funeral.

Inform the family of your position and assist them as needed: funeral arrangements, flowers, cemetery marker, announcement in paper, special wishes for service, notifying friends, relatives, employer, etc. If the person left any written instructions, this will be much easier on everyone.

■ Find the Trust Document.

Read it for any specific instructions, and to find out if you will be able to write checks and sell assets with just your signature. If there is a Co-Trustee, notify him/her as soon as possible.

■ Contact Attorney to Review Trust Document, Process.

Contact an attorney and schedule an appointment to go over the Trust document, the assets, and your responsibilities as soon as possible. It will also be comforting for you to know there is someone you can call if you have questions. You do not have to use the attorney who prepared the Trust, although he/she will probably be more familiar with the document.

If this person has a surviving spouse, and the estate is more than the federal estate tax exemption or the Trust document has an A-B or A-B-C provision, the attorney will probably need to do some estate tax planning. For information about this process, see page 208.

■ **Keep Beneficiaries Informed.**

Give copies of the Trust document to all Beneficiaries, and make sure you keep them fully informed throughout the process.

■ **Order Death Certificates.**

Order at least 12 certified death certificates (you can usually get these from the funeral home). You will need these to transfer titles, collect benefits, and conduct other business as Trustee. Multiple copies will help speed things up, since you won't have to wait to get copies back in order to give them to someone else.

■ **Put Together Team of Advisors.**

Depending on the values of the assets, you may want to put together a team of professionals—like the attorney, accountant, banker and/or trust officer, financial advisor, and/or insurance advisor—to advise you and the Beneficiaries. Talk to them before you sell any assets or change any investments—they may have some suggestions that will save taxes.

■ **Inventory Assets/Determine Current Values.**

Before you meet with the attorney, it would be a good idea to put together a preliminary list of the assets and their estimated values. Later on, you'll need to determine exact values for accounting and tax purposes.

The attorney, accountant or trust officer will need this "quick estimate" to know which tax returns will need to be filed (remember, a federal estate tax return is required if the gross value of the estate is more than the estate tax exemption in effect at that time) and to be able to advise you.

Determining the values of assets is also important because they receive a new basis when the owner dies. If assets have appreciated, this can save a considerable amount in capital gains tax when they are eventually sold. (Remember, if an asset was jointly owned—for example, if a married couple had one Living Trust together and this is the first spouse to die—*only the interest of the deceased spouse* receives a new basis. However, as discussed in Part Six, if they jointly owned an asset since before 1976 in a noncommunity property state, *both* interests may get a new basis when the first spouse dies.)

If the deceased was the second spouse to die, you will also need to know if the assets had been placed in multiple trusts for tax planning or other purposes (through A-B or A-B-C provisions).

Hopefully, the person organized this information as we suggested. But if not, you'll need to start a list of the assets, where they are located, account numbers, current values, phone numbers, and your contact persons. You'll also need the actual title documents. (The Organizer in the back of this book will be helpful in this process.)

If you don't know what the assets are, your advisors, the Beneficiaries, and close friends of the deceased may be able to help. Look for bank and brokerage account statements. Is there a safe deposit box or a safe? Last year's income tax return may also be helpful.

If there is any real estate, make sure you have keys, the insurance is in force, and the mortgage is paid. Make arrangements to keep the utilities on (or turn them off), etc.

How to Determine Values

It is important that current values are appropriately determined—otherwise the IRS will not accept them. The IRS has specific rules that must be followed in establishing "fair market value" when an estate tax return is required or when calculating basis for income tax purposes. In other words, a "ballpark" estimate by a neighbor who happens to be a real estate agent—or your best guess—usually will not do.

Your banker and broker can provide you with the values of accounts on the day your spouse died. *The Wall Street Journal* for that day can also be a good source for values of stocks and mutual funds. Some items (especially real estate and collectibles) will need to be appraised—this should be done as soon as possible. Your attorney or trust officer can recommend a reputable appraiser. There are also companies that do estate valuations—your attorney or trust officer will know about them, too.

■ Notify the Bank, Others.

Notify the bank, brokerage firm, and others that you are now the Trustee. They will probably want to see a certified death certificate, a copy of the Trust document, and your personal identification. Remember, you are conducting business as a Trustee now—not as an individual—and you will sign checks and papers as the Trustee.

■ **Make Partial Distributions if Needed.**

If the surviving spouse or other Beneficiary needs money to live on, you can make some partial distributions. If the gross value of the estate is more than the federal estate tax exemption, check with the attorney before you make any distributions, especially within the first six months after the death. You'll want to make sure you keep enough to pay expenses (including taxes and known creditors). And be sure to have the Beneficiary sign a receipt.

■ **Collect Benefits.**

Notify Social Security, life insurance companies, retirement plans, associations, and any others that will provide a death benefit. Put these in an interest bearing account (titled in the name of the Trust) until distributed.

■ **Take Care of Recordkeeping/Tax Returns.**

Keep good records of final medical and funeral expenses. (They may be deductible.) File medical claims promptly. Start a ledger of bills to be paid and income received.

Contact an accountant for preparation of the final income tax return as soon as possible. Remember, if the gross value of the estate is more than the federal estate tax exemption in effect at that time, a federal estate tax return (IRS Form 706) must be filed within nine months after the death. (An attorney or accountant with experience in federal estate taxes will be very helpful.) A state inheritance tax return may also have to be filed.

■ **Pay Bills/Final Accounting.**

Verify and pay all bills and taxes. Make a final accounting record of all assets and bills paid. Give a copy to all Beneficiaries when the assets are distributed.

■ **Distribute Assets.**

To distribute the assets, you will need to change titles from the Trust to the Beneficiaries (or to the Trustee, if the assets are to stay in Trust). Part Six will give you a general idea of how this is done. Basically, the process is reversed—instead of putting assets into the Trust, you will be taking them out. Make sure you get a receipt signed by each Beneficiary stating that he/she has received the assets.

Distribute the assets in the following order.

1. Assets on Special Gifts Lists, if any.

2. Remaining personal property—hold estate sale if necessary.

3. If there is a Children's Trust, transfer assets to the Trustee.

4. If the assets are to be fully distributed, divide cash and transfer titles of assets according to Trust instructions. Nothing else needs to be done— the Trust has been dissolved.

5. If the assets are to stay in the Trust and will be distributed to the Beneficiaries later—for example, if the Beneficiaries will receive their inheritances in installments—the Trust will need a new tax identification number, and proper bookkeeping and reporting procedures will need to be established. (If separate Trusts are to be established, each will need its own tax ID number, and separate bookkeeping and reporting procedures will need to be followed.) Each year, the Trust will file IRS Form 1041 and Form K1 to report any income earned.

It is very important that the bookkeeping be set up properly from the beginning, with a complete listing of the assets and their values. The Trustee is responsible for accurate accounting—but, remember, that doesn't mean you have to do it all yourself. A bookkeeper, accountant or Corporate Trustee can help. (A Corporate Trustee can invest the Trust assets and do the accounting.)

Remember, if you feel you simply cannot handle these responsibilities due to work or family demands—or for any other reason—you can resign and let the next Successor Trustee step in. If no other Successor Trustee has been named, or none are willing or able to serve, a Corporate Trustee can usually be named.

I'm The Successor Trustee.
What Do I Do at the Grantor's Death?

☐ **Assist with the Funeral.**

☐ **Find the Trust Document.**

☐ **Contact Attorney to Review Trust Document, Process.**

☐ **Keep Beneficiaries Informed.**

☐ **Order Death Certificates.**

☐ **Put Together Team of Advisors.**

☐ **Inventory Assets/Determine Current Values.**

☐ **Notify the Bank, Others.**

☐ **Make Partial Distributions if Needed.**

☐ **Collect Benefits.**

☐ **Take Care of Recordkeeping/Tax Returns.**

☐ **Pay Bills/Final Accounting.**

☐ **Distribute Assets.**

SUMMARY

We know that was a lot of information, but it should be very helpful to your family and/or Successor Trustee when something happens to you. And we hope the checklists have enlightened you and will help motivate you to continue putting things in order.

Remember, if your Trust has been properly prepared and funded, it will work even if you don't do any of the things we have suggested in this section. However, if you take the time now to:

■ organize your financial information as we suggest,

■ make sure your spouse and/or Successor Trustee(s) know where this information and these checklists are, and

■ review your Trust and information each year and keep it current,

then you will be able to relax and get on with living, knowing you have done the best you can do for the people you care about. And that will give you the best benefit of all—tremendous peace of mind.

Part Eight

. . . .

INCOME TAX ISSUES AFTER YOU DIE

Part Eight—
INCOME TAX ISSUES AFTER YOU DIE

As we have explained, your Living Trust has no effect on your income taxes while you are living. You continue to report your income and pay taxes as you always have. As long as you are a Trustee, you file your regular 1040, using your social security number.

But what happens *after* you die? Income that is earned on your assets from the time you die until the assets are distributed to your Beneficiaries is still subject to income taxes. (This should come as no surprise. *Any* time income is earned, it is subject to taxes.) However, different tax rules apply during this time.

In the past, there were even different rules depending on whether the income was earned by assets in a Trust or by assets in a probate estate. Most of these differences had little, if any, impact on most families. Even so, pro-Trust attorneys pushed (for several years) to make the taxation of Trusts and probate estates equal. Finally, in *The Taxpayer Relief Act of 1997,* the last remaining differences were all but eliminated.

In this section, we explain how income earned on your assets after you die will be taxed, how the rules were different, and how they are now virtually the same.

If you plan to keep assets (and income) in your Trust for some time after you die, you may want to read this section now. If not, you can probably skip over it for now and come back later (if you want to). At least you'll know where to find the information if you need it!

INCOME TAX RATES FOR TRUSTS AND PROBATE ESTATES

At one time, the income received by some Trusts and probate estates was taxed at a lower rate than income received by individuals. As a result, some people set up Trusts specifically to save income taxes. Instead of the Beneficiaries reporting the income and paying taxes at their higher rates, the Trust reported the income and paid taxes at its lower rate.

Naturally, Congress caught on and passed a series of laws that increased the tax rates for Trusts and probate estates.

So, now, the income received by many Trusts (those in which the Trustee can decide whether or not to distribute the income or to keep it in the Trust) and the income received by *all* probate estates is taxed at a *higher* rate than the income received by most individuals.

In 1998, if one of these Trusts, or a probate estate, has income over $6,100, the income will be taxed at a rate of 36%. If the income is over $8,350, the tax rate is 39.6%. To put this in perspective, the following chart shows the level of income when these rates apply for Trusts and estates as compared to married taxpayers filing jointly and to individuals.

Taxable Income Comparison (1998 Estimated Tax Rates)

Tax Rate	Level of Taxable Income Probate Estates & Trusts	Level of Taxable Income Married, Filing Jointly	Level of Taxable Income Individual
15%	$0 to $1,700	$0 to $42,350	$0 to $25,350
28%	$1,701 to $4,000	$42,351 to 102,300	$25,351 to $61,400
31%	$4,001 to $6,100	$102,301 to $155,950	$61,401 to $128,100
36.0%	$6,101 to $8,350	$155,951 to $278,450	$128,101 to $278,450
39.6%	$8,351 and above	$278,451 and above	$278,451 and above

Because the tax rates apply to lower levels of their income, probate estates and Trusts pay more in taxes than individuals on the income they receive after you die. As a result, most Trustees will distribute the income to the Beneficiaries or invest in assets that produce little, if any, income. (Note: These numbers are estimates. The official 1998 tables had not been released by the IRS at the date of publication.)

Now, remember, *these higher rates do not apply to your Living Trust while you are living*. They only apply *after* you die, *if* your assets are earning income and *if* the income stays in the Trust.

In many cases, these higher tax rates will not apply after you die because the income will be distributed to the surviving spouse (for example, if you have a B Trust or C Trust) or to other Beneficiaries. This is one reason why it is important to give the Trustee some flexibility in how to distribute the income.

If, for some reason, you did not want the income distributed—for example, a Beneficiary is a minor, is irresponsible, or has special needs (like a disabled child or elderly parent), the Trustee can avoid the higher tax rates by investing in tax-exempt investments or in assets that will appreciate in value but produce little, if any, income. (So you want to give your Trustee some flexibility in how to invest the Trust's assets.)

These tax rates do not apply to your Living Trust while you are living

PREVIOUS INCOME TAX DIFFERENCES BETWEEN TRUSTS AND PROBATE ESTATES

Even though the tax *rates* are the same for Trusts and probate estates, as we mentioned earlier there used to be some different rules for how the taxes were determined. Most families were not affected by these differences. Even so, in *The Taxpayer Relief Act of 1997*, the laws were changed to all but eliminate these differences and put Trusts and probate estates on more equal footing.

Here is a brief summary of these issues—how they were different and, now, how they are virtually the same.

Living Trust Can Be Treated The Same As Probate Estate

One of the provisions in *The Taxpayer Relief Act of 1997* states that if the Trustee of a Revocable Living Trust decides it would be advantageous to have the Trust treated as a probate estate for income tax purposes, the Trustee (along with the Executor, if any, of the probate estate) can choose to do so by making a one-time, irrevocable election.

If a probate is opened after you die (for example, if an asset was inadvertently left out of your Trust or if a shorter creditor claims period is desired, as explained in Part Two), the election can be made during this proceeding.

If there is no need for a probate (for example, if no assets were left out of your Trust or if a shorter creditor claims period is not needed), the general consensus is that the Trustee should be able to make this election without having to open a probate.

Here's what you get if the Trustee decides to have the Trust treated as a probate estate for income tax purposes.

■ Calendar Year vs. Fiscal Year

With few exceptions, a Trust has been required to report income on a calendar year basis (January 1 through December 31) just like most Beneficiaries. A probate estate, however, can elect to report income on a calendar year *or fiscal* year basis—in other words, its year can be any 12-month period, as long as it ends at the end of a month. This often results in a short first year.

For example, let's say Grandpa dies on March 1, 1998. A fiscal year ending January 31 is chosen. So the first fiscal year will begin March 1, 1998 and end on January 31, 1999. The second year (and subsequent years, if his estate continues in probate) will be February 1-January 31.

In most cases, any income you receive in a calendar year must be reported on that year's tax return. But if an heir receives income from a probate estate that has elected a fiscal year, the heir may not have to report the income until the *following* year's tax return is filed.

In the example given above, the income the heirs receive between Grandpa's death and December 31, 1998 will not be reported by the heirs on their 1998 tax returns. That's because the estate does not report the income as having been distributed until the end of *its fiscal year*, which is January 31, 1999. The heirs, then, report the income they received from Grandpa's estate from March 1, 1998 through January 31, 1999 on their income tax returns for 1999—which are due the following April. So the heirs will not pay taxes on income they receive from the estate in 1998 until they file their tax returns in April, 2000.

The ability to choose a fiscal year over a calendar year sometimes gave a probate estate a slight advantage. However, in most cases, the ability to delay taxes on income for one year hardly justified having to go through probate. Also, if the heirs were required to file quarterly income tax payments, they probably did not see much of a benefit because the estimated taxes had to be paid in the year the income was received.

Now, however, the Trustee of a Living Trust can also have the option to elect a fiscal year.

■ Annual Personal Exemptions

A probate estate is entitled to a $600 annual exemption from income taxes— in other words, each year $600 of income produced by the assets in a probate estate are exempt from income taxes.

Generally speaking, if a Trust is required to distribute all the income each year, it is allowed a $300 annual exemption. If the Trust is not required to distribute all the income each year, it is allowed a $100 annual exemption. However, if the Trust distributes any principal (regardless of whether it is required to distribute the income), it is only allowed a $100 annual exemption for that year.

Since many Trusts these days distribute the income, you are only looking at a $300 difference in the amount of the exemption (when principal is not distributed). And even in a 39.6% tax bracket, that produces a tax savings of *less than $120* a year—a very insignificant savings compared to the expenses of probate.

Now, however, a Living Trust can also be entitled to a $600 exemption.

■ Amounts "Set Aside" for Charity

In both a Will and a Trust, you can specify that a certain asset is to be given to a charity. Sometimes, the distribution may not occur immediately after you die, and the asset is "set aside" during the administration process (the time from the date you die until your assets are distributed).

Any income that is generated by the asset before it is distributed to the charity is not included in the taxable income of either the probate estate or the Trust. However, if the asset is sold before it is transferred to the charity, the tax on the gain is handled differently for probate estates and Trusts.

A probate estate can keep the gain in the estate until the administration is complete and the full proceeds from the sale are distributed to the charity. A

Trust, however, must distribute the gain to the charity in the year the asset is sold—otherwise, the Trust will have to pay a capital gains tax on the gain.

Now, a Living Trust can elect the same treatment as a probate estate.

■ Passive Losses on Rental Real Estate

While you are living, if your Adjusted Gross Income (as defined on IRS Form 1040) is less than $150,000 and you actively participate in the management of rental real estate (approve repairs and new tenants, write checks, make management decisions, etc.), you can deduct up to $25,000 in net losses each year from your ordinary income. (If your AGI is more than $100,000, the $25,000 is gradually phased out so that, by the time the AGI is $150,000, the amount of passive net losses that can be deducted from ordinary income is reduced to "0.")

A probate estate can continue to deduct these losses (up to $25,000 per year) for up to two tax years. If the surviving spouse also has rental real estate (separate property or property that was jointly owned), the $25,000 maximum will be reduced by the amount the spouse uses within the estate's tax year.

The Trustee of your Trust can now elect the same treatment as a probate estate.

However, if the election is not made and the Trustee actively participates in the management of the property as you did, it may still be possible for your Trust to deduct from ordinary Trust income the net losses that occur between the date of your death and when the property is transferred to your Beneficiary(ies).

If that is not possible, the deductions still will not be lost—your Beneficiary(ies) will get to use them later. The net losses that occur between the time you die and when the property is distributed will be added to the cost basis of the property when it is distributed to your Beneficiary(ies). So, when the property is sold, the cost basis will be higher. This means your Beneficiary(ies) will have less "profit" (as far as the IRS is concerned) and will pay less in capital gains tax.

Other Differences Eliminated
Here are other differences that were recently eliminated.

■ Sixty-Five Day Rule
This is a tax-planning opportunity that previously was available only to certain Trusts—those that let the Trustee decide whether to pay income to the Beneficiaries or to keep the income in the Trust. Basically, it gives the Trustee 65 extra days in which to decide if it is better for the Trust or for the Beneficiaries to pay the income tax.

If the Trustee realizes after the end of the year that the Trust has too much income, the Trustee has 65 days in the new year (until around March 5) to distribute income to the Beneficiaries—and the income will be considered as having been distributed in the previous year.

Here's an example. In February, 1998, while reviewing the 1997 year-end accounting for a Trust, the Trustee realizes that the Trust has more than $8,100 in income and would have to pay income taxes at the highest tax rate (39.6%). The Beneficiaries, however, are in a lower tax bracket, so they would pay less in taxes if they had received the income. On February 28, 1998, the Trustee distributes the income to the Beneficiaries. As far as the IRS is concerned, the income was distributed to the Beneficiaries on December 31, 1997. So the Beneficiaries include this income on their 1997 tax returns.

This option is also available now to probate estates.

■ Throwback Rule Repealed
When Trusts had a lower tax rate than individuals, it sometimes made sense to accumulate income in the Trust from one year to the next, with the Trust paying the income tax each year at its lower tax rate.

Of course, Uncle Sam wanted to make sure he got as much tax as possible. So, the purpose of the Throwback Rule was to make sure that when the income was eventually distributed, it would be "thrown back" and taxed as if the Beneficiary had received it in the year it was earned. If it turned out that the Trust had already paid *more* in income taxes than the Beneficiary would have paid, Uncle Sam would not issue a refund.

This law applied only to Trusts and not to probate estates. However, since the tax rates on Trusts are now higher than those that apply to most individuals, there is no longer an advantage to accumulating income in a Trust. In most cases, it made more sense to pay the income to the Beneficiary in the year it was generated and have the Beneficiary pay the tax—and not even deal with the Throwback Rule.

Congress agreed. This law was repealed for domestic Trusts (except for certain Trusts created before March 1, 1984) in *The Taxpayer Relief Act of 1997*.

■ Recognition of Losses

In the past, probate estates and Trusts have handled losses on assets differently. For example, let's say you leave $25,000 to a Beneficiary. Your Trust says the Beneficiary can receive this amount in cash or in assets of the same value. (This is called an "in kind" distribution.) The Beneficiary decides on some stock that was valued at $30,000 when you died, but is now worth $25,000.

When the stock is distributed to the Beneficiary, your Trust cannot claim the $5,000 loss on its income tax return. But the deduction is not lost—the Beneficiary will use it later. The $5,000 loss is added to the cost basis of the asset when it is distributed to the Beneficiary. So instead of having a $25,000 cost basis, the cost basis is now $30,000.

If the Beneficiary later sells the asset for, let's say, $40,000, the taxable gain will be $10,000 ($40,000 sales price less $30,000 cost basis equals $10,000 taxable gain). If the asset is sold at a loss, say $20,000, the Beneficiary will be able to report the $10,000 capital loss on his/her income tax return.

By contrast, in a probate estate, when the stock was distributed the estate could take the $5,000 loss on its income tax return—or, in the final year of the probate, the loss could be distributed to the heirs so they could take it on their income tax returns.

The difference was that the probate estate could deduct the loss when the stock was distributed. But this meant all the heirs would share the loss (even though, in the example above, only one received the asset). With a Trust, the Beneficiary who receives the asset gets the full benefit of the loss (when it is added to the cost basis), but only *sees* the benefit when the asset is sold.

In *The Taxpayer Relief Act of 1997*, this law was changed so that probate estates now handle losses the same way as Trusts—but *only* if the heir is to receive a *percentage* of assets (say, 10% of your stock portfolio). If the heir is to receive a *specific dollar amount* of assets, as in the example above, the old rules (as explained above) still apply. (This is called *tax simplification*?!) Please note that the law only changes how *losses in a probate estate* are handled. There was *no change* for Trusts.

■ Gain on the Sale of Depreciable Assets

If you sell a depreciable asset for a price that is greater than its depreciated cost basis, the difference is a taxable gain.

For example, let's say you buy a car for $15,000. Each year you own it, you depreciate $2,000 of its value on your income tax return. In the fifth year after you bought the car, you sell it for $10,000. In the four years you have owned it, you have depreciated $8,000 of its value ($2,000 times four years equals $8,000 total depreciation), so its depreciated cost basis is now $7,000 ($15,000 purchase price less $8,000 in total depreciation). You now have a taxable gain of $3,000 ($10,000 sales price less $7,000 depreciated cost basis equals $3,000 taxable gain).

If a Trustee sells a depreciable asset (or makes an exchange) to a Beneficiary, any gain is taxed as ordinary income. If the Executor for a probate estate did the same, the gain was taxed as capital gains income. However, if the Trustee or the Executor elected not to recognize the gain (which either one could do), the Beneficiary would recognize the gain later when the asset was sold.

The reason for the different tax treatment was that, as far as the IRS was concerned, a Trustee and the Beneficiaries of the Trust were and are considered "related parties," while a probate estate and the heirs were not.

In *The Taxpayer Relief Act of 1997*, this law was changed so that a probate estate and the heirs are also considered "related parties." So now the gain will be taxed the same way as in a Trust (as ordinary income instead of capital gains)—but *only* if the heir is to receive a *percentage* of assets. If the heir is to receive a *specific dollar amount* of assets, as in this example, the old rules (as explained above) still apply. (Again, please note that the law only changes how gains on depreciable assets are handled *in a probate estate*. There was *no change* for Trusts.)

■ Two-Year Exemption from Estimated Tax Payments

In the past, only a probate estate was allowed this exemption. But now, both probate estates and Living Trusts are exempt from having to make quarterly estimated tax payments for the first two years.

SUMMARY

Income earned by your assets from the time you die until the assets are transferred to your Beneficiaries is subject to income tax. While the tax *rates* are the same for Trusts and probate estates, until recently there were different rules for how the taxes were determined. Now, with recent changes in the tax laws, those differences have been virtually eliminated.

Part Nine

. . . .

ADDITIONAL TAX- SAVING STRATEGIES

Part Nine—
ADDITIONAL
TAX-SAVING STRATEGIES

You may be wondering, "Once I have a Living Trust, have I finished my estate planning?"

The answer is "Not necessarily." A Living Trust is the perfect foundation for most estate plans. And, packaged with the appropriate "support" documents (Pour Over Will, Durable Power of Attorney for Asset Management, and Health Care documents explained in Part Six), it *will* be all many families need.

However, depending on the size of your estate, your family situation, the amount of your income and your goals, your attorney may suggest some additional strategies to save you and your family as much as possible in taxes, give you more control, and to create and preserve your wealth.

In this section, we give you an introduction to some of the most popular (and proven) strategies. These descriptions are—out of necessity—brief and fairly general in nature. You will, of course, need to find out more about the strategies that interest you, and how they would apply in your situation, before you jump into anything. This section will, however, give you some great ideas of what can be done.

Most of these are *irrevocable*. Up until now, we have been discussing a Living Trust which is *revocable*—it can be changed or cancelled at any time as your needs change. But an Irrevocable Trust usually cannot be changed or cancelled once the final document has been signed. If you decide to use one of these in your tax planning, make sure you read the document very carefully and that you completely understand it before you sign anything.

MAKE GIFTS TO REDUCE YOUR ESTATE

One thing you can do to save estate taxes—whether you are married or single—is start giving away some of your assets *now* to the people or organizations who will eventually receive them after you die.

This is an excellent way to reduce estate taxes—because you are reducing the *size* of your taxable estate. (Just make sure you don't give away any assets you may need later.) But even more satisfying to many people is that you can *see* the results of something that may not have happened without your help.

As we mentioned earlier, you can currently give up to $10,000 per recipient each year. (If you are married, you and your spouse can *each* give $10,000, for a total of $20,000 per recipient per year.) You can also give an *unlimited* amount for tuition and medical expenses if you make the gifts directly to the educational organization or health care provider.

Gifts do not have to be in cash. For example, if you want to give your son some land worth $40,000, you can give him a $10,000 "interest" in the property each year for four years.

As long as the gift is within these limits, you don't have to report it to Uncle Sam. Just the same, it's a good idea to get appraisals (especially for real estate) and document these gifts in case the IRS later tries to challenge the values.

What if you want to give someone *more* than $10,000 in one year? You can—it just starts using up your federal estate tax exemption. That's because the federal estate tax exemption is a *combined gift and estate tax* exemption. Under current law, it's the same tax—if you transfer the asset while you are living, it's called a *gift* tax. If the transfer is made after you die, it's called an *estate* tax. So you can either use part or all of the exemption now while you are living, or you can use it later after you die.

If your gift exceeds the $10,000 limit, you need to let Uncle Sam know—by filing an informational gift tax return (IRS Form 709) for the year the gift is made. The gift is applied to your federal gift and estate tax exemption. So you only pay a gift tax after you have used up your exemption.

Note: Beginning in 1999, the amount of tax-free gifts (currently $10,000) will be tied to inflation. However, the amount will only be increased in increments of $1,000, and it will be rounded *down* instead of up. So, for example, if adjustments for inflation would increase the amount to $10,999, it would remain at $10,000. With current inflation rates, it will probably be several years before the amount of tax-free gifts is increased to $11,000.

Making gifts now can reduce your estate taxes later

Pay The Tax Now—And Save

Once your exemption is used up, you will have to pay a gift tax if you make any more taxable gifts (currently, those more than $10,000) while you are living. Or, you could wait and have your estate pay an estate tax after you die.

The tax *rate* is the same, whether you pay it now or after you die. But, *it costs you less to pay the gift tax now* than to pay the estate tax after you die.

As we explained in Part Three, after you die, taxable gifts you have made since 1976 are added back into your estate before estate taxes are calculated. (This is so Uncle Sam can calculate your estate taxes at the highest tax rate.) The amount you have paid in gift taxes is then subtracted from the estate taxes due. (Think of the gift tax as a prepayment of the estate taxes you will owe.)

But the amount you've already paid in gift taxes is not in your taxable estate when you die. You've already paid it to Uncle Sam. *Making the gift now lets you forever remove the amount paid in gift tax from your taxable estate.*

If, on the other hand, you keep the asset in your estate until you die, the amount you would have paid in gift taxes is still in your estate. This makes your taxable estate larger and increases the amount of estate taxes your estate will have to pay. *Keeping the asset in your estate until after you die forces you to pay estate taxes on the amount you would have paid in gift tax.* In effect, you're paying a tax on the tax!

This is best explained with an example. Let's assume you have used up your federal gift and estate tax exemption through prior gifts and, as a result, you are now in a 50% gift and estate tax bracket.

If you give your children $1 million as a gift (while you are living), the gift tax will be $500,000. You, the donor (not your children), pay the gift tax. So your children would receive the full $1 million, and an additional $500,000 would be removed from your taxable estate (because you would pay the gift tax). So, it would cost you $500,000 to give your children $1 million .

If, on the other hand, you wait until after you die, it would cost you $1 million to give them $1 million (50% estate tax on $2 million leaves $1 million). That's *$500,000 more* than if you gave them the $1 million while you were living!

Of course, there is an exception you need to be aware of. Any gifts you make within three years of your death will be included in your estate—and so will any gift tax you pay on them. This is to prevent you from making enormous gifts "from your deathbed" so you can get the gift tax out of your estate. (Yes, Uncle Sam already figured that one out!)

Which Assets Are The Best To Gift?

It can be especially smart to give away assets that are appreciating in value—because any income and appreciation that occurs *after* the gift is made are also removed from your taxable estate.

But you also have to look at the estate tax savings compared to what the recipient may have to pay in capital gains tax if the asset is later sold. Remember, when you give away an appreciated asset, it keeps your original cost basis (plus any gift tax paid). And if the recipient decides to sell it, he/she will have to pay capital gains tax on the difference between the selling price and what you paid for it.

If, on the other hand, you don't give it away and it stays in your estate, the asset will receive a full step up in basis as of the date of your death (saving capital gains tax). But, depending on the size of your estate when you die, there may be estate taxes. So it's a trade off.

Currently, the maximum federal long term capital gains rate (for assets held longer than 18 months) is 20%, while estate taxes *start* at 37%. But it isn't always better to give away an asset and let the recipient pay the lower capital gains tax. Among other things, you have to consider what you paid for the asset, what it's worth now, what you think it will be worth when you die and if the recipient plans to sell or keep it.

Making Gifts From Your Living Trust

You may have heard that you should remove an asset from your Living Trust *before* making the gift. For example, if you wanted to give your son a $5,000 gift in cash and your checking account is titled in the name of your Trust, you would make the check payable to yourself, cash it, then make the gift in cash or use a cashier's check.

That's because, in the past, if the Grantor died within three years of making a gift directly from his/her Living Trust, the IRS tried to include the gift—even annual tax-free gifts—in the Grantor's taxable estate.

You don't have to play this "shell game" anymore. *The Taxpayer Relief Act of 1997* says that gifts made directly from a Revocable Living Trust are considered the same as if they were made directly from you, even if they are made within three years of your death.

IRREVOCABLE LIFE INSURANCE TRUST

If you are single and your net estate (including your life insurance) is more than the federal estate tax exemption ($625,000 in 1998), or if you are married and your total net estate is more than two exemptions ($1.25 million in 1998), an Irrevocable Life Insurance Trust can reduce your estate taxes.

Remember, life insurance proceeds for which you have any "incidents of ownership" (policies you can borrow against, assign, or cancel, or for which you can revoke an assignment, or name or change the Beneficiary) are included in your taxable estate when you die. And estate taxes start at 37% of every dollar over $625,000 (in 1998) and quickly increase to 55%.

Very simply, a Life Insurance Trust owns your insurance policies *for* you. And since you don't personally own the insurance, it will not be included in your taxable estate. So your estate will pay less in estate taxes—and more of your estate will go to your family.

Of course, you could have another person (like your spouse or an adult child) own your insurance for you. That would also keep it out of your estate—but you would not have as much control over the policy. This person could change

A Life Insurance Trust removes insurance proceeds from your taxable estate

243

the Beneficiary, take the cash value or even cancel the policy. With an Insurance Trust, the Trustee you select (it must be someone other than you) must follow the instructions in your Trust.

An Insurance Trust also gives you more control over how the proceeds are used. For example, you could direct the Trustee to make the funds available to pay estate taxes and other final expenses. You could provide your surviving spouse with a lifetime income and keep the proceeds out of *both* your estates. You could also keep the proceeds in Trust and provide periodic income to your children or other loved ones—without giving them the full amount.

Existing policies can be transferred into an Insurance Trust—but if you die within three years of making the transfer, the death benefits of the policies will be taxed as part of your estate. There may also be a gift tax.

The Trustee can also purchase a new policy. But it must be done in a special way so you don't incur a gift tax. Each year, using annual tax-exempt gifts, you can give up to $10,000 ($20,000 if married) to one or more Beneficiaries of the Insurance Trust. (The actual amount given will depend on the premium for the policy.) But instead of giving this money directly to the Beneficiaries, you give it to the Trustee *for* them.

The Trustee then notifies each Beneficiary that a gift has been received on his/ her behalf and, unless the Beneficiary elects to receive the gift now, the Trustee will invest the funds—by paying the premium on the insurance policy. Of course, for this to work, the Beneficiaries must understand not to take the gift now. (By the way, the written notification to the Beneficiaries is known as a "Crummey letter," named after the man who first tested it and had it approved by the IRS.)

CHARITABLE REMAINDER TRUST

You might be interested in a Charitable Remainder Trust if you own investment assets that have appreciated significantly since you purchased them and you would like to enjoy the profits, but you have been hesitant to sell the assets because you would have to pay capital gains tax.

When you set up a Charitable Remainder Trust, you transfer the appreciated asset to an Irrevocable Trust. This removes the asset from your estate, so estate taxes are reduced when you die. You also reduce your current income taxes with a charitable income tax deduction.

The Trustee then sells the asset at full market value—paying no capital gains tax—and reinvests in income-producing assets. For the rest of your life, the Trust pays you an income. (Or, the Trust can be set up to exist for a set number of years, up to 20.) When you die, the remaining Trust assets will go to one or more charities you have chosen. (That's why it's called a *Charitable Remainder* Trust.)

Of course, this means that your children or other Beneficiaries will not receive this asset when you die. If you are concerned about this, you can use the income tax savings and part of the income you receive from the Charitable Remainder Trust to fund an Irrevocable Life Insurance Trust. The Trustee can then purchase enough life insurance to replace the full value of the gifted asset.

CHARITABLE LEAD TRUST

A Charitable Lead Trust is, in some ways, similar to a Charitable Remainder Trust. You transfer an asset to the Trust, which reduces your taxable estate and saves estate taxes.

But with a Charitable Lead Trust, the charity receives the income and your Beneficiaries will eventually receive the principal. And since the Beneficiaries must wait a while before they can receive the asset, its value is reduced for gift tax purposes. So you will pay substantially less in gift tax than if you left the asset to them outright.

A Charitable Lead Trust would be appealing if you currently do not need the income, or if you have current charitable commitments you would like to continue in the future, and you want someone other than the charity (perhaps your spouse, children or grandchildren) to eventually have the assets.

For example, Jacqueline Kennedy Onassis included a Charitable Lead Trust provision in her estate plan. The assets in the Trust would benefit charities for 24 years, then go to her grandchildren. Unfortunately (for the charity), the Trust was optional—no assets were transferred into it.

PRIVATE CHARITABLE FOUNDATION

Instead of giving all that tax money to Uncle Sam after you die and letting Congress decide how to spend it, you can set up your own charitable foundation, donate your assets to it and keep some control over how the money is spent! (The IRS does have a few restrictions on how the money is used.)

You can set up the foundation while you are living, or it can be established after you die. To qualify, a small percentage of the Trust assets must be distributed to charity each year. But you can name whomever you wish to run the foundation—including your children—and the foundation can pay them a reasonable salary. You can be very specific about which charities you want to support, or you can leave that up to the Trustees of the foundation to decide (within the IRS guidelines, of course).

The tax benefits of setting up your own foundation can be substantial—you can save estate, capital gains and ordinary income taxes:

- The assets you give to the foundation will be removed from your taxable estate. So, for example, if you give your entire estate to the foundation—or the entire amount over the estate tax exemption—your estate will pay no estate taxes!
- There will be no capital gains tax when the assets are sold by the foundation, so it's great for appreciated assets.
- And, currently, if you donate publicly traded securities to a private foundation, you can get a charitable income tax deduction for their *full fair market value*—up to 30% of your adjusted gross income. (The deduction is less than the 50% limit for standard charitable contributions because this is a *private* charitable foundation.) By the way, Congress has extended this deduction every year for the last several years. Eventually, it will probably be gone, but for now it's available.

PERSONAL RESIDENCE TRUST

A Personal Residence Trust lets you continue to live in your home but transfer it to your children now so you will save estate taxes when you die.

When you set up a Personal Residence Trust, you transfer your home or vacation home to an Irrevocable Trust. For a specified period of time (often 10 to 15 years), you retain the right to use and live in the residence. After that time, the residence transfers to your Beneficiaries (usually your children).

In effect, you are giving your home to your children today. But because your children will not receive it until sometime in the future, the value of this gift is discounted (reduced). This uses less of your federal gift and estate tax exemption than if you had kept the home (and any future appreciation) in your estate.

If you die before the term of the Trust is over, there is no penalty—your home will just be included in your taxable estate, which is what would happen anyway without the Trust. If you live longer than the duration of the Trust and want to keep living there, you will have to pay rent (at fair market value).

And, of course, the house will not receive a stepped-up basis when you die. So you will want to see whether it's better for your Beneficiaries to save the capital gains taxes or to save the estate taxes.

GRANTOR RETAINED ANNUITY TRUST (GRAT) AND GRANTOR RETAINED UNITRUST (GRUT)

GRATs and GRUTs have much in common with the Personal Residence Trust. The main difference is that a GRAT or GRUT lets you transfer *any* asset—not just your home—out of your taxable estate. And, with a GRAT or GRUT, you receive an income, instead of continuing to live in your home, for a set number of years.

When you set up a GRAT or GRUT, you transfer an income-producing asset (like a family business, stocks or real estate) into an Irrevocable Trust for a set number of years. During this time, the Trust pays you an income.

If the income you receive is a set dollar amount and does not fluctuate each year, the Trust is a GRAT (that's why it's called a Grantor Retained *Annuity* Trust). If the income is a percentage of the Trust assets and the amount of income you receive fluctuates each year, the Trust is a GRUT.

At the end of the Trust term, the asset will be owned by the Beneficiaries of the Trust (usually your children) and will not be included in your estate when you die. However, if you die before the Trust term is over, the asset will be taxed as part of your estate.

Like the Personal Residence Trust, the Beneficiaries will not receive the asset until sometime in the future (when the Trust term is over). So the value of the gift you are making (transferring the asset to the Trust is considered a gift) is reduced. This uses less of your federal gift and estate tax exemption than if you had kept the asset (and any future appreciation) in your estate.

A GRAT or GRUT can be a great way to save estate taxes by transferring an asset (especially a business) and any future appreciation, to your children at a discounted value—especially if you want (or need) the income.

FAMILY LIMITED PARTNERSHIP

A Family Limited Partnership is a way you can remove assets (like a family business, stocks, real estate or insurance) and any future appreciation on them from your taxable estate *without* giving up control. It is especially useful when real estate or a family business might otherwise have to be liquidated to pay estate taxes.

When you set up a Family Limited Partnership, you transfer the assets into the partnership in exchange for partnership shares. You keep the *general partner* shares and, over time, gift *limited* partnership shares to your children, removing the value of the gifted partnership interests from your estate.

As the general partner, you have full control—you determine how the assets are managed, when income is distributed and how the partnership is run. Limited partners (you and/or your children) are *passive*—they have no say in how the partnership is managed. Losses and profits are allocated among the partners, but no income is distributed unless you, as the general partner, decide to do so. Also, the Agreement can be written so that shares cannot be sold or transferred without your approval.

Because there is no market for these shares, their value is highly discounted. (What would someone pay for minority shares in assets over which they would have no control?) So you are able to transfer these assets to your children, removing them from your taxable estate, at a discounted value—*all without losing control.*

If you gift shares in increments of $10,000, there is no gift tax. (Larger gifts can be applied to your federal estate tax exemption.) And since you are making gifts based on current value—not the appreciated value when you die—this lets you, in effect, freeze the value of your estate at the time the gifts are made.

A Family Limited Partnership gives you more control than a corporation, in which even minority stockholders (either your children or their creditors) can have substantial voting rights and can force sales, distributions or even liquidations. You also have some protection from your children's creditors. If a creditor is awarded a limited partnership interest, the creditor has no more rights than the previous limited partner.

ASSET PROTECTION TRUST

Because malpractice and liability insurance costs are so high—and lawsuits are so common—more people are turning to Asset Protection Trusts as a way to protect their assets and still keep control. Those who are at a higher risk include lawyers, doctors, architects, entrepreneurs, contractors, property developers and accountants.

Asset Protection Trusts are often called Offshore Trusts, because they are created under the laws of a foreign country—often the Isle of Man, Cayman Islands, or the Cook Islands—that does not enforce the judgments of other countries.

A common way to set up an Asset Protection Trust is to transfer your assets to a limited partnership. As the general partner, you could keep only 1% of the shares—but full control. The other 99% of the shares would be transferred to the foreign Trust. Your assets, however, do not have to leave the country until they are actually threatened. Even so, to be on the safe side, your attorney may suggest that you transfer your assets now to your offshore Trustee.

If you are sued in this country and a judgment is awarded, it has no effect in the country where title of your assets is held (in your foreign Trust). The case would have to be retried in the foreign country. But first a local attorney would have to be hired and the witnesses would have to go there to convince the court to even accept jurisdiction over the case. This is usually a good deterrent.

An Asset Protection Trust cannot be set up after someone has filed suit against you or a lawsuit is imminent—that would be considered a fraudulent transfer. So it must be set up before then.

Also, an Asset Protection Trust does not affect your taxes—you would still pay income, gift and estate taxes as you do now. But it can potentially save money by reducing the need for insurance. Eliminating your insurance "deep pockets" and having your assets held by a foreign Trust can go a long way toward discouraging lawsuits.

Of course, an Asset Protection Trust is not without risk. It is subject to foreign rules, which can change at any time. Also, a foreign Trustee must be involved.

LAND TRUST

For privacy, some people set up what is called a Land Trust or a Title Holding Trust, especially for real estate.

The concept is very simple. You transfer title of the property to a Corporate Trustee or corporation, yet you keep full control over how the property is managed. However, since the title is in the name of the Corporate Trustee or corporation, no one will ever know that it is yours. In all financial transactions and dealings, your personal name never comes up.

Land Trusts are valid in most states and the cost to have an outside Trustee administer them is very low. However, it is becoming more difficult to find a Corporate Trustee who is willing to act as Trustee because of the liabilities associated with contaminated property.

PROTECT AGAINST THE GENERATION SKIPPING TRANSFER TAX

If some or all of your estate bypasses your children and goes directly to a grandchild, there could be another tax called the generation skipping transfer tax (GSTT). This can happen intentionally, if you "skip" the living parent (your child) and leave an inheritance directly to your grandchildren.

It can also happen unintentionally. For example, if the inheritance is in a Trust for your child, he or she dies after you but before receiving the full amount and, under the terms of the Trust, your grandchildren will receive their parent's remaining inheritance, it could then be subject to the GST tax.

Why do we have this tax? Well, in the past, Generation Skipping Trusts were common, especially among the wealthy. The grandfather would set up a Trust that distributed only income (no principal) to his children. The Trust principal would be distributed later to his grandchildren and future generations.

This allowed the Trust assets to grow tax-free and appreciate in value. And it avoided the heavy taxation that would have occurred if each generation had been taxed on the full inheritance. The Rockefellers are one family who used this concept to great advantage, building (and retaining) considerable wealth for several generations.

Eventually, of course, Uncle Sam decided he wanted his share of taxes, just as if each generation had received its inheritance and paid taxes on it. So, if you leave substantial assets to your grandchildren and future generations— bypassing your children's generation—these assets may be subject to the Generation Skipping Transfer Tax. (This tax also applies if you leave assets to a non-relative who is more than 37 1/2 years younger than you.)

The bad news is that this is a *very* expensive tax. It is equal to the *highest* federal estate tax rate in effect at the time—so currently it is 55%. And it is *in addition to* the federal estate tax, which can also be as high as 55%.

So if, for example, $10 million of a $15 million estate was left directly to the grandchildren with no estate planning, $5.5 million would be paid in estate taxes and another $2,475,000 (55% of the remaining $4.5 million) would be paid in GST taxes—leaving only $2,025,000 for the grandchildren.

Now the good news is that most people won't be affected by the GST tax— because everyone has a $1 million exemption from this tax. So, you and your spouse together can leave up to $2 million to your grandchildren and future generations without having to pay the Generation Skipping Transfer Tax. But just like the federal estate tax exemption, you have to plan ahead so you don't waste one of these GST tax exemptions.

One common way is with the A-B-C Living Trust (as we explained in Part Three). When one spouse dies, the estate can be divided in half. The deceased spouse's $1 million GST tax exemption can be applied to his/her half (Trust B + Trust C). And when the surviving spouse dies, his/her $1 million GSTT exemption can be applied to Trust A. This makes full use of both exemptions. Your attorney, of course, may suggest other planning options.

> **Note:** Beginning in 1999, the amount of the GSTT exemption (currently $1 million) will be tied to inflation. However, the amount will only be increased in increments of $10,000, and it will be rounded *down* instead of up. So, for example, if adjustments for inflation would increase the amount to $1,009,999, it would remain at $1 million.

QUALIFIED DOMESTIC TRUST

Using a Qualified Domestic Trust is the only way your estate will be allowed to use the marital deduction if your spouse is not a U.S. citizen. That's because Uncle Sam doesn't want noncitizen spouses to inherit sizeable estates and then return to their homelands without paying any estate taxes.

Remember, the marital deduction lets you leave your spouse an unlimited amount of assets with no estate taxes when you die. Uncle Sam plans to collect the taxes when your surviving spouse dies. But if your spouse takes the assets and leaves the country, Uncle Sam is left empty handed. So, in 1988, Congress decided to eliminate the unlimited marital deduction for noncitizen spouses.

This means that, when you die, everything in your estate over the federal estate tax exemption will be taxed—unless your Living Trust plan includes a Qualified Domestic Trust (QDOT or QDT).

The QDOT works a little like the C Trust we explained in Part Three. The assets that are transferred to this Trust (probably all of your assets over the federal estate tax exemption) are not taxed when you die, so the entire estate is available to provide for your surviving spouse. The Trust (not your spouse) owns the assets, but your spouse can receive income from it and, with the Trustee's approval, may also receive principal.

To make sure estate taxes are paid when your spouse dies, at least one Trustee of the QDOT must be a U.S. citizen or U.S. corporation. (Sometimes a surviving spouse wants to return to his/her homeland and finds it would be easier to have the Trust administered there. But some countries do not authorize Trusts or allow Trusts to have U.S. Trustees. For these situations, Congress recently passed legislation that will allow the requirement for a U.S. Trustee to be waived and will allow a similar legal arrangement to be used instead of a Trust.)

The income your spouse receives from the QDOT is taxed as ordinary income in the year it is received. But any principal your spouse receives (unless the distribution is due to "hardship" as defined by the IRS), plus assets remaining in the QDOT when your spouse dies, will be taxed as if they were part of your estate when you died (at your highest estate tax rate).

Without a QDOT, these estate taxes would have to be paid when you die. But *with* a QDOT (just like a C Trust), the taxes are delayed until your surviving spouse dies. So more is available to provide for your spouse.

Of course, if your spouse becomes a U.S. citizen before the assets are transferred to the QDOT, you would not need one.

SUMMARY

If some of these tax-saving strategies sound interesting to you, you may want to ask your attorney if they could be helpful in your situation. Remember, these strategies are *in addition to* your Living Trust—and most are irrevocable. So, you'll want to do your homework and make sure this is what you want—*before* you put one in place.

Also, many of these strategies can be complicated, and most are loaded with tax traps and pitfalls that can cost you a bundle if they are not done correctly. You simply cannot afford to use an inexperienced attorney for one of these. Make sure you find someone who is well qualified, has experience with the strategy(ies) you are interested in and knows what he/she is doing. If you're not sure where to begin, see "How To Find The Right Attorney" in Part Five.

Part Ten

. . . .

THE PERSONAL AND FINANCIAL ORGANIZER

Part Ten—
THE PERSONAL AND FINANCIAL ORGANIZER

INSTRUCTIONS FOR COMPLETING THE PERSONAL AND FINANCIAL ORGANIZER

To set up your Living Trust, your attorney will need to know some basic information about you and your family, your assets, and your decisions about your Trust—who you want to be your Trustee, Successor Trustee(s), and your Beneficiaries, and how you want your Beneficiaries to inherit from you.

Our Personal and Financial Organizer gives you one place to write down all this information as you prepare to meet with your attorney. Being organized will undoubtedly save you time and money. And actually writing this information down will help you to think seriously about your plan.

In this section, we'll help you complete the Organizer with the following step-by-step instructions.

General Instructions

1. Print or write *legibly*. Using a pencil is a good idea, since you will probably make some changes. (It's okay to make a couple of copies of the Organizer for your own personal use. However, since it is copyrighted, professionals must call us for approval before making copies.)

2. We suggest that you complete the Organizer as much as possible *before* you meet with your attorney. Of course, we realize that you will probably

have some questions you will want to ask him/her before actually making some decisions. Just make notes in the appropriate sections or write your questions down in Section 7 so you won't forget about them.

3.   If you don't have enough room on the Organizer to put all the information requested, use a separate sheet of paper and attach it to that page. If a question doesn't apply to you, mark "N/A" for "not applicable" rather than leaving it blank—this way your attorney will know that you did not overlook the question or forget to answer it.

4.   *Take your time* completing this Organizer—these are *serious* personal decisions. (You may want to re-read sections of the book that apply to each decision, so we've included page numbers whenever appropriate.)

5.   And, finally, be thorough. Remember, your attorney can only plan with the information you provide him/her. If you withhold information about your assets or personal situation, you could end up paying too much in taxes or your plan may not work the way you want it to work.

Now, let's complete the Organizer.

SECTION

1   GENERAL INFORMATION

Be sure to date the Organizer and mark your marital status. If you are single, you only need to complete the sections that apply to you. If you are married, you and your spouse need to complete this entire section.

The information in the box on the right will help your attorney plan for some special circumstances. For example, if your spouse is not a U.S. citizen, your attorney may need to include an additional provision (QDOT) in your Trust document. Your attorney also needs to know (for tax planning purposes) if you expect to receive money or other assets from an outside source.

If you have a previous Will or Trust that this Living Trust will replace, make sure you take a copy with you when you meet with your attorney.

SECTION

2 | ABOUT YOUR CHILDREN

This section requests some basic information that will help introduce your family situation to your attorney—how many children, stepchildren, or grandchildren you have, their ages, where they live, if they are dependent on you, and if any of them require special care.

SECTION

3 | FINANCIAL INFORMATION

This section requests information about the current values of what you own and what you owe. Remember, your attorney is not being nosey. He/she needs this information to know if you will need tax planning in your Living Trust.

Your attorney also needs to know about your assets so he/she can advise you about transferring them into your Trust. This section will be a good check list for you, too, when making sure all appropriate titles and beneficiary designations are changed.

You'll notice we have included space for you to write down in whose name each asset is titled—this information is important for both tax planning and funding purposes. For example, if you are married but you and your spouse own substantial assets separately, your attorney may recommend that you have separate Living Trusts in addition to, or instead of, one Living Trust.

Questions 1, 5, and 7 have a place for you to list the purchase price of these assets (remember, this is your cost basis). Depending on what you paid for these assets and what the current values are, your attorney may recommend some additional tax planning options for you to consider (some of these are explained in Part Nine).

You'll also notice on Questions 1 and 2 that we've included a "formula" to help you determine the net value (equity) in these assets. Remember, estate taxes are based on the *net* value of your estate. As we explained in Part Three, if the net value of your estate is more than the federal estate tax exemption in effect when you die, estate taxes will have to be paid. So you will list the current market value of each asset, and subtract from that the remaining mortgage or loan value, which gives you the net value (equity) of that asset.

You may need to have some current appraisals done if some assets have not been appraised recently. For these purposes, a formal appraisal of your home is not necessary—it's okay to have a real estate agent give you a general idea of its value, based on recent sales of comparable homes in your area.

It is very important that you fully complete this section. Remember, your attorney can only plan with the information you provide him/her. If you omit assets or undervalue them, you could end up paying too much in taxes. If you need more room to answer any of the questions in Section 3, list them on a separate sheet of paper and attach it to these pages.

SECTION

4 TRUST DECISIONS: YOUR LIVING TRUST TEAM

Okay, so far this has been pretty straightforward. Beginning in this section, you will need to start making some decisions about your Living Trust.

1. Trustee(s)

See pages 111 and 115 for more information.

The Trustee is responsible for management of your Trust now. You can be your own Trustee if you want to. If you are married, you and your spouse can be Co-Trustees. You can also name someone else as your Trustee or Co-Trustee—an adult son or daughter, another relative, or a Corporate Trustee. You should probably consider naming someone else as your Trustee or Co-Trustee if you don't have the time, ability, or desire to manage your own affairs anymore or if you and/or your spouse are ill. (Remember, until you become incapacitated or die, you can always change your Trustee.)

2. Successor Trustee(s)

See pages 113 and 115 for more information.

Your Successor Trustee will step in and take control for you if you become physically or mentally incapacitated and are no longer able to handle your own affairs. When you die, your Successor acts just like an Executor named in a Will—pays your final bills, has tax returns prepared, and distributes your assets according to the instructions in your Trust—but without court supervision. If you have a Co-Trustee (perhaps your spouse), he/she will assume these responsibilities until his/her own incapacity or death, at which time your Successor Trustee will take over.

You will probably want to name two or three Successor Trustees if, for whatever reason, the first is not available. They should be people you know and trust, whose judgment you respect, and who will also respect your wishes. They do not have to live in the same state as you do, although it would be helpful if they live close to you. If you have adult children, they can be named as Successor Trustees.

If you wish, you can name two or more Successor Trustees to jointly share the responsibilities (for instance, you may want two of your adult children to act together). You may also want to consider naming a third impartial Co-Successor Trustee (like a Corporate Trustee) to prevent deadlocks or major disagreements. If you do want to name two or more to act together, just cross out "1st choice," "2nd choice," and "3rd choice" and write in "Co-Trustees."

If you don't feel you have good candidates for your Successor Trustee—your family lives too far away, they're too busy, or aren't responsible enough, or if you feel you have no one you can trust—you should definitely consider a Corporate Trustee.

Note: If you name a Corporate Trustee as a Trustee or to act alone as your Successor Trustee, you do not need to name any other Successor Trustees.

3. Guardians For Minor Children
See page 121 for more information.
If you have minor children, you will need to select a Guardian for them. This is a very important decision. The person you name will be *responsible for raising* your children if both parents become incapacitated or die. Guardians must be adults. You will, of course, want to choose someone who respects your values and standards (moral, ethical and religious) and will raise your children the way you would want.

Remember, the court must still approve your selection. If you are a single parent with custody and really don't want your "ex" to be Guardian, go ahead and name your preference anyway. While the other natural parent is almost always the court's preferred choice, your choice will probably receive careful consideration. It's possible that the other parent may not be able to take the responsibility (or won't want it), or the court could agree with you that he/she is not a suitable choice. In these situations, the judge would want to know your preference.

4. Trustees For Minor Children

See page 122 for more information.

Remember, the Guardian is only responsible for *raising* your children and does not control the inheritance. You also need to name a Trustee for your Children's Trust—someone who will be responsible for the safekeeping of their inheritance, and will provide the money for education, medical care, maintenance and other needs from the assets in the Children's Trust.

You can name the same person as Trustee and Guardian, making it convenient for one person to take care of your children. However, remember that the person you want to raise your children may not be your best choice to manage the money—and vice versa. The Trustee can be a different individual, a Corporate Trustee or, if you wish, you can name two as Co-Trustees.

Grandparents (and others) who leave assets to minor children: You will also need to name a Trustee to manage the inheritance in the Children's Trust.

5 BENEFICIARIES

Your Beneficiaries are the persons and/or organizations who will receive your assets when you die. Most people prefer to pass their assets down to family members, but you can leave them to any person or organization you wish. If you are married and you want to make sure the Beneficiaries you have named cannot be changed if you die first, ask your attorney about including an A-B provision in your Living Trust (see Part Three for more information).

1. Special Gifts To Organizations

See pages 120 and 133 for more information.

This is an excellent time to think about giving to a charity or organization that has special meaning to you. There are many excellent ones and they are all in need of funding to continue their work. In addition to the tax benefits of charitable donations, you will have the satisfaction of knowing that your contribution will make a difference. Your gift can be as specific or as general, as large or as small, as you want to make it. The charity or foundation of your choice will be glad to make suggestions.

2. Special Gifts To Individuals

See page 120 for more information.

You probably will want to leave specific items to certain individuals—a favorite piece of jewelry or antique that you want a special friend or relative to have. Remember, in most states, you just need to make a list of these Special Gifts on a separate sheet of paper, have it notarized, and keep it with your Living Trust document. If you change your mind, you can usually just make a new list and have it notarized. You may want to make a separate list for each of your children or grandchildren.

Use the space on this Organizer to start getting your Special Gifts lists organized. This way, if you have any questions, you will be prepared when you meet with your attorney.

3. Beneficiaries

See page 120 for more information.

Who do you want to receive the rest of your assets after your Special Gifts have been distributed? For most people, this will probably be the bulk of your estate—your home, other real estate, investments, etc.—everything that you did not list as a Special Gift. Remember, it's usually better to specify a percentage rather than a dollar amount.

4. Inheriting Instructions

See page 125 for more information.

When do you want your Beneficiaries to inherit? If your Beneficiaries are younger, you may want to keep "strings" on their inheritances until each one reaches an age at which you feel he/she will be mature enough to have outright control, such as age 21, 25, 35. Some parents specify a certain amount at certain ages (some at 21, some at 25, etc.) or at certain intervals (some every three to five years). You may want to keep the assets in Trust indefinitely. It's completely up to you. You just need to specify how long you want the Trustee(s) to keep control.

5. Dependents Who Require Special Care

See pages 128-133 for more information.

If you have a disabled spouse, parent, child, or other loved one who requires special care, your attorney will need to know how you want to provide for them and any other special instructions you may have. Under "Explanation," briefly explain the situation. Include whether this person is currently receiving government benefits or may need to qualify for them in the future.

6. Alternate Beneficiaries

See page 133 for more information.

Who do you want to have your assets if all of your Beneficiaries die before you? Many people specify their church, a favorite charity, or foundation.

7. Disinheriting

See page 133 for more information.

Are there any persons that you specifically want to exclude? Make sure you write them down.

SECTION 6 — SPECIAL INSTRUCTIONS AT INCAPACITY

This is a very appropriate time to think about what you would want to happen to you and your assets if you were to become physically or mentally incapacitated and unable to handle your own affairs. You may have some specific requests and/or instructions if this should happen to you—and your Co-Trustee or Successor Trustee(s), family members, and physicians should know your wishes.

1. Keeping/Selling Assets

If you become incapacitated, it may become necessary to sell some of your assets to pay for your care. Do you have a preference for which ones are sold first? Are there others you don't want sold unless absolutely necessary? Do you have any special instructions you want followed? Are there any potential buyers you would want contacted? You may also want some special gifts distributed at this time.

2. Medical Care

You may have specific requests regarding your medical care. For example, you may want to be cared for in a specific hospital or nursing home (or maybe there's one you *don't* want to be in). You may also have some definite ideas about the type or extent of care you receive at this time—life support, blood transfusions, organ transplants, etc.

3. Living Will

See page 157 for more information.

A Living Will is a document that lets you express your wishes about life support in certain terminal situations. It is available in just about all states, but its practical use is limited.

4. Durable Power of Attorney for Health Care

See page 158 for more information.

A Durable Power of Attorney for Health Care (also called a Health Care Proxy or Medical Power of Attorney) is a document that lets you appoint someone (usually called an "Agent") to make *any* health care decisions (including the use of life support) for you if you are unable to make them yourself. This keeps these personal decisions out of the courts. You can choose your spouse, trusted friend or another relative as your Agent. You should list at least two choices, in case your first is unavailable.

SECTION

7 QUESTIONS TO ASK YOUR ATTORNEY ABOUT YOUR LIVING TRUST

This is where you can list the questions you have about your Living Trust, so you won't forget to ask your attorney.

SUMMARY

There—now you've got your information all organized. That was a big step. Now it's time to see a qualified estate planning attorney who can answer your questions and prepare your Living Trust document for you. (Remember to take this book and your completed Personal and Financial Organizer with you.) We suggest that you re-read Part Five if you don't yet have an attorney selected.

Good luck—and good for you for taking care of this now!

PERSONAL AND FINANCIAL ORGANIZER FOR YOUR LIVING TRUST

1 GENERAL INFORMATION

Home Phone _____ Date _____

Marital Status: ☐ Married ☐ Single ☐ Divorced ☐ Widowed

Your Legal Name _____

Spouse's Legal Name _____

Street Address _____

City _____ State _____ ZIP _____

Mailing Address (if different) _____

Your Employer _____

Address _____

Your Occupation _____ Work Phone _____

Spouse's Employer _____

Address _____

Spouse's Occupation _____ Work Phone _____

	You	Your Spouse
Social Security #		
Date of Birth		
U.S. citizen?	Yes No	Yes No
Currently have Will or Trust? If so, give year & state in which prepared.	Yes No Yr. _____ State _____	Yes No Yr. _____ State _____
Expect to receive money or other assets from (circle all that apply):	Gift Inheritance Lawsuit Other	Gift Inheritance Lawsuit Other
If so, approximately how much?	$	$

2 ABOUT YOUR CHILDREN

1. _____

Legal Name _____ Date of Birth _____

Goes By _____ Soc. Sec. # _____

Street Address _____

City _____ State ____ ZIP ____ Phone _____

☐ Natural ☐ Legally Adopted ☐ Foster

☐ Married ☐ Needs Special Care ☐ Dependent

Related To:

☐ You Only   ☐ Spouse Only   ☐ Both

2. _____

Legal Name _____ Date of Birth _____

Goes By _____ Soc. Sec. # _____

Street Address _____

City _____ State ____ ZIP ____ Phone _____

☐ Natural ☐ Legally Adopted ☐ Foster

☐ Married ☐ Needs Special Care ☐ Dependent

Related To:

☐ You Only   ☐ Spouse Only   ☐ Both

3. _____

Legal Name _____ Date of Birth _____

Goes By _____ Soc. Sec. # _____

Street Address _____

City _____ State ____ ZIP ____ Phone _____

☐ Natural ☐ Legally Adopted ☐ Foster

☐ Married ☐ Needs Special Care ☐ Dependent

Related To:

☐ You Only   ☐ Spouse Only   ☐ Both

How many grandchildren do you have? _____ Yours Only _____ Your Spouse's Only _____ Both

1. Do you own a **home** or any **other real estate**?

Description and Location	Titled in whose name	Purchase Price	Current Value	(-) Mortgage	(=) Equity
				Total Net Value=	

2. Do you own any **other titled property** such as a car, boat, etc.?

Description	Titled in whose name	Current Value	(-) Loan	(=) Equity
			Total Net Value=	

3. Do you have any **checking accounts**?

Name of Institution	Account Number	Titled in whose name	Approx. Balance
		Total Value=	

4. Do you have any **interest bearing accounts** (savings, money market) and/or **CDs**?

Name of Institution	Account Number	Titled in whose name	Approx. Balance
		Total Value=	

5. Do you own any **stocks, bonds or mutual funds** (including company stock)?

# of Shares	Description	Account Number	Titled in whose name	Purchase Price	Current Value
				Total Value=	

6. Do you have any **profit sharing, IRAs or pension plans**?

Description/Location	Beneficiary	Current Value
	Total Value=	

7. Do you or your spouse own a **business** or have any **partnership interests**?

Description	Type of Ownership	Purchase Price	Current Value
		Total Value=	

8. Do you have any **life insurance** policies and/or **annuities**?

Name of Company	Policy Owner	1st Beneficiary	2nd Beneficiary	Death Benefit
			Total Value=	

9. Does anyone owe you money?

Description	Approx. Value
Total Value=	

10. Do you have any **special items of value** such as coin collections, antiques, jewelry, etc.?

Description	Approx. Value
Total Value=	

11. What is the approximate total value of all your remaining **personal property**—whatever you own that has not been included above? (clothes, furniture, etc.) Just estimate. .... $ _____

12. Do you have any **debts** other than mortgage(s) and loans listed above (credit cards, personal loans, etc.)?

	Amount owed
Total Debt=	

13. Total value of everything you (and your spouse) own (add totals of lines 1 thru 11 above) $ _____

14. Total amount you (and your spouse) owe (total of line 12 above) .... _____

15. Subtract line 14 from line 13.   269   **NET ESTATE = $** [_____]

15. Do you have a **safe deposit box**?

Location	Titled in whose name

4 TRUST DECISIONS: YOUR LIVING TRUST TEAM

1. Trustee(s)—Manages your trust now; usually you (and your spouse) and/or a Corporate Trustee.

_____

2. Successor Trustee(s)—Steps in at your incapacity or death. Can be adult children, trusted friend, and/or a Corporate Trustee.

#1 Choice: Name _____ Phone _____

Address _____

#2 Choice: Name _____ Phone _____

Address _____

#3 Choice: Name _____ Phone _____

Address _____

3. Guardian For Minor Children—Responsible adult who will raise your minor children if something happens to you.

#1 Choice: Name _____ Phone _____

Address _____

#2 Choice: Name _____ Phone _____

Address _____

4. Trustees For Minor Children— Manages inheritance. Can be same person as Guardian, another adult and/or a Corporate Trustee.

#1 Choice: Name _____ Phone _____

Address _____

#2 Choice: Name _____ Phone _____

Address _____

5 BENEFICIARIES

1. Special Gifts To Organizations

Do you want to make a gift (cash or a specific item) to a charity, foundation, religious or fraternal organization?

Name of Organization	Address	Description of Gift

2. Special Gifts To Individuals

Do you want to give any specific items to a family member or other individual? (For example: wedding ring to your daughter, gun collection to a son or nephew, etc.)

Name of Person	Address	Description of Gift

3. Beneficiaries

Who do you want to receive the rest of your estate after these special gifts have been distributed? You can designate a dollar amount or a percentage.

Name of Person/Organization	Address	Amount/Percentage

4. Inheriting Instructions

Do you want your Beneficiaries to receive their inheritances in installments, at certain ages, or all at once?

_____

_____

_____

_____

_____

5. Do you provide for someone who requires special care?

Do any of your dependents (aging parents, disabled child) require special care? Are they currently receiving government benefits? Is there someone else you want to provide for who is not related to you (significant other, special friend, pet)?

Name	Age	Relationship	Explanation

6. Alternate Beneficiaries

Who do you want to receive your estate if you (and your spouse) outlive the Beneficiaries you've named above?

Name of Person/Organization	Address	Amount/Percentage

7. Disinheriting

Are there any relatives that you specifically do not want to receive anything from your estate?

_____

_____

SPECIAL INSTRUCTIONS AT INCAPACITY

1. Keeping/Selling Assets:

If it becomes necessary to sell assets to pay for your or your spouse's care, are there certain ones you prefer to be sold first? Are there potential buyers you want contacted? Are there certain assets you prefer not be sold unless absolutely necessary?

_____

_____

_____

_____

2. Medical Care:

Do you prefer (or want to avoid) a certain hospital/nursing home? Do you have strong feelings about blood transfusions, life support, etc.?

You _____   **Your Spouse** _____

_____   _____

_____   _____

_____   _____

	You		Your Spouse	
3.	Yes	No	Yes	No
4.	Yes	No	Yes	No

3. Do you want a **Living Will**? This lets others know how you feel about life support treatment if you become terminally ill ....

4. Do you want a **Durable Power of Attorney for Health Care**? ....

This document lets you choose the person you want to make any health care decisions (including life support) for you if you are unable to make them for yourself, keeping these personal decisions out of the courts. You can choose anyone you trust: your spouse, friend or other relative, etc. List your choices below:

You

#1 Choice: Name _____

Address _____

_____

Phone _____

#2 Choice: Name _____

Address _____

_____

Phone _____

Your Spouse

#1 Choice: Name _____

Address _____

_____

Phone _____

#2 Choice: Name _____

Address _____

_____

Phone _____

QUESTIONS TO ASK YOUR ATTORNEY ABOUT YOUR LIVING TRUST

_____

_____

_____

_____

_____

_____

_____

_____

_____

A memo from Vickie and Jim...

"We'd love to hear from you!"

Dear friend,

Since we published the first edition of *Understanding Living Trusts*® in 1988, we have received scores upon scores of letters from the over 300,000 readers of our book.

Believe us, these letters make all the hard work of writing this book worth it. They have been truly inspirational. People have told us how much they appreciate our accurate, objective, and easy-to-understand information on the often complex subject of estate planning and Living Trusts. And they have told us how this information has changed their lives for the better—and given them peace of mind.

We'd also love to hear from you. Please feel free to write to us (or e-mail us) with any of the following in mind:

- How has the book helped you?
- What is your opinion of our book?
- Do you have a specific question on estate planning or Living Trusts? If so, what is it?
- Do you need more information on a particular Trust or strategy? If so, which one(s)?
- Have you had any frustrations or problems regarding your Living Trust (for example, in finding the right attorney or transferring assets)? If so, what happened?
- Is there any other way we can help you?

As you can see, we are 100% dedicated to helping you save unnecessary legal fees and taxes, avoid problems with probate, and enjoy peace of mind. While we can't answer each letter or message personally, please know that we do read them. And we keep them as ideas for future editions of this book and our other publications. We hope you'll find time to write or e-mail us at the address below.

Sincerely,

Vickie Jim Schumacher

P.S. Your letters "keep us in touch" with your questions, concerns, and needs on the subject of estate planning and Living Trusts. We'd like to hear from you today!

The Schumachers
P.O. Box 64395
Los Angeles, CA 90064-0395
comments@www.estateplanning.com

IN CONCLUSION

Our goal in writing this book has been to give you accurate and understandable information about Living Trusts and estate planning.

It's now up to you to use this knowledge and turn it into wisdom.

When is the best time to set up your Living Trust? *Right now*—while you are healthy and you don't think you need one.

If you think a Living Trust would probably be a good idea, but you just haven't gotten around to it yet, here are some things to keep in mind:

■ You write a check every year for car insurance and for homeowner's insurance to protect you against a loss that, odds are, won't even occur. The cost to set up a Living Trust is a one-time cost. It protects *all* your assets—not just one or two. And, unless you know something that we don't, dying is something that *will* happen to all of us some day!

■ Perfection is impossible. Don't postpone getting your Trust because you are trying to come up with the perfect plan that covers every conceivable possibility.

■ Your Trust is a snapshot of you, your family and your assets *right now*—not one year, five years, or twenty years from now. No one can predict what your personal, family, or financial future will be. Go ahead and set up your Trust now—then change it as your situation changes.

■ None of us likes to think about our own mortality—which is why so many families are caught off guard and unprepared when incapacity or death strikes. But remember, a Living Trust is *not* about dying. It's about doing what's best for you and your family, so *you* can enjoy peace of mind *now—while you're living*.

Please—act now.

DEFINITIONS

We may have introduced some legal terms that are new to you, so we've put together this handy reference. There are also some legal terms that we have purposely *not* used in this book because we wanted to keep it easy to understand. But, since you will probably feel more comfortable dealing with an attorney if you know some of their "legalese," we've included some of it here.

A Trust—The surviving spouse's portion of an A-B Trust. Also called Marital Trust or Survivor's Trust.

A-B Trust—A Living Trust with a provision that lets you provide for your surviving spouse, keep control over who will receive your assets after your spouse dies, and leave up to $1.25 million (in 1998) to your Beneficiaries, estate-tax free. (This amount will increase over the next several years as the federal estate tax exemption increases. By the year 2006, an A-B Living Trust will let you and your spouse leave your Beneficiaries up to $2 million estate-tax free, and with no probate.)

Administration—The court-supervised distribution of an estate during probate. Also used to describe the same process for a Trust after the Grantor dies.

Administrator—Person named by the court to represent a probate estate when there is no Will or the Will did not name an Executor. Female is Administratix. Also called Personal Representative.

Alternate Beneficiary—Person or organization named to receive your assets if the primary Beneficiaries named in your Trust die before you do.

Ancillary Administration—An additional probate in another state. Typically required when you own real estate in another state that is not titled in the name of your Trust.

Annual Exclusion—Amount you can give someone each year without having to file a gift tax return or pay a gift tax. Currently, $10,000 per recipient ($20,000 if married). Tied to inflation starting in 1999.

Assets—Basically, anything you own, including your home and other real estate, bank accounts, life insurance, investments, furniture, jewelry, art, clothing, and collectibles.

Assignment—A short document that transfers your interest in assets from your name to another. Often used when transferring assets to a Trust.

B Trust—The deceased spouse's portion of an A-B Trust. Also called Credit Shelter or Bypass Trust.

Basis—What you paid for an asset. The value that is used to determine gain or loss for income tax purposes.

Beneficiaries—In a Living Trust, the persons and/or organizations who receive the Trust assets (or benefit from the Trust assets) after the death of the Trust Grantor.

By-Pass Trust—Another name for the "B" part of an A-B Living Trust because the assets in this Trust bypass federal estate taxes.

C Trust—See "QTIP."

Certificate of Trust—A shortened version of a Trust that verifies the Trust's existence, explains the powers given to the Trustee, and identifies the Successor Trustee(s). Does not reveal any information about the Trust assets, Beneficiaries, or their inheritances.

Children's Trust—A Trust included in your Living Trust. If, when you die, a Beneficiary is not of legal age, the child's inheritance will go into this Trust. The inheritance will be managed by the Trustee you have named until the child reaches the age at which you want him/her to inherit.

Codicil—A written change or amendment to a Will.

Co-Grantors—Two or more persons who establish one Living Trust together.

Co-Trustees—Two or more individuals who have been named to act together in managing a Trust's assets. A Corporate Trustee can also be a Co-Trustee.

Common Trust—One Living Trust established by two or more individuals (usually a married couple).

Community Property—Assets a husband and wife acquire by joint effort during marriage if they live in one of the eight community property states. (Wisconsin also has a similar law, but does not use the term "community property.") Each spouse owns half of the assets in the event of divorce or death.

Conservator—One who is legally responsible for the care and well-being of another person. If appointed by a court, the Conservator is under the court's supervision. May also be called a Guardian. (Duties and titles can vary by state. For example, in Missouri, there is a Guardian of the person and a Conservator of the estate.)

Conservatorship—A court-controlled program for persons who are unable to manage their own affairs due to mental or physical incapacity. May also be called a Guardianship.

Contest—To dispute or challenge the terms of a Will or Trust.

Corporate Trustee—An institution, like a bank or trust company, that specializes in managing Trusts.

Credit Shelter Trust—Another name for the B Trust in an A-B Living Trust because this Trust "shelters" or preserves the federal estate tax "credit" of the deceased spouse.

Creditor—Person or institution to whom money is owed.

Custodian—Person named to manage assets left to a minor under the Uniform Transfer to Minors Act. In most states, the minor receives the assets at legal age.

Deceased—One who has died.

Deed—A document that lets you transfer title of your real estate to another person(s). Also see warranty deed and quitclaim deed.

Disclaim—To refuse to accept a gift or inheritance so it can go to the recipient who is next in line.

Discretion—The full or partial power to make a decision or judgment.

Disinherit—To prevent someone from inheriting from you.

Distribution—Payment in cash or asset(s) to one who is entitled to receive it.

Durable Power of Attorney for Asset Management—A legal document that gives another person full or limited legal authority to sign your name on your behalf in your absence. Valid through incapacity. Ends at death.

Durable Power of Attorney for Health Care—A legal document that lets you give someone else the authority to make health care decisions for you in the event you are unable to make them for yourself. Also called a Health Care Proxy or Medical Power of Attorney.

Equity—The current market value of an asset less any loan or liability.

Estate—Assets and debts left by an individual at death.

Estate Taxes—Federal or state taxes on the value of assets left at death. Also called inheritance taxes or death taxes.

Executor—Person or institution named in a Will to carry out its instructions. Female is Executrix. Also called a Personal Representative.

Family Business Exclusion—An additional estate tax exemption for family-owned businesses and farms that qualify. When added to the individual exemption, the total exempt amount is $1.3 million.

Federal Estate Tax Exemption—Amount of an individual's estate that is exempt from estate taxes. From 1987 through 1997, it was $600,000. It was increased to $625,000 in 1998 and will gradually continue to increase to $1 million by the year 2006.

Fiduciary—Person having the legal duty to act primarily for another's benefit. Implies great confidence and trust, and a high degree of good faith. Usually associated with a Trustee.

Funding—The process of transferring assets to your Living Trust.

Gain—The difference between what you receive for an asset when it is sold and what you paid for it. Used to determine the amount of capital gains tax due.

Generation Skipping Transfer Tax—A steep (55%) tax on assets that "skip" a generation and are left directly to grandchildren and younger generations. Everyone has a $1 million exemption from this tax.

Gift—A transfer from one individual to another without fair compensation.

Gift Tax—A federal tax on gifts made while you are living. Currently $10,000 per person per year is exempt from gift tax. Also see "Annual Exclusion."

Grantor—The person who sets up or creates the Trust. The person whose Trust it is. Also called Creator, Settlor, Trustor, or Donor.

Gross Estate—The value of an estate before debts are paid.

Guardianship—See "Conservatorship."

Health Care Proxy—See "Durable Power of Attorney for Health Care."

Heir—One who is entitled by law to receive part of your estate.

Holographic Will—A handwritten Will.

Homestead Exemption—Portion of your residence (dwelling and surrounding land) that cannot be sold to satisfy a creditor's claim while you are living.

Incapacitated/Incompetent—Unable to manage one's own affairs, either temporarily or permanently. Lack of legal power.

Independent Administration—A form of probate available in many states. Intended to simplify the probate process by requiring fewer court appearances and less court supervision.

Inheritance—The assets received from someone who has died.

Inter vivos—Latin term that means "between the living." An inter vivos Trust is created while you are living instead of after you die. A Revocable Living Trust is an inter vivos Trust.

Irrevocable Trust—A Trust that cannot be changed (revoked) or cancelled once it is set up. Opposite of Revocable Trust.

Intestate—Without a Will.

Joint Ownership—When two or more persons own the same asset.

Joint Tenants with Right of Survivorship—A form of joint ownership in which the deceased owner's share automatically and immediately transfers to the surviving joint tenant(s).

Liquid Assets—Cash and other assets (like stocks) that can easily be converted into cash.

"Living Probate"—The court-supervised process of managing the assets of one who is incapacitated.

Living Trust—A written legal document that creates an entity to which you transfer ownership of your assets. Contains your instructions for managing your assets during your lifetime and for their distribution upon your incapacity or death. Avoids probate at death and court control of assets at incapacity. Also called a revocable inter vivos Trust. A Trust created during one's lifetime.

Living Will—A written document that states you do not wish to be kept alive by artificial means when the illness or injury is terminal.

Marital Deduction—A deduction on the Federal Estate Tax Return that lets the first spouse to die leave an unlimited amount of assets to the surviving spouse free of estate taxes. However, if no other tax planning is used, and the surviving spouse's estate is more than the amount of the federal estate tax exemption in effect at the time of his/her death, estate taxes will be due at that time.

Marital Trust—See "A Trust."

Medicaid—A federally-funded health care program for the poor and minor children.

Medicare—A federally-funded health care program, primarily for Americans over age 65 who are covered by Social Security or Railroad Retirement benefits.

Minor—One who is under the legal age for an adult, which varies by state (usually age 18 or 21).

Net Estate—The value of an estate after all debts have been paid. (Federal estate taxes are based on the net value of an estate.)

Net Value—The current market value of an asset less any loan or debt.

Payable-on-Death Account—See "Totten Trust."

Per Capita—A way of distributing your estate so that your surviving descendents will share equally, regardless of their generation.

Per Stirpes—A way of distributing your estate so that your surviving descendents will receive only what their immediate ancestor would have received if he/she had been living at your death.

Personal Property—Movable property. Includes furniture, automobiles, equipment, cash and stocks. Opposite of real property that is permanent (like land).

Personal Representative—Another name for an Executor or Administrator.

Pour Over Will—A short Will often used with a Living Trust. It states that any assets left out of your Living Trust will become part of (*pour over* into) your Living Trust upon your death.

Power of Attorney—A legal document giving someone legal authority to sign your name on your behalf in your absence. Ends at incapacity (unless it is a *durable* power of attorney) or death.

Probate—The legal process of validating a Will, paying debts, and distributing assets after death.

Probate Estate—The assets that go through probate after you die. Usually this includes assets you own in your name and those paid to your estate. Usually does not include assets owned jointly, payable-on-death accounts, insurance and other assets with beneficiary designations. Assets in a Trust also do not go through probate.

Probate Fees—Legal, executor, and appraisal fees and court costs when an estate goes through probate. Probate fees are paid from assets in the estate before the assets are fully distributed to the heirs.

Qualified Domestic Trust (QDOT)—Allows a non-citizen spouse to qualify for the marital deduction.

Qualified Terminable Interest Property (QTIP)—A Trust that delays estate taxes until your surviving spouse dies so more income will be available to provide for your spouse during his/her lifetime. You can also keep control over who will receive these assets after your spouse dies.

Qualifying Subchapter S Trust (QSST)—Trust that meets certain IRS qualifications and is allowed to own Subchapter S Stock.

Quitclaim Deed—Document that allows you to transfer title to real estate. With a quitclaim deed, the person transferring the title makes no guarantees, but transfers all his/her interest in the property.

Real Property—Land and property that is permanently attached to land (like a building or a house).

Recorded Deed—A deed that has been filed with the county land records. This creates a public record of all changes in ownership of property in the state.

Revocable Trust—A Trust in which the person setting it up retains the power to change (revoke) or cancel the Trust during his/her lifetime. Opposite of Irrevocable Trust.

Required Beginning Date (RBD)—The date you must begin taking required minimum distributions from your tax-deferred plans. Usually, it is April 1 of the calendar year following the calendar year in which you turn age 70 1/2. If your money is in a company-sponsored plan, you may be able to delay your RBD beyond this date if you continue working (providing you are not a 5% or greater owner of the company).

Required Minimum Distribution (RMD)—The amount you are required to withdraw each year from your tax-deferred plan after you reach your Required Beginning Date. It is determined by dividing the value of your tax-deferred accounts by the life expectancy of you and your Beneficiary. The intent is that, by the time you and your Beneficiary are both expected to die, your tax-deferred savings will be fully withdrawn.

Separate Property—Generally, all assets you acquire prior to marriage and assets acquired by gift or inheritance during marriage.

Separate Trust—A Trust established by one person. A married couple has separate Trusts if each spouse has his/her own Trust with its own assets. In contrast, see "Common Trust."

Settle an Estate—The process of handling the final affairs—valuation of assets, payment of debts and taxes, distribution of assets to Beneficiaries—after someone dies.

Settlor—See "Grantor."

SPARRS—Schumacher Publishing's Attorney Rating and Review Site. Exclusive on-line database of estate planning attorneys, unique because it contains ratings and reviews from the attorneys' clients. Accessible at no cost to consumers through Schumacher Publishing's Web Site: **www.estateplanning.com.**

Special Gifts—A separate listing of special assets that will go to specific individuals or organizations after your incapacity or death. Also called Special Bequests.

Special Needs Trust—Allows you to provide for a disabled loved one without interfering with government benefits.

Spendthrift Clause—Protects assets in a Trust from a Beneficiary's creditors.

Spouse—Husband or wife.

Stepped-up Basis—Assets are given a new basis when transferred by inheritance (through a Will or Trust) and are re-valued as of the date of the owner's death. If an asset has appreciated above its basis (what the owner paid for it), the new basis is called a stepped-up basis. A stepped-up basis can save a considerable amount in capital gains tax when an asset is later sold by the new owner. Also see "Basis."

Subchapter S Corporation Stock—Stock in a corporation which has chosen to be subject to the rules of subchapter S of the Internal Revenue Code.

Surviving Spouse—The spouse who is living after one spouse has died.

Survivor's Trust—See "A Trust."

Successor Trustee—Person or institution named in the Trust document who will take over should the first Trustee die, resign, or otherwise become unable to act.

Tax-Deferred Plan—A retirement savings plan (like an IRA, 401(k), pension, profit sharing, or Keogh) that qualifies for special income tax treatment. The contributions made to the plan and subsequent appreciation of the assets are not taxed until they are withdrawn at a later time—ideally, at retirement, when your income and tax rate are lower.

Taxable Gift—Generally, a gift of more than $10,000 in one year to someone other than your spouse. The value of the gift is applied to your federal gift and estate tax exemption, and no gift tax is required to be paid until the exemption has been exhausted.

Tenants-in-Common—A form of joint ownership in which two or more persons own the same property. At the death of a tenant-in-common, his/her share transfers to his/her heirs.

Tenants-by-the Entirety—A form of joint ownership in some states between husband and wife. When one spouse dies, his/her share of the asset automatically transfers to the surviving spouse.

Testamentary Trust—A Trust in a Will. Can only go into effect at death. Does not avoid probate.

Testate—One who dies with a valid Will.

Title—Document proving ownership of an asset.

Transfer Tax—Tax on assets when they are transferred to another. The estate tax, gift tax and generation skipping transfer tax are all transfer taxes.

Trust—An entity that holds assets for the benefit of certain other persons or entities.

Trust Company—An institution that specializes in managing Trusts. Also called a Corporate Trustee.

Trustee—Person or institution who manages and distributes another's assets according to the instructions in the Trust document.

Trustor—See "Grantor."

Totten Trust—A "pay-on-death" account. A bank account that will transfer to the Beneficiary who was named when the account was established. The terms "transfer on death" ("TOD"), "in Trust for" ("ITF"), "as Trustee for" ("ATF"), and "pay on death" ("POD") often appear in the title.

Unified Credit—The amount each person is allowed to deduct from any estate taxes owed after death. In 1998, the credit is $202,050—the amount of estate taxes owed on the first $625,000 in assets.

Uniform Transfer to Minors Act (UTMA)—Law enacted in many states that lets you leave assets to a minor by appointing a Custodian. In most states, the minor receives the assets at legal age.

Unfunded—Your Living Trust is unfunded if you have not transferred assets into it.

Warranty Deed—Document that allows you to transfer title to real estate. With a warranty deed, the person guarantees that the title being transferred is clear (free of any encumbrances). If the title is defective, the person making the transfer is liable. Compare to quitclaim deed.

Will—A written document with instructions for disposing of assets after death. A Will can only be enforced through the probate court.

INDEX

A

AARP, 16, 17, 67
A-B Living Trust
    explanation of, 82,96
    providing for surviving spouse with, 87
    keeping control with, 87
    dividing assets, 89, 209
    common vs. separate, 82, 83, 91
    if spouse is incapacitated, 92
    Medicaid and, 93
    if spouse is not U.S. citizen, 95
    if not married, 95
    at death of first spouse, 208
A-B Trust in a Will, 92
A-B-C Living Trust
    explanation of, 100, 104
    additional control with, 100
    delaying estate taxes with, 102
    providing for surviving spouse with, 102
    dividing assets, 103, 209
    at death of first spouse, 208
Annual personal exemptions, 231
Asset Protection Trust, 249
Assignment, 162
Automobiles, 174
Attorney
    fees in probate, 16, 17
    where to get referrals for, 142
    certification of, 143
    how to evaluate, 145
    meeting with to prepare Trust, 151
    assistance with funding, 150, 161
Attorney rating and review site, 142
ATM withdrawals, 64

B

Bankruptcy protection, 63
Bar associations, 143, 144
Basis
    explanation of, 31, 206, 219
    stepped-up, 31, 92, 163, 206, 219, 242
Beneficiaries
    explanation of, 42
    controlling when they inherit, 49, 125
    who can be, 42, 120
    determining amount of inheritance, 125
    distribution options for, 50, 125

    irresponsible, 128
    protecting assets from creditors of, 47, 127, 129
    with special needs, 129-133
    charities as, 42, 133, 244-246
Beneficiary designations
    problems with, 33
    why change to Living Trust, 47
    time required to change, 59
    for IRA and other tax deferred plans, 48, 180-187
Boats, 174
Bonds, 172, 174

C

Calendar year vs. fiscal year, 230
California, 30, 48, 62, 166
Capital gains tax, 31, 206, 242
    on sale of personal residence, 167
CERCLA, 65
Certificate of Trust, 156, 169, 173
Certificates of Deposit, 170
Certified copy of Trust, 156
Changing titles (see "Funding")
Charitable foundation, 185, 246
Charitable Lead Trust, 245
Charitable Remainder Trust, 185, 244
Charitable "set aside," 231
Charities (as Beneficiaries), 42, 133, 244-246
Checking Accounts, 169
Children's Trust
    in a Will, 26, 45
    in a Living Trust, 44
Club memberships, 179
Common trust, 82-83, 91, 96
Community property
    listing of states, 30
    retaining status in Living Trust, 163
Conservatorship, 22
Contesting, 20, 51, 136
Copyrights, 179
Corporate Trustee
    explanation of, 41, 115
    when to use, 111, 113-115, 128, 131
    benefits of, 53, 117
    safety of trust assets with, 118
    fees, 59, 118
    disadvantages of, 119
    how to evaluate, 119

N

Net estate, 74, 79
Notice of Trust, 48

O

Oil and gas interests, 179
Onassis, Jacqueline Kennedy, 19, 245
Organizing information for your family, 194

P

Passive losses on rental real estate, 167, 232
Patents, 179
Partnerships
    general, 178
    limited, 178
    family limited, 248
Payable-on-death accounts, 169
Pennsylvania, 166
Pension plans, 48, 180
Per capita, 133-135
Per stirpes, 133-135
Personal (untitled) property, 175
Personal Residence Trust, 246
Pour Over Will, 150, 154
Power of attorney, 23
Pre-nuptial protection, 51
Prepaid legal services plans, 144
Private foundation, 185, 246
Private letter ruling, 188
Probate
    explanation of, 12
    why we go through, 13
    what assets go through, 13, 61
    what happens in, 13-15
    small estates and, 16
    informal, 16
    expense of, 16-18, 58, 59
    time involved with, 18
    lack of privacy with, 18-20
    loss of control with, 20
    multiple, 18, 49
    court supervision with, 60
    as big business, 16, 67
Professional corporation, 189
Profit sharing plans, 48, 180
Property taxes, 63, 166

Q

Qualified Domestic Trust, 95, 252
Qualified Subchapter S Trust (QSST), 178
QTIP, 103, 106

R

Real estate
    contaminated, 65, 168
    rental, 167, 232
    how to transfer to Trust, 164
    refinancing, 60, 165
    out of state, 18, 48, 164
Recognition of losses, 234
Required minimum distribution, 180-187
Rollover, 181-187
Roth IRA, 187
Royalties, 179

S

Safe Deposit Box, 172
Saving Accounts, 169
Savings Bonds, 174
Section 1244 stock, 189
Separate Trusts, 82, 83, 91, 98
Sixty-five day rule, 233
Sole Proprietorship, 177
SPARRS, 142
Special gifts, 120, 208, 222
Special Needs Trust 130-133
Spendthrift clause, 128
Spousal consent form, 186
Spouse's responsibilities at incapacity/death, 199-212
Stepped-up basis, 32, 92, 163, 206, 219, 242
Stocks, 78, 172
Stretch out, 181-187
Subchapter S corporation, 177
Successor Trustee
    explanation of, 42
    as fiduciary, 44
    responsibilities of, 42, 44, 112, 213, 214, 218
    who can be, 113
    choosing yours, 112-114
    Corporate Trustee as, 113, 114

T

Tax identification number, 52, 56, 211, 222
Tax-deferred annuities, 187
Tax-deferred savings plans, 48, 180-187
Taxpayer Relief Act of 1997, 66, 75, 167, 227, 229, 234, 235

LIKE THE BOOK? SEE THE MOVIE!

This power-packed video makes the information come alive!

13 of the Most Common and Costly Estate Planning Mistakes

13 OF THE MOST COMMON AND COSTLY ESTATE PLANNING MISTAKES

One-Hour Seminar Edition

Presented by: Vickie and Jim Schumacher

VIDEO

In this information-packed, entertaining video, you'll get a front-row seat at Jim and Vickie Schumacher's exclusive estate planning seminar! Lively, easy-to-understand, and filled with the Schumachers' personal experiences and anecdotes, it's the perfect complement to their book, *Understanding Living Trusts.*®

In just 70 minutes, you'll learn concrete strategies to shield your estate from 13 critical mistakes…errors and oversights that can cost you thousands of dollars, and cause your estate to crumble into conflict, confusion and endless probate. More importantly, this videotape provides answers—the specific steps you need to take to ensure that the courts, the IRS, unethical attorneys or unwanted heirs can't loot your estate or override your expressed wishes.

Order today! Just call toll-free **1-800-728-2665** for immediate service. (Prefer to order by mail? Send check to address below.) **This exceptional video presentation is not available in book or video stores**. It's an easy way to share the information with children, family and friends, and is an essential addition to your personal library!

You'll discover...

- ✔ Why the courts can ignore specific, written instructions in your Will …and the simple solutions that can ensure it won't happen to you.
- ✔ The huge mistake that has caused thousands of people to unintentionally disinherit their own children. Have you made this mistake, too?
- ✔ Think your Will has you covered? Wrong! 4 huge legal loopholes that make Wills ineffective.
- ✔ "Uncle Sam" will be your biggest heir, if you make this common, expensive estate planning error.
- ✔ How to protect your family's privacy. Make this error, and your personal and financial information will be made public…available to any "interested party" who wants to see it!
- ✔ Find out how you can <u>guarantee</u> your estate won't be plundered by your children's creditors…unethical attorneys and the courts…greedy in-laws…the IRS…and more!
- ✔ Miss this critical extra step, and your carefully crafted Living Trust could become a waste of time, money and effort.
- ✔ A little-known fact about life insurance ... and how it can shrink your loved ones' insurance proceeds in a flash!
- ✔ 5 critical documents you must have. Check your records immediately. Do you have all five?
- ✔ And much more!

Unconditional Lifetime Guarantee

If you are not completely satisfied with this video, we will refund your money in full, at any time, with no questions asked.

Vickie & Jim Schumacher

Vickie & Jim Schumacher

Express Credit Card ✆ Order Line!

1-800-728-2665 ext. 13

✉ **or send your check for $34.95 ($37.42 if CA) to:**

≡ **Schumacher Publishing**
3000 Ocean Park Blvd., Suite 1070-V
Santa Monica, CA 90405

Location: http://www.estateplanning.com

CLICK HERE TO ENTER...
NEW The Learning Center
ON-LINE EDUCATION

Educate yourself! Save time and money! Avoid probate and reduce/eliminate estate taxes! If this sounds good to you, come visit *The Learning Center* at our Web Site: **www.estateplanning.com**.

Find an Attorney in Seconds!
Skip the fear and anxiety of locating an attorney. SPARRS (Schumacher Publishing's Attorney Rating and Review Site) will help you find a consumer-reviewed attorney in your area—in just seconds!

Estate Tax & Probate Calculator!
See your own bottom line! The Estate Tax and Probate Calculator lets you fill in your own numbers and estimate your probate and estate tax liability instantly!

FAQs

Frequently Asked Estate Planning Questions!
Immediate answers to your questions! We've worked with thousands of consumers and know what's puzzling you. The answers are here—in plain, easy-to-understand English.

Your Own Private Seminar!
Have a seat for our on-line seminar—at your own pace, at your convenience, in the privacy of your home!

Up-to-the-Minute News That Affects You!
Learn the legislative and legal news that impacts your financial decisions—before it costs you time, money and aggravation!

Get a FREE "Learning Center Kit" Today!
Is your Internet connection slow? Don't have time to learn on-line? Not to worry. We'll send you a FREE Learning Center Kit with our on-line information and more!

Visit *The Learning Center* on-line at our Web Site: **www.estateplanning.com**

Here's how you can order additional copies of *Understanding Living Trusts*® at special savings...

...and share the peace of mind, tax savings, and financial security a Living Trust offers with your friends and loved ones.

1 If you received *Understanding Living Trusts*® from a professional, ask him or her how you can get additional copies.

2 Check with your local bookstore (they can order additional copies if they are sold out).

3 Or, you can order directly from us by using the "Special Savings Certificate" below.

- -

Special Savings Certificate

☐ **YES**, I want to purchase additional copies of *Understanding Living Trusts*® and share with my friends and loved ones the peace of mind, tax savings, and financial security a Living Trust offers.
30-day Money-Back Guarantee.

QTY	Price per book	Shipping/Handling	Total (circle)
1	$24.95	$4.00	$28.95
2	$19.95	$5.00	$44.90
3	$18.95	$6.00	$62.85
CA residents add 8.25% sales tax			.
Total of payment enclosed			$.

SAVE $6.00!

SHIP TO:
Please print clearly.

Mr./Mrs./Ms. _____

Company _____

Address _____ Apt./Suite _____

_____
City   State   Zip

Telephone ( ) _____ (We may have questions about your order.)

METHOD OF PAYMENT: ☐ Check enclosed

☐ Mastercard [MasterCard]   ☐ Discover [DISCOVER]

☐ VISA [VISA]   ☐ American Express [AMERICAN EXPRESS]

Account # _____ Exp. Date _____

Signature _____

SEND THIS CERTIFICATE AND PAYMENT TO:

Schumacher Publishing
P. O. Box 64395
Los Angeles, CA 90064-0395

Save time. Call TOLL-FREE
1-800-728-2665 ext.11
(M-F, 7 am-5 pm, Pacific Time)

Please allow 2-3 weeks for delivery.

Larger quantity discounts are available. Call or write for information.

ULT/5th ed.

PEEKABOO
PLANET

A COLLECTION OF ROSE IS ROSE® COMICS
CREATED BY PAT BRADY, BY DON WIMMER

Andrews McMeel
Publishing, LLC

Kansas City • Sydney • London

Rose is Rose® is distributed internationally by United Feature Syndicate, Inc.

Peekaboo Planet copyright © 2009 by United Feature Syndicate, Inc. All rights reserved. Printed in China. No part of this book may be used or reproduced in any manner whatsoever without written permission except in the case of reprints in the context of reviews. For information, write Andrews McMeel Publishing, LLC, an Andrews McMeel Universal company, 1130 Walnut Street, Kansas City, Missouri 64106.

09 10 11 12 13 TEN 10 9 8 7 6 5 4 3 2 1

ISBN-13: 978-0-7407-8545-0
ISBN-10: 0-7407-8545-1

Library of Congress Control Number: 2009921632

www.andrewsmcmeel.com

Cover design, cover art, and flip book by Pat Brady

Other *Rose is Rose*® Books

She's a Momma, Not a Movie Star

License to Dream

Rose is Rose 15th Anniversary Collection

The Irresistible Rose is Rose

High-Spirited Rose is Rose

Rose is Rose Right on the Lips

Rose is Rose Running on Alter Ego

Red Carpet Rose

The Enchanting Rose

100% Whole Grin Rose is Rose

FLIP THE PAGE CORNERS
FROM FRONT TO BACK AND
WATCH BOTH SIDES TOGETHER!

I HAVE BEEN UNLAWFULLY FORCED TO BATHE EVERY NIGHT THIS WEEK!

MY CONSTITUTIONAL RIGHT TO BE DIRTY HAS BEEN VIOLATED!

SHOW ME JUST ONE INDIVIDUAL WHO HAS ENDURED MORE BATHING THAN ME!

SCRUB SCRUB

EXHIBIT "A"!

NO FAIR! HE NEVER GETS OUT OF HIS BATH!

I'M GRATEFUL FOR THAT!

WHAT'S WITH THE WORRIED FACE, ROSE?

IF I TELL YOU, YOU'LL JUST ROLL YOUR EYES!

ROSE, I'M MATURE ENOUGH TO CONTROL MY EYE MOVEMENTS!

YOU KNOW HOW EYE-ROLLS BUG ME?!

YES!

SERIOUSLY... I WANT A NON-EYE-ROLL REACTION!

OKAY! GIVE ME A SECOND!

I THINK THIS PROVES HOW SERIOUS I AM!

OH, JUST FORGET IT!

I'M SENSING MAJOR EYE-ROLLING!

FLOP FLOP FLOP FLOP FLOP FLOP FLOP FLOP FLOP FLOP FLOP FLOP FLOP FLOP FLOP FLOP FLOP FLOP FLOP FLOP FLOP

HOW DO YOU LIKE YOUR NEW FLIP-FLOPS, MIMI?

DARE AWL FWOP EN NO FWIP!

The **Butterfly** CHRONICLES "THE CHASE"

HER SPEED AND AGILITY WERE NO MATCH FOR MY TIRELESS DELICATE WINGS!

UGH!

HUFF HUFF HUFF HUFF HUFF

The **Butterfly** CHRONICLES "THE LITTLE GIRL"

SHE DIDN'T WANT TO CHASE ME... SHE WANTED TO **BE** ME! FOR A MOMENT EVEN **I** BELIEVED SHE COULD **FLY!**

The **Butterfly** CHRONICLES "THE LANDING"

HIS MOOD WAS SULLEN, BUT WITH A SIMPLE GESTURE I'D LIKE TO THINK I MADE A DIFFERENCE IN HIS DAY!

11

C'MON! LET'S MAKE SOME **BIG** WAVES!

THERE'S NO EXCESSIVE SPLASHING IN THE POOL!

WHO'S GONNA KNOW?

HANDS **ABOVE THE WATER,** CLEM! **THIS** LIFEGUARD DOESN'T MISS MUCH!

PASQUALE, WILL YOU COUNT HOW MANY SECONDS I CAN HOLD MY BREATH **UNDERWATER?**

UH... CLEM...

I'M NOT SURE THE LIFEGUARD WILL CONSIDER THAT **SAFE POOL PLAY...**

START COUNTING!

GLUB

TWEET TWEET TWEET

OKAY! I'M **ABOVE** WATER!

ALMOST A SECOND, CLEM!

IT'S NICE TO BE BACK AT MY "LET THINGS BE" TREE!

AFTER A SHORT VISIT AND A GENTLE LEAN... I AM ABLE TO RELAX AND JUST LET THINGS BE!

IT'S MORE THAN A TREE... IT'S A STEADFAST FRIEND WHO IS ALWAYS HERE FOR ME!

NOW I FEEL GUILTY!

ME TOO! LET'S NOT TAKE THIS TREE FOR GRANTED ANYMORE!

DO YOU SEE WHAT I SEE?!

I CERTAINLY DO!

THAT IS ONE **FINE** COLLECTION OF **WORMS**!

THERE MUST BE **DOZENS** OF THEM!

WHAT'S THE **FAIREST** WAY TO SPLIT THEM UP?!

WELL... SHE SHOULD GET **FIRST DIBS!**

A SPIRITED SPRINT THROUGH THE BLISTERING MIDDAY SUN...

A FLAWLESS HANDOFF...

THANK YOU! THANK YOU! THANK YOU! THANK YOU! THANK YOU!

A **GRATEFUL GARDENER!**

STAND UP, ROSE, AND I'LL SHOW YOU MY GARDENING TECHNIQUE!

YOU HAVE A GARDENING TECHNIQUE? **THIS** I **HAVE** TO SEE!

ALLOW ME TO DEMONSTRATE!

=SMOOCH=

KEEPING THE GARDENER **HAPPY** IS AN **EXCELLENT** GARDENING TECHNIQUE!

AFTER A LONG DAY OF TOILING IN THE SOIL...

AND YOU'VE GATHERED UP THE SHOVELS, RAKES, ETC...

DOUBLE CHECK TO MAKE SURE NOTHING ELSE OF VALUE WAS LEFT IN THE GARDEN!

ROSE! ALL OF THIS CAME OUT OF OUR GARDEN?

ISN'T IT AMAZING!

DO YOU REALIZE THAT THERE'S A MARKET FOR HOME-GROWN PRODUCE?!

HA!

JIMBO, I DO THIS BECAUSE I ENJOY IT! I'M NOT INTERESTED IN GARDENING FOR PROFIT!

THAT'S GOOD NEWS FOR US!

=MUNCH=

=MUNCH=

HADAZE DA PWULL GEZZ VUREE KWOWDID!

YES, MIMI! ON HOT DAYS THE POOL DOES GET VERY CROWDED!

15

16

AUNTIE ROSE, WOULD YOU CONSIDER BECOMING A CORPORATE SPONSOR FOR MY "SNACK AND SWIM" ENTERPRISE?

TELL ME ABOUT IT!

FOR A **SMALL** FEE CLIENTS TAKE A REFRESHING DIP FOLLOWED BY A TASTY TREAT!

AND WHAT ARE **MY** RESPONSIBILITIES AS A CORPORATE SPONSOR?

I'D SAY PROVIDING ACCESS TO **YOUR** KIDDIE POOL AND BAKING A TRAY OR **TWO** OF YOUR **DELICIOUS** BROWNIES WOULD APPEASE **OUR** CUSTOMERS!

CAN WE SWIM NOW?

HEY! WHAT ABOUT THE SNACK?!

I SEE THAT OLDER COUPLE HERE **EVERY** DAY!

IT'S SO NICE HOW HE WAITS FOR HER TO CATCH UP... OR SHE'LL ADJUST HER SPEED FOR HIM!

I **HOPE** THAT WILL BE **US** SOMEDAY!

IT WILL BE, ROSE...

BUT WE'LL START **SLOW**... AT OUR OWN PACE!

AND I'LL **DEFINITELY** NEED FASTER RUNNING SHOES!

:DIP:
:DIP:
:DIP:

=PWHHHT=
=PWHH= =PHFWIT=
=PWW=

WHAT'S THE PROBLEM, MIMI?

BWUBULL MAKUR EZ BWOOKN!

18

DO YOU STILL HAVE ICE CREAM EATING CONTESTS?

SURE! WE HAD ONE LAST WEEK!

IN FACT... WE'RE ASKING FOR HELP TO IDENTIFY THE WINNER!

WOULD YOU MIND TAKING A LOOK?

HE DIDN'T EVEN OFFICIALLY REGISTER! HE SIMPLY WALKED IN AND WIPED US OUT OF RASPBERRY SWIRL IN RECORD TIME!

WHO IS THIS??

TIME TO GO, PASQUALE!

HE LOOKS JUST LIKE MY COUSIN CLEM!

HE STANDS TALL WHERE OTHERS WOULD RUN FOR COVER... REFUSING TO RETREAT... HANGING IN THERE UNTIL THE TASK IS COMPLETE!

I HAVE TO WONDER IF I'LL HAVE WHAT IT TAKES...

...TO BE AN ALL-WEATHER GRILLER?!

AAUUUGGHH

SSSS

SINCE MY DADDY IS WORKING LATE, MOMMA IS LETTING ME HAVE MY DINNER OVER THE SINK, MIMI!

ET EEZ WUDE, GWOOZ EN DEZKUSTEN!

WELL OF COURSE IT'S RUDE, GROSS AND DISGUSTING! THAT'S WHY GUYS DO IT!

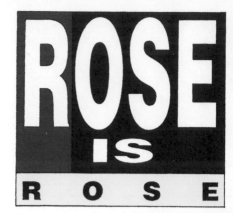

THIS PARTICULAR SCENARIO WASN'T DISCUSSED DURING MY KITTEN SURVIVAL TRAINING!

CHASING A BIRD HAS LEFT ME BALANCING ON A BEACH BALL ABOVE THIS TUB OF WATER!

SO I MUST **GENTLY** LIFT MYSELF UP AND DISMOUNT!

WHOA WHOA WHOA

I'VE HEARD THAT THIS PILATES POSE IS GREAT FOR THE LOWER BACK!

CHASING A BIRD HAS PUT ME IN THIS PRECARIOUS POSITION! I MUST REMAIN STILL OR RISK BEING **DUNKED!**

I'LL HAVE TO RELY ON THE KINDNESS OF A PASSERBY TO RESCUE ME!

I'LL BET MY FIRST MORNING **WORM** SHE FALLS IN.

YOU'RE ON!

21

THIS IS WHAT I GET FOR TRYING TO NAB A BIRD PERCHED ON A BEACH BALL!

I'M DESPERATELY HOLDING ON TIGHT TO AVOID ANY FURTHER **HUMILIATION!**

OF COURSE THERE'S ALWAYS A CHANCE THAT I HAVEN'T BEEN NOTICED YET!

GRACIE! GET THE KIDS! THEY'RE GONNA WANT TO SEE THIS!

HOLD ON, PEEKABOO! I'LL **RESCUE** YOU!

HOW DID YOU END UP STRANDED ON A BEACH BALL?!

WELL... YOU CAN RELAX NOW... YOU'RE SAFE.

HOLD ME! I HAD A **NEAR-AQUATIC EXPERIENCE!**

HE'S ALWAYS BEEN SO KIND TO ME... BUT **THIS** IS OVERWHELMING!

LOOK AT HIM SLOWLY MOVE PAST MY BOWL WITH GRACEFUL FLOWING MOTIONS...

AND HE **EVEN** HAS PROPS TO ADD **AUTHENTICITY!** I'M TOUCHED THAT HE WOULD PUT IN **SO** MUCH EFFORT...

...TO MAKE MY LITTLE WORLD APPEAR SO MUCH **BIGGER!**

23

WE'RE OUT OF LIMA BEANS **AND** BRUSSELS SPROUTS?!

:TOSS:

SOME OF MY LOYAL CUSTOMERS GET **TWO** WISHES FOR THE PRICE OF **ONE!**

ROSE, YOU ARE A BEAUTIFUL AND VIBRANT WOMAN! BUT... THE COSMETIC INDUSTRY WOULD HAVE YOU QUESTION THOSE **UNIQUE** TRAITS!

THEY ARE SUBTLY IMPLYING THAT **TRUE** HAPPINESS CAN ONLY BE ATTAINED BY USING **THEIR** LINE OF PRODUCTS!

THEY ARE **EXPLOITING** OUR INSECURITIES FOR THEIR OWN RUTHLESS QUEST FOR FINANCIAL GAIN!

IT'S LIP GLOSS...I'M NOT BEING EXPLOITED!

SURE! THEY LURE YOU IN WITH LIP GLOSS!

I THINK IT'S TIME TO CHANGE THE BIRD-BATH WATER!

:SPLASH:

I HOPE THE BIRDS **APPRECIATE** THIS!

SIP SIP SIP

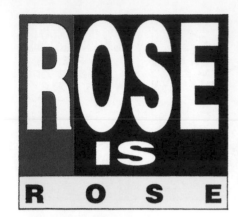

WELL, WELL... YOU'VE MADE YOURSELF QUITE A NICE GETAWAY!

IT'S MY BACKYARD BEACH! ALL THE AMENITIES OF A SHORE TRIP WITH NONE OF THE HASSLES!

EXCEPT IF...

THE TIDE COMES IN FAST!

AT LEAST THIS IS A REFRESHING HASSLE!

IT'S HARD TO BELIEVE THAT MILLIONS OF PARTICLES OF BROKEN STONE CAN OFFER SUCH A UNIQUE EXPERIENCE!

THIS IS WHY PEOPLE FLOCK TO THE BEACHES! THE SENSATION OF SAND BETWEEN YOUR TOES!

DADDY! YOUR LEGS ARE TAKING UP THE WHOLE SANDBOX!

OF COURSE... BACKYARD BEACHES HAVE LESS SAND TO GO AROUND!

WHILE MANY DISMISS ITS RELIEF AS FLEETING AND INSIGNIFICANT, LAUNDRY FOLDING SHADE DOES HAVE ITS ARDENT FOLLOWERS!

THEY REALLY NEED TO ADD SOME SARDINES TO THE ACT!

WOOK WAT KWEM MAYD!

I SEE WHAT CLEM'S MADE, BUT ITS NOTHING TO WORRY ABOUT!

CUZ ETKANT GETTUS?

NO... IT CAN'T GET US, MIMI!

WAWTA BWOON TU BEEG TO FWROW!

THAT WATER BALLOON IS WAY TOO BIG TO THROW!

UGH!

I COULD USE A LITTLE HELP HERE!

UH-OH! THERMAL READINGS REGISTER APPROACHING LIFE FORM!

WHOA! STARBOARD WING SENSORS ARE INDICATING ADDITIONAL WEIGHT!

I'M BEING PULLED DOWN! MY SHIP'S STABILITY IS BEING COMPROMISED! COMMAND CENTER, PLEASE ADVISE!

DREAMSHIP PILOT AWAITING INSTRUCTIONS...

I'D EMPLOY UNSNAGGING MANEUVERS IMMEDIATELY!

THAT APPEARS TO HAVE THE PROPER DEPTH AND A NATURAL CONTOUR!

WHEN THEY'RE TOO IMPATIENT TO WAIT FOR THE NEXT RAIN...

SPLASHERS RELY ON A PUDDLE SPECIALIST!

MOMMA! LOOK WHAT CAME IN THE MAIL! IT'S A POSTCARD FROM THE PARKERS!

LET'S SEE!

"GUMBOS—OUR CARIBBEAN CRUISE HAS BEEN DELIGHTFUL! ONE SPECTACULAR SUNSET AFTER ANOTHER! IT LOOKS LIKE GLORIOUS WEATHER WILL FORCE US TO EXTEND OUR TRIP A FEW MORE WEEKS!"

SO THEY SENT IT TO REMIND YOU WHERE THEY ARE?

IT'S MOSTLY TO REMIND ME WHERE I'M NOT!

WHAT ARE YOU JUMPING ON, ROSE?

STOMP STOMP STOMP STOMP

A POSTCARD FROM THE PARKERS! THEY'RE ON A CARIBBEAN CRUISE!

ISN'T THAT NICE!

HOW THOUGHTFUL OF THEM TO THINK OF US ON THEIR VACATION!

THOUGHTFUL?

POSTCARDS ALLOW US TO SHARE IN EACH OTHER'S ADVENTURES!

MAYBE THEY'D ENJOY A POSTCARD FROM OUR LAUNDRY ROOM!

THIS IS NICE, HUH, ROSE? JUST YOU AND ME... A LITTLE TIME ALONE!

UH-HUH.

TEN MINUTES IS HARDLY ENOUGH TIME THOUGH!

I AGREE!

THE OIL CHANGE IS DONE, MR. GUMBO... WILL THAT BE ALL?

OIL and LUBE 10 MINUTES

DO THE TIRE ROTATION, RICHIE! WE'RE MAKING A NIGHT OF IT!

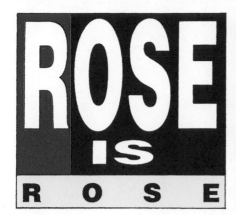

READY?

YEAH...JUST GIVE ME A SEC!

♪

OH, MY!

THAT WAS WONDERFUL!

HUH?

ALL YOU DID WAS CLEAR YOUR THROAT!

THANKS!

ANYTHING WE DO IS MUSIC TO HER EARS!

CLEM! CLEM! WE'RE HERE!

Wilson's Pond

WHOA! IS THAT YOUR TOY BOAT?!

ACTUALLY... IT'S A SHIP!

SHE RUNS ON TWO HUNDRED AND SIXTY-FOUR "C" BATTERIES!

MINE JUST FLOATS.

THERE AREN'T ANY TO PICK?

NOT EVEN ONE! AND THE SEASON IS OVER!

I'LL SEE YA LATER, MOMMA!

UH... OKAY, PASQUALE!

♪

THANK YOU SO MUCH!

DON'T THANK ME...

IT JUST WASN'T THE PROPER SOIL TO GROW LIMA BEANS!

SO I SHOULD BE THANKING THE DIRT?!

WHOA! THAT PILOT IS FLYING PRETTY **LOW**! OH... HE'S PULLING ONE OF THOSE **SKY BANNERS**!

WHEN HE GETS A BIT CLOSER I'LL BE ABLE TO MAKE OUT WHAT IT SAYS!

Hey, Cutie!

SO MANY **STARS**! AND I **IMAGINE** THAT THE VIEW IS EVEN NICER **OUTSIDE**!

I **WILL** STAND BENEATH THE **HEAVENS**!

JOIN ME, ROSE! DON'T LET ME EXPERIENCE THIS **ALONE!**

AFTER ALL THESE YEARS TOGETHER...

WHY CAN'T HE SIMPLY ASK FOR HELP TAKING OUT THE TRASH?

DON'T FORGET TO LOOK UP!

OUR LIVES ARE SO **HECTIC**...

IT'S **CRUCIAL** TO OUR RELATIONSHIP THAT WE SPEND QUALITY TIME **ALONE** WITH EACH OTHER!

I AGREE!

IF HE AGREES... **WHY** ISN'T HE GIVING US OUR TIME **ALONE**?

38

LET'S TRY THIS AGAIN, GUYS! AND BELIEVE IN THE WORDS YOU SAY THIS TIME!

YOU MAY LAUGH AT THE LOCKS I LACK... BUT I KNOW THEY WILL GROW BACK!

CURRENT MEMBERS OF THE **HARROWING HAIRCUTS COMMITTEE** GATHER FOR AN EMERGENCY SESSION!

LET'S SEE... BIG DRAGON ON THE LOOSE... VILLAGERS LIVE IN FEAR... BRAVE KNIGHT VOLUNTEERS HIS SERVICES...

=YAWN= =YAWN=

=YAWN=

HUGE BATTLE... HERO RETURNS... VILLAGERS REJOICE!

THAT WAS ONE OF YOUR SHORTER BEDTIME STORIES!

WHEN HE'S THAT TIRED... I JUST GIVE HIM THE HIGHLIGHTS!

YES! THE COOL WATER BECKONS THEM TO SPLASH AND FROLIC!

THOSE FEATHERED BEAUTIES ARE FORTUNATE THAT I AM **TEMPORARILY** DETAINED...

WET WINGS WILL PROBABLY SLOW DOWN THEIR TAKEOFFS CONSIDERABLY!

SORRY YOU HAVE TO GO, ABBY./ WELL, MIMI IS READY FOR HER NAP./ :YAWN:

UH-OH! MIMI LEFT HER TIARA...

I'LL HAVE TO GET THIS BACK TO HER...

RIGHT AFTER SHE WAKES UP!

♪ DING DONG ♪ DING DONG

DID YOU HAPPEN TO FIND MIMI'S TIARA? UHHH... DARETT IZZ!

THERE ARE TIMES WHEN YOU CAN BE TOO THOUGHTFUL, ROSE!

YEAH, MOMMA! HOW MUCH LONGER? MY ARMS ARE GETTING TIRED!

I'M SORRY! DAMP SHEETS AND TOWELS ARE NO REASON TO INTERRUPT A CONCERT!

42

THERE ARE DAYS WHEN IT'S BEST TO CUT TO THE **KISS!**

MIX-UP AT THE **NOTE IN A LUNCH BOX** DISTRIBUTION CENTER!

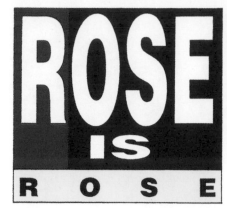

ROSE IS ROSE

LESS THAN A MINUTE TO GO, PASQUALE!

THE MOST EXCITING PART IS COMING UP!

TEN SECONDS!

NINE...EIGHT... SEVEN...SIX... FIVE...FOUR... THREE... TWO...

THERE GOES THE BUZZER!

BZZZZZ

I CAN'T LOOK, PASQUALE! WHAT'S HAPPENING NOW?!

THE OFFICIAL IS COMING ON THE FIELD!

I HAVE TO GET IN THERE TO MAKE MY RULING!

BAKING...IS... COMPLETE!

SHE'S NUMBER ONE! SHE'S NUMBER ONE!

DURING THE BROWNIE PLAY-OFFS... I ALWAYS HAVE TO BE ON MY BEST GAME!

WHENEVER YOU'RE READY!

YOU'VE MET YOUR MATCH!

=ACK= =ACK= BLAHHHHH!

THE STALE WALNUTS vs. SPICY SARDINES BREATH-OFF ENDS IN A PUNGENT TIE!

=POP= =POP= =POP= =POP=

HOW LONG CAN THEY KEEP UP THIS PACE?

OH, THIS IS ONLY THE BEGINNING!

ONCE THEY START BUBBLING... THERE'S NO STOPPING THEM!

HERE, MIMI! CLOSE YOUR EYES. TOSS THE COIN IN AND MAKE A WISH!

'KAY.

SO...WHAT WAS YOUR WISH? TU GHET DA KOYN EEN!

YOUNG WISHERS KEEP IT SIMPLE!

DURING RECENT MONTHS I'VE DEVELOPED SOME USEFUL SKILLS...

LIKE BECOMING QUITE ADEPT AT READING BODY LANGUAGE...

AND HIS POSTURE SUGGESTS "NO LAP TODAY!"

THAT'S SOMETHING WE DON'T SEE EVERY DAY!

YEAH! BUT I'M NOT SURPRISED...

SHE'S ALWAYS BEEN AN EQUAL OPPORTUNITY CROSSER!

:HONK:
:HONK:
:HONK:
:HONK:

IF GIVEN THE CHANCE...I WOULDN'T CHANGE A SINGLE THING IN MY LIFE!

I'M WITH YOU! WHY MESS WITH PERFECTION?

AND WE BOTH SAID IT WITHOUT SO MUCH AS A SMIRK!

IT TOOK ALL THE FACIAL MUSCLE CONTROL I COULD MUSTER!

HAHA
HAHAHA
HAHAHA

EXCUSE ME! I BUMPED MY ARM AND IT HURTS!
:SNIFF:
:SNIFF:

LET'S SEE, PASQUALE... I BELIEVE A FEW MINUTES WITH AN ICE-PAK WILL DO THE TRICK!

FEELING BETTER?
YES, BUT I DIDN'T BRING ANY MONEY!

I'M HERE FOR YOU AT NO CHARGE!
WHOA!

SCHOOL NURSE
IT'S LIKE HAVING A PRIVATE DUTY MEDICAL MOMMA!

:SWAT:

:KLUNK:

:SMACK:

:ROLL:
:ROLL:
:ROLL:

HEY! SHE CRACKED THE SHELL OF MY WALNUT!

THANK YOU!

OKAY! I'M GOOD!

AREN'T THERE MIRRORS TO CHECK FOR FOOD CAUGHT IN BETWEEN YOUR TEETH?!
YEAH... BUT YOUR SWORD HAS AWESOME MAGNIFICATION!

HI, PEEKABOO! HOW WAS YOUR LUNCH?

MEEEOOOWWW
:SNIFF:
:SNIFF: :SNIFF:
EEEEWWW!

SERIOUSLY! HE ACTED AS IF HAVING SAVORY SEAFOOD BREATH WAS A BAD THING!

THIS JUST IN: HUGGING CONGESTION REPORTED AT THE KITCHEN AND LIVING ROOM INTERSECTION! EXPECT DELAYS!

THAT SOUNDS FAMILIAR!

IT SURE DOES!

SHE'S GOT A SONG-BIRD SINGING AS HER RINGTONE!

IT SOUNDED LIKE MY AUNT AGNES!

52

HE'S NOT IN HERE!

HE COULD BE HIDING!

PASQUALE, CLOSET MONSTER ACADEMY IS IN FULL SESSION! ALL OF THEM ARE IN CLASS!

THEY HAVE TO LEARN HOW TO SCARE?!

SNEAK UP ON THE KID AND ROAR!

AHHH...

WHICH ONE IS ME?!

YOU JUMP OUT...HE'LL SCREAM IN TERROR... YOU RETURN AND I'LL GRADE YOUR PERFORMANCE!

OKAY, DAD!

THIS IS MY CHANCE TO PROVE I HAVE CLOSET MONSTER POTENTIAL!

WHAT IS HE DOING UP THERE? HOW LONG DOES IT TAKE TO SCARE A KID?

THESE RANGER RORY COMIC BOOKS ARE AMAZING!

:EERP:

:GAK:

:TWPT:

THOSE AREN'T VERY SCARY CLOSET MONSTER FACES!

I'VE GOT ONE MORE!

TERRIFYING FLAPPING EARS!

GET BACK IN HERE!

WE'RE LOSING DARKNESS! GET OVER THERE AND SCARE THAT KID!

HE'S SLEEPING SO PEACEFULLY!

UHHHHH...

HE FRIGHTENED ME, DADDY! HE YAWNED!

I ADMIT THERE IS SOME SKILL INVOLVED...

AND THREE WALNUTS ISN'T BAD... BUT...

BE MORE IMPRESSED IF HE WAS JUGGLING SARDINES!

THE FIRST PART SOUNDED LIKE...

NO... IT WAS MORE LIKE...

AND THEN IT WENT...

CAN YOU SING THAT ONE AGAIN?

I DIDN'T RECOGNIZE A SINGLE NOTE! WHEN IN DOUBT... WE DO A MEDLEY OF OUR HITS!

=BEEP= =BOOP= =BOP= =BEEP= =BEEP= =BOP=

MEEMAW! DON'T FORGET YOU'RE THE GUEST READER FOR MY CLASS TODAY!

UH...WHY DO YOU WANT ME TO LOOK OUT THE WINDOW?

WE HAVE TO PICK OUT A BOOK!

OH, PASQUALE! THIS IS GOING TO BE FUN!

I'VE GOT THE BOOK, MEEMAW!

I HOPE SHE REMEMBERS HOW TO GET THERE!

IF SHE GETS LOST...WE'LL HAVE NO PROBLEM FINDING HER!

GRANDCHILD ON BOARD!

GUEST READER AT MY GRANDSON'S SCHOOL!

IT'S STORY TIME... MOM'S READING TO PASQUALE'S CLASS!

=TICK= =TICK= =TICK=

I HOPE SHE'S NOT TOO NERVOUS! I KNOW HOW I GET IN FRONT OF CROWDS!

AT A NEARBY PUBLIC SCHOOL...

"...AND THE LITTLE CHICKS DRIFTED OFF TO SLEEP!"

I BELIEVE MY WORK HERE IS DONE!

SHE READ JUST LIKE MY NANA!

Panel 1: LET SOMEONE ELSE DO THAT ROSIE! / WHO? JIMBO'S AT WORK AND...

Panel 2: RAKES AT THE READY, PLEASE! / MOM... WHO ARE YOU TALKING...

Panel 3: A GRANDMOTHER'S GENTLE REQUEST CAN BE VERY PERSUASIVE!

Panel 4: ROSIE! ARE YOU THROWING AWAY THAT BALL OF YARN? / UH... I GUESS NOT!

Panel 5: LET'S SEE IF WE CAN PUT THIS OLD YARN TO GOOD USE!

Panel 6: KNIT KNIT KNIT / I MAY HAVE JUST ENOUGH...

Panel 7: NOW... PULL THIS OVER YOUR HEAD! / MOM!

Panel 8: HOW DOES SHE DO IT? / I'M A MOTHER!

Panel 9: TOO MANY CHOICES!

Panel: STRETCHABILITY IS A MUST WHEN FACED WITH A "MULTIPLE OPEN LAPS" OPPORTUNITY!

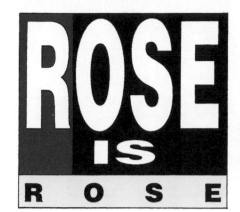

ROSE IS ROSE

ROSE! I'VE GOT A MEETING IN TWENTY MINUTES!

I KNOW! BUT WHAT CAN I DO?!

TAP TAP

YOU'VE GOT TO ASK HER TO STOP, SO I CAN LEAVE!

ME?! WHY CAN'T YOU ASK HER?

SHE'S YOUR MOM...IT WOULD BE BETTER COMING FROM YOU!

OKAY.

SHE JUST WANTS YOU TO BE WARM!

SHE'S GOT A HEART OF GOLD... BUT IT'S EIGHTEEN MINUTES AND COUNTING 'TIL MY MEETING!

UH, MOM... IT'S NOT THAT JIMBO DOESN'T APPRECIATE YOUR THOUGHTFULNESS...

SIXTEEN MINUTES!

...BUT HE REALLY HAS TO GO TO WORK NOW!

OH, IT'S FINE, DEAR... I'LL FINISH THE LAST FEW FEET TONIGHT!

LOOK, JIMBO! MOM MADE SOME FRESH COFFEE FOR YOU TO BRING TO WORK!

UH...THAT WAS SWEET OF HER...

BUT I'LL NEVER DRINK TWO GALLONS OF COFFEE!

DON'T FORGET YOUR SANDWICH, JIMBO!

BOOM CHUKA BOOM
BOOM CLANG TING TING

BOOM CHUKA CHUKA BOOM CLANG

AREN'T YOU GOING TO ASK YOUR MOM TO STOP?

YEAH...IN A SECOND...

BOOM BOOM

I LOVE THIS PART! CLANG

RATTA-TAT RATTA-TAT TAT

FOR YOU, PEEKABOO!

I GOT SO CAUGHT UP IN HER ENERGETIC PERFORMANCE... I DIDN'T NOTICE THAT SHE WAS SERVING ME THE BARGAIN BRAND CAT FOOD!

ALL OF HER WISHES ARE FOR HER KIDS AND GRANDKIDS!

THE SCRAMBLED EGGS WERE SENSATIONAL! I'M STUFFED!

ME TOO!

HOW ABOUT THE BISCUITS? I COULDN'T EAT ANOTHER BITE!

THE NEXT COURSE IS READY!

ANY TAKERS FOR SOME OF MY FAMOUS FLAPJACKS?!

MEEMAW, IS IT TRUE THAT YOU WERE A CHAMPION...

SLICE SPIN SPIN SLICE SLICE SPIN SLICE

SHAKE SHAKE SHAKE SHAKE SHAKE SHAKE SHAKE

SLICE CUT CUT CUT SLICE SAW CHOP SAW

PUMPKIN CARVER?!

63

YOU HAVE A **VERY** GUILTY LOOK ON YOUR FACE...

... AS IF YOU'RE HIDING SOMETHING...

BUT WHAT SECRET COULD A PUMPKIN POSSIBLY HAVE?

THANKS, PAL!

PAT PAT

WHOA!

MOMMA... I'M DEFINITELY GOING TO NEED A SMALLER-SIZED ICE CREAM CONE COSTUME!

I GUESS A CHERRY ON TOP IS OUT!

IT LOOKS LIKE WE WON'T BE SEEING HIM FOR A WHILE!

HAVE A GREAT HALLOWEEN, DADDY!

ICE CREAM! ICE CREAM!

IT'S ONLY A COSTUME!

Jimbo's ice cream

64

WE TRAVEL IN VERY DIFFERENT **SOCIAL CIRCLES!**

AND FOR THE SAKE OF BOTH OF OUR REPUTATIONS...IT'S BEST IF WE GO OUR SEPARATE WAYS!

AHEM!

EXACTLY HOW MANY SARDINES WILL IT TAKE FOR YOU GUYS **TO FORGET** WHAT YOU'VE SEEN HERE TODAY?

GET READY TO **SCAMPER!** LOOK WHO'S HEADING OUR WAY!

HOLD ON! SHE'S NOT COMING FOR US!

IS SHE **BEING CHASED** BY A **PUPPY?**

STOP FOLLOWING ME!

BARK BARK

SHE SEEMS MORE ANNOYED THAN SCARED!

NO LUCK FINDING YOUR PUPPY, HUH?

NO... I'M STILL LOOK...

DID YOU HEAR THAT?

—BARK—

I'D RECOGNIZE THAT **BARK** ANYWHERE!

BARK BARK BARK

YOUR KITTEN LEAD HIM BACK TO ME!

I'LL BET YOU HAD QUITE THE ADVENTURE WITH THAT LITTLE GUY!

BARK

PLEASE TELL ME THAT I **DON'T** SMELL LIKE **DOG!**

ROSE
IS
ROSE

IT'S WORTH A TRY!

:GLUG:
:GLUG:

SWISH SWISH   GARGLE GARGLE

UCH!   GAK!

BLEECCCH

SPIT   SPIT

LATER THAT EVENING...

MOMMA! WE'RE OUT OF MOUTHWASH!

THAT WAS A BRAND NEW BOTTLE!

DO YOU SUPPOSE THE DRAIN MONSTER USED IT ALL UP?!

OF COURSE! HE'S PROBABLY GOT HIMSELF A GIRLFRIEND!

OOOFF! WHAT HAPPENED TO THE FOUL-BREATHED CREATURE THAT I FELL FOR?!

THE MINTY FRESHNESS SHOULD WEAR OFF SOON!

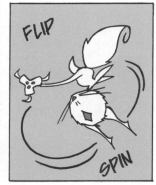

AGAIN?! HOW DO YOU MANAGE SO MANY CLAW SNAGS?!

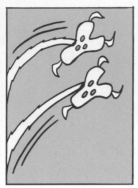

THEY JUST SORT OF HAPPEN!

EASY, JIMBO! YOU'RE PUSHING YOURSELF TOO HARD!

RAKE RAKE RAKE

I KNOW, CORKY... BUT THERE'S SO MUCH TO DO!

THEY'RE ONLY LEAVES, MY FRIEND! YOU'LL FINISH EVENTUALLY... LEARN TO PACE YOURSELF!

OKAY, CORKY!

CORKY REALLY PUTS IT ALL IN PERSPECTIVE!

WHIRRRRR

ANUDDA WUN?

MISTAH TWEE... YUR DWOPPIN ALL YUR WEEVES!

HE'LL GET ALL NEW LEAVES IN THE SPRING, MIMI!

DATS NO WEESON TU MAKA MESS!

YOU'RE NOT FOOLING ANYONE! I CAN SEE YOU!

THE TREE-SHEDDING SEASON LEAVES ME COMPLETELY FEELING EXPOSED!

:SNIFF:

:SNIFF:
:SNIFF:
:SNIFF:

:ACK:

UGGGH! HOW CAN A PILE OF LEAVES EMIT SUCH A FOUL AND OFFENSIVE ODOR?!

DO THESE LEAVES HAVE A BAD SMELL?

NO... WHICH MEANS YOUR PUMPKIN SEEDS BREATH IS WORSE THAN I THOUGHT!

IT TAKES A BRIEF MESSAGE WITH A GENTLE TOUCH...

A COOPERATIVE BREEZE...

A SMOOTH LANDING...

AND A CURIOUS RECIPIENT...

FOR THE PERFECT LOVE LEAF DELIVERY!

HUMANS REALLY KNOW HOW TO CELEBRATE A HOLIDAY...

STYLISH ATTIRE... FANCY DINNERWARE... AN ABUNDANCE OF TASTY DELICACIES... AND ONE OF THE HALLMARKS OF A **CIVILIZED SOCIETY**...

THE **PERSONALIZED PLACE CARD!**

Peekaboo

YOU CERTAINLY SEEM TO BE IN A **RUSH!**

SNIFF

LONG-DISTANCE WILL NOT DISSUADE A **PEPPERMINT CHEWING GUM BREATH AFICIONADO** FROM BEING THERE FOR THE FIRST FRESH WHIFF!

YEWUU... GWEEN... BWUU... PURRPUL...

BWOWN... PURRPUL... WED... WED...

WED... GWEEN... BWUU!

WYKE A **WEEF WAINBOW!**

YES, MIMI! JUST LIKE A **LEAF RAINBOW!**

I'VE GOT THE SHOE BOX!

HERE'S THE STYROFOAM BALL, PAINTS, BRUSHES STRING AND GLUE!

THE TAPE IS **EXACTLY** WHERE I SAID IT WOULD BE!

PERHAPS YOU'D LIKE ME TO DO THE MERCURY DIORAMA FOR YOU?!

SORRY, MOMMA... I HAVE TO DO THIS SCIENCE PROJECT **ENTIRELY** ON MY OWN!

WHAT'S THE STYROFOAM BALL FOR, PASQUALE?

IT'S PART OF MY SCIENCE PROJECT ON MERCURY!

I'M GOING TO PAINT IT AND...

WE CAN MAKE A ROCKET SHIP FOR EXTRA CREDIT!

MOMMA WARNED ME NOT TO MENTION PROJECTS INVOLVING SPACE TO HIM!

MERCURY'S SURFACE IS MADE UP OF...

:YAWN:

ANYONE CAN GET FACTS ABOUT A PLANET FROM A BOOK...

GOING DIRECTLY TO THE SOURCE WILL GIVE ME A UNIQUE PERSPECTIVE!

IT SEEMS A LOT OF STUDENTS HAD THE **SAME IDEA!**

MERCURY INFORMATION CENTER

79

DID YOU **SEE** THE **ARGYLES** AT THE PARTY LAST NIGHT?

UH-HUH.

DID THEY LOOK LIKE THEY HAD **WORK** DONE?

HA! YES!

THE NEW STITCHING WAS OBVIOUS!

ANY IDEA WHEN HIS SOCK PUPPET SHOW WILL END?

WHEN HIS FEET GET COLD!

SHHHHH!

WE WRAP IT SNUGLY WITH BURLAP... BUT **NOT TOO** TIGHT!

NOW IT'LL BE PROTECTED FROM HARSH WEATHER!

I HOPE ALL OF THE TREES DON'T CLOSE FOR THE WINTER!

...TWO...THREE... FOUR...

UGH!

YAAAAA!

OOOFF!

I SAID A **SLIGHT CHANCE** OF FLURRIES!

SNOW WARRIORS ARE AN OPTIMISTIC BREED!

80

OH! A FRESH BLANKET OF SNOW!

PRISTINE... UNTOUCHED... NOT A SINGLE TRACK!

THIS FRAGILE CANVAS SILENTLY AWAITS THE DISTINCTIVE MARKINGS OF PAWS, HOOVES AND FEET!

TODAY IT WILL BE A PINK SLIPPER THAT MAKES THE FIRST IMPRESSION IN THE SNOW!

BEEP! BEEP! COMING THROUGH!

OR... A HERD OF TRAMPLING TOBOGGANERS!

GIFT-GIVING HAS GOTTEN OUT OF HAND, HASN'T IT, JIMBO?

UH-HUH.

I DON'T WANT TO BE SO SHALLOW THAT MY POSSESSIONS DEFINE WHO I AM!

I AGREE!

NOW... IF I WERE A SHALLOW PERSON... THAT'S THE SWEATER I'D WANT TO BE SHALLOW IN!

THERE'S A CORDLESS DRILL OVER IN HARDWARE WITH SHALLOW WRITTEN ALL OVER IT!

AUNTIE ROSE, WOULD YOU MIND MAKING A BATCH OF YOUR DELICIOUS BROWNIES TO WELCOME A NEW FAMILY TO OUR NEIGHBORHOOD?

CLEM, THAT'S A THOUGHTFUL AND TOTALLY UNSELFISH IDEA!

SO... CAN YOU START BAKING NOW?

BECAUSE I'M NOT SURE HOW LONG THEY'LL BE STAYING!

I'M NOT MAKING BROWNIES FOR A SNOW FAMILY, CLEM!

WHY NOT, AUNTIE ROSE?

BECAUSE... YOU KNOW, AS WELL AS I DO, CLEM... YOU'LL BE THE ONLY ONE EATING THE BROWNIES!

DO YOU GUYS HAVE ANY OBJECTIONS TO SHARING YOUR BROWNIES?

OBVIOUSLY THEY'RE TOO POLITE TO OBJECT IN FRONT OF YOU!

ONCE A YEAR I LET HER GLITZ ME UP FOR HOLIDAY WISHERS!

HUMPF!

:KISS:
:KISS:

HA.

FORGET IT, JIMBO!

C'MON, ROSE! YOU HAVEN'T EVEN GIVEN IT A CHANCE!

PARSLEY WILL NEVER REPLACE MISTLETOE!

EDDIE! WHY ARE WE MOVING?!

THIS MUST BE SOME KIND OF MIGRATING TREE!

ROSE IS ROSE

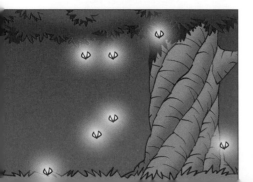

THEY ARE **ANNOYING** LITTLE CRITTERS...

BUT I DO ADMIRE A CULTURE WHICH IS SO RICH WITH UNIQUE AND EXCITING **TRADITIONS**...

LIKE THE ANNUAL MIDNIGHT DROPPING OF THE WALNUT!

FOUR!... THREE!... TWO!...

EXPERT ADVICE FOR A SUCCESSFUL START TO THE NEW YEAR:

FIND A COMFORTABLE PACE THAT WILL COMPLEMENT YOUR CURRENT MOOD!

UNCLE JIMBO, AFTER THAT **HUGE** BLIZZARD LAST NIGHT... I FELT THAT I SHOULD OFFER **FREE ESTIMATES** FOR SNOW SHOVELING!

OKAY, CLEM!

I'LL INCLUDE THE DRIVEWAY, SIDEWALK, FRONT AND BACK PORCH...AND WHEN I FACTOR IN YOUR AGE, WEIGHT AND GENERAL HEALTH...

I BELIEVE IT'LL TAKE YOU JUST UNDER THREE HOURS! I'LL CHECK IN LATER TO SEE **HOW CLOSE** MY ESTIMATE WAS!

BEING AN **ALL-ACCESS** WISHING WELL WOULDN'T BE POSSIBLE WITHOUT A **DEDICATED** SUPPORT SYSTEM!

HOLD STILL!

MIMI! MR. DUCK'S MEASURING STICK SAYS YOU'VE GROWN **HALF** AN INCH!

DAT'S ALL?

GROWING TAKES TIME... WE HAVE TO BE PATIENT!

WEE KOOD GETTA FASTA DUK!

LUCKY ME!

THIS IS JUST WHAT I NEEDED TO PICK UP MY SPIRITS!

HA! HA! HA! HA! HA! HA! HA!

I WOULDN'T BE SMILING! THIS **CLAW SNAG** MAKES BOTH OF US LOOK SILLY!

HEH-HEH

93

AND HOW ARE **YOU** FEELING TODAY, DOCTOR?

UH... I'M **FINE**... THANKS FOR ASKING...

IN FACT, PASQUALE... YOU'RE THE **FIRST** PATIENT TO INQUIRE ABOUT **MY HEALTH!**

I ASSURE YOU THAT YOUR INFORMATION WILL BE KEPT COMPLETELY CONFIDENTIAL!

PASQUALE, DO YOU HAVE ANY QUESTIONS?

JUST ONE...

IS THERE **ANY** SCIENTIFIC RESEARCH TO SUPPORT MY THEORY THAT **BROCCOLI** IS AN **UNNECESSARY** PART OF OUR DIET?

BROCCOLI IS HIGH IN **VITAMIN C** AND CONTAINS A VARIETY OF NUTRIENTS...

SO THE MEDICAL COMMUNITY THINKS YOU SHOULD EAT IT! IF OUR OPINION CHANGES... I'LL BE SURE TO CALL YOU!

CALL HER! SHE BUYS THE BROCCOLI!

YOU'RE IN GREAT SHAPE, YOUNG MAN! HELP YOURSELF TO A LOLLIPOP!

THANK YOU!

UH, DOCTOR... WOULD IT BE POSSIBLE TO HAVE ANOTH...

YES! YOU MAY TAKE ONE FOR YOUR **FATHER!**

94

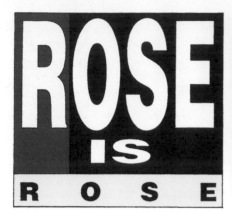

ROSE IS ROSE

ADMIRE THE PRISTINE BEAUTY OF FRESHLY FALLEN SNOW, WHILE SNUGLY WRAPPED IN A QUILT MADE BY GREAT AUNT BETTY'S OWN HANDS...

FIND THE **PERFECT POSITION** FOR QUIET CONTEMPLATION...AND THEN CONTEMPLATE ABSOLUTELY **NOTHING AT ALL...**

BECOME **THOROUGHLY** ABSORBED BY THE THRILLING ADVENTURES OF COMIC BOOK LEGEND, **RANGER RORY...**

TAKE A **THIRD EXTENDED NAP** BY A WARM FIRE...

INTENTIONALLY DO NOT WIND THE MANTEL CLOCK ALL WEEKEND!

EASY-TO-DO WINTER INACTIVITIES!

I WAS PLANNING TO ASK YOU TO **MARRY ME** ON A MOONLIT NIGHT...

BUT WHEN I SAW YOU IN THE DAYLIGHT THAT AFTERNOON... I COULDN'T WAIT!

>SMACK<

I NEVER GET TIRED OF HEARING THAT STORY!

LET ME CATCH MY BREATH... I MAY TELL IT AGAIN!

WHA?!

:TUG:

SLED STOWAWAYS.

I USUALLY LIKE TO HAVE MY "GARBAGE MOMENT" ALONE... BENEATH THE STARS... ENJOYING THE QUIETUDE BY MYSELF!

BUT IF **ANYONE** CAN APPRECIATE THE PEACEFUL BEAUTY OF STILLNESS... IT WOULD BE **HIM!**

SO TONIGHT I'LL SHARE MY MOMENT AND MY GARBAGE!

TAKING TIME TO BREAK IN SOME NEW STRINGS!

THE WIND... THE ICY SNOW... THE BITTER COLD...

WHY DOES HE DO IT, MOMMA?

HE BELIEVES BEING A WINTER GRILLER IS HIS CALLING!

I'D WAIT FOR A WARMER CALL!

MY VEGGIE BURGERS!

SNACK TIME! COME IN AND GET IT!

ARE YOU SURE THE INVITATION INCLUDED US, MARTY?

WHAT RESPECTABLE ESTABLISHMENT WOULD EXCLUDE SQUIRRELS?!

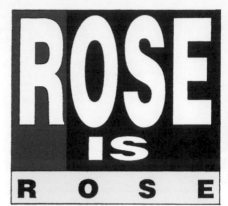

OH, GOOD! PASQUALE'S HOME!

TELL ME ALL ABOUT YOUR DAY!...DOWN TO THE **LAST DETAIL!**

WHY, MOMMA?

I'VE DECIDED TO WRITE DOWN SOME OF YOUR CUTE AND HILARIOUS STORIES IN MY JOURNAL!

SINCE **WE'LL BOTH BE IN** IT...WE CAN READ FROM YOUR JOURNAL **EVERY NIGHT!**

UH-UH! DEAL'S **OFF!**

THE OUTDOORS MAY PROVIDE ME WITH AN INTERESTING JOURNAL ENTRY!

OH! A WILDLIFE ENCOUNTER! THAT'S WORTH NOTING.

DON'T BE SCARED, LITTLE GUY...YOU'RE GOING TO BE IN MY JOURNAL!

THE RAVENOUS SQUIRREL FORAGED UNTIL HE FOUND THE **PRECIOUS WALNUT!**

IT WAS JUST LYING ON THE GROUND!

HOW WAS WORK?

OKAY.

THAT'S **IT?** I'LL NEED MORE IF YOU WANT TO BE INCLUDED IN **MY JOURNAL!**

ROSE! THE **WHOLE POINT** OF KEEPING A JOURNAL IS TO RECORD **YOUR** EXPERIENCES... NOT **MINE!**

GOT A LONG-WINDED LECTURE ON **JOURNALING INTEGRITY** FROM "MR. JOURNAL" HIMSELF!

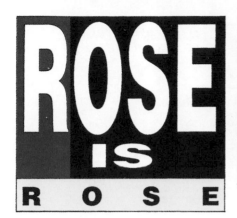

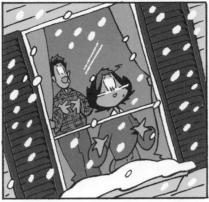

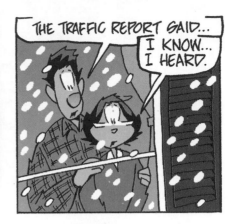

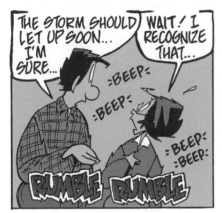

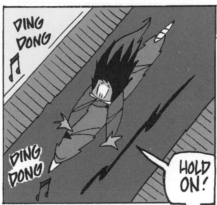

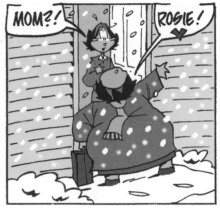

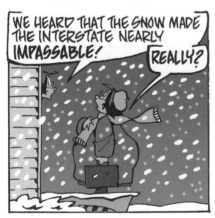

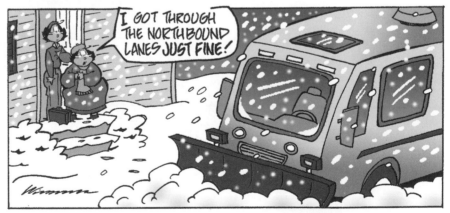

105

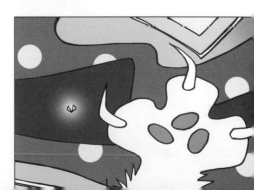

I JUST HAVE TO BE A LITTLE PATIENT...THEN I'LL MAKE MY MOVE!

FORTUNATELY, I WON'T HAVE TO WAIT TOO LONG TO POUNCE...

TIME OUT!

ARE YOU THINKING WHAT I'M THINKING?

YEAH... LET'S EAT!

...BECAUSE IN THE GAME OF WALNUT HOCKEY...

THE PUCK NEVER MAKES IT THROUGH THE FIRST QUARTER!

IT LOOKS LIKE OUR WALNUT HOCKEY GAME IS GOING TO BE DELAYED!

GULP!

DON'T PANIC!

SLIP SLIP SLIP SLIP SLIP

AREN'T KITTENS SUPPOSED TO BE AGILE?

SHE SHOULD FIRE HER STUNT COORDINATOR!

THIS ICE HAS NO POWER OVER ME! I SHALL PREVAIL!

UGGGH!

YES! I.... BELIEVE... I'VE...

FLAP FLAP FLAP SLIP SLIDE SLIP SLIP FLAP FLAP SLIDE SLIP

WHO KNEW KITTENS COULD DO PHYSICAL COMEDY?!

I WONDER IF SHE DOES KID'S PARTIES?

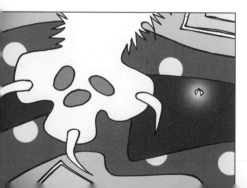

108

MY "ABOUT TO KNOCK OVER FRAGILE ITEMS" FACE GAVE ME AWAY!

JIMBO...

I'M ON IT ROSÉ!

-PUSH-

-SMACK-

HOW ABOUT SOME HOT COCOA?!

LOVE SOME!

OH! THAT SOUNDS...

HOGBOARDING

-ROLL- -ROLL- -ROLL-

WEENEE WODESIGH SISTENTS!

YES, YOU DO NEED ROADSIDE ASSISTANCE!

110

TAP TAP TAP
TAP TAP
TAP

I'VE GOT THIS, JIMBO...KEEP GOING!

WE'RE READY FOR THE HOSE!

OKAY, DADDY!

MOMMA! I'M HANDLING THE WATER!

GREAT, PASQUALE! I'VE GOT THE SEED!

SHOULD I GET THE LADDER?

NO, MOMMA! I CAN REACH IT!

SEE! I TOLD YOU THEY'D BE READY FOR US!

THIS RESORT MUST HAVE AN INCREDIBLE STAFF!

Rose's
EFFECTIVE KISSING SOLUTIONS: "LIPS AT DAWN" THIS MORNING MOTIVATOR FUELS BOTH BODY AND SOUL!

IT'S TIME TO GET UP, JIMBO!

ROSE, I HAVE ABSOLUTELY **NO ENERGY!**

:KISS:

I'LL GO FIX US SOME BREAKFAST!

AS LONG AS YOU'RE **UP!**

Rose's
EFFECTIVE KISSING SOLUTIONS: "LIPS AT FULL SPEED" THE SHEER IMPACT OF THIS GREETING IS SAID TO **EXPEL NEGATIVE THOUGHTS!**

OH! LOOK AT THAT GRUMPY FACE!

UGH! WAIT 'TIL YOU HEAR ABOUT MY DAY!

HOLD ON, JIMBO!

SMACK

LET'S GO INSIDE AND YOU CAN TELL ME ALL ABOUT YOUR DAY!

HUH? DAY?

Rose's
EFFECTIVE KISSING SOLUTIONS: "POLITICAL UNREST CARESS" WHEN THE CONVERSATION TURNS TO POLITICS... ELIMINATE THE CONVERSATION!

...BACK TO THE CAMPAIGN TRAIL!

I WANT THE ISSUES TO BE DEBATED! MY VOTE WILL GO TO THE...

SMOOCH

NOW I'VE LOST MY TRAIN OF THOUGHT!

:CLICK:

Rose's EFFECTIVE KISSING SOLUTIONS: *"SNAP-OUT-OF-IT SMOOCH"* THIS FULL-BODY DIP AND LIP-LOCK HAS BEEN KNOWN TO PREVENT **HASTY DECISIONS!**

ALL THESE EXTRA FEES ON OUR PHONE BILL! LET'S CANCEL OUR SERVICE AND START WRITING LETTERS INSTEAD!

I GUESS I COULD TRY AND FIND THE HUMOR IN SOME OF THESE ADDITIONAL COSTS!

USAGE FEE?!

IT'S FEBRUARY 29TH, MIMI! IT'S A **LEAP YEAR!** WE GET A WHOLE EXTRA DAY!

DO YOU KNOW WHAT THAT MEANS FOR US?!

EXTRA SLEEP! EXTRA PLAY! EXTRA DESSERT!

MEENS AN **XTRA BAFF!**

OH, YEAH... I GUESS IT DOES MEAN AN EXTRA BATH!

I THOUGHT I WAS FAMILIAR WITH **MOST SPORTING EVENTS...**

...BUT THIS IS MY FIRST EXPERIENCE WITH **EXTREME KITE FLYING!**

HOLD ON, PASQUALE!

I'M TRYING!

Free Family Fun Ideas: "SOCK NIGHT" SPEND AN ENTERTAINING EVENING REUNITING SEPARATED COMPANIONS!

117

HOW DID **BOTH OF YOU** END UP WITH A CLAW SNAG?

THANKS FOR STOPPING BY, MOM! I HOPE YOU HAD A NICE TIME!

IT WAS **WONDERFUL!** I WOULDN'T HAVE CHANGED A THING!

SCHOOL ENTHUSIASTS OFTEN CARRY THE BURDEN OF THE HIGH ACADEMIC EXPECTATIONS OF **OTHERS!**

FLIP THE PAGE CORNERS
FROM FRONT TO BACK AND
WATCH BOTH SIDES TOGETHER!

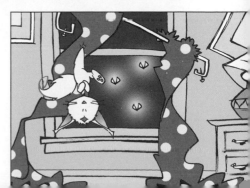